Freeing Tammy

THE WOMEN, POVERTY, AND VIOLENCE TRILOGY

Jody Raphael

Saving Bernice: Battered Women, Welfare, and Poverty (2000)

Listening to Olivia: Violence, Poverty, and Prostitution (2004)

Freeing Tammy: Women, Drugs, and Incarceration (2007)

THE NORTHEASTERN SERIES ON GENDER, CRIME, AND LAW

Editor: Claire Renzetti

For a complete list of books in this series, please visit www.upne.com and
www.upne.com/series/NGCL.html

Jody Raphael

Freeing Tammy

WOMEN,

DRUGS, AND

INCARCERATION

Northeastern University Press • BOSTON

Published by University Press of New England
Hanover and London

Northeastern University Press
Published by University Press of New England,
One Court Street, Lebanon, NH 03766
www.upne.com
© 2007 by Northeastern University Press
Printed in the United States of America
5 4 3 2 1

Library of Congress Cataloging-in-Publication Data

Raphael, Jody.
Freeing Tammy : women, drugs, and incarceration / Jody Raphael. — 1st ed.
    p.   cm. — (Northeastern series on gender, crime, and law)
Includes bibliographical references and index.
ISBN-13: 978–1–55553–672–5 (cloth : alk. paper)
ISBN-10: 1–55553–672–7 (cloth : alk. paper)
ISBN-13: 978–1–55553–673–2 (pbk. : alk. paper)
ISBN-10: 1–55553–673–5 (pbk. : alk. paper)
  1. Abused women—United States—Case studies. 2. Women—Drug use—United States—Case studies. 3. Female offenders—United States—Case studies. I. Title.
HV6626.2.R364 2007   ·
365'.43092—dc22   2006037673

For Claire Renzetti

Contents

Freeing Tammy

Prologue

I have come to believe over and over again that what is
most important to me must be spoken, made verbal and
shared, even at the risk of having it bruised or misunder-
stood. That the speaking profits me, beyond any other
effect.

— AUDRE LORDE

Tammara (Tammy) Johnson stands before fifty men in an in-patient
drug treatment program in south suburban Chicago.[1] An ex-addict with
a nineteen-year heroin habit and a felony record, Tammy is the program's job development trainer. The African American, with her styl-
ized helmet of Black hair, stands poised with a proud carriage and an
exquisitely groomed appearance. Now in her 50s, Tammy is beautiful—
movie star beautiful—but that wouldn't be relevant except for the fact
that it played such an important part in the choices she made as a teen.
Today Tammy's job is to help prepare the men for the world of work,
a difficult assignment since about 80 percent have criminal records and
she has only about three or four sessions with them before the program
will release them.

Hard to tell, too, that only five years ago, then newly released from
prison, Tammy sat in her dark basement, still confined by her feelings
of worthlessness. Only her own ferocious determination to recover
from her nightmare and find a place in society propelled her out of
that basement prison back into the light.

Her mission today is to instill some hope into the men, who make
clear that they don't believe they can be hired because of their criminal records and past addiction. Tammy explains.

A lot of prisoners believe, "This is my life and it is never going to be any different." Low expectations and no hope. They accept it, "This is what I am." Absolutely, just accept it, "no big deal."

Tammy is here to change the men's thinking. Pacing back and forth, she delivers a staccato lecture. They can find employment and they will need education. The way to do it is to be upfront with employers. Don't wait to be asked about it; put it out there as a positive. Walk in there with your resume and be prepared to discuss your criminal record and how it will make you a valuable employee. But be realistic. If you have been convicted of retail theft, for example, don't apply to Walmart.

The men—about equal number of Blacks and whites—appear skeptical, but, hanging on every word, they are remarkably attentive. It's clear, though, that they don't have a clue about using external resources. Most can't use a computer or the Internet to research programs, opportunities, or job postings. Nor do they have the basic tool for job hunting, a resume.

So Tammy operates a resume preparation service. The men fill out a form, Tammy puts the information into her computer, and presto! change-o! a professional-looking resume pops out of the printer. In eight months Tammy has completed 225 resumes, many of them produced after hours because there is always a long line of people waiting to see her during the day. Shari Zavala, clinical supervisor of the men's residential treatment program, tells me how spectacular the process is.

> Even having a resume gives them hope. They never had a
> resume before in their life. Most people don't even know
> how to do a resume, and if you wanted to pay for it,
> they don't have the money to pay for it. The interesting
> part is that they will leave here and come back to get it;
> that is a miracle. She has never done one that they haven't
> come back for. That's awesome.[2]

Although it's a lot of work, Tammy wouldn't have it any other way.

> *When you get that kind of response, it makes it all worthwhile. I don't want anyone to have to go through what I*

went through. That was painful. There was no one to hold
my hand. So I try to offer what I didn't have. If I would
have had someone to tell me, "Oh you can do it, don't listen
to these people." "You can't do this"—that's all I heard. It
was a self-fulfilling prophesy. So that's why I try to tell
them, "Don't let anybody tell you that."

This book, the third in a trilogy about Chicago women, is the story of
Tammy's metamorphosis. What was the process by which childhood
sexual assault, and later domestic violence, led to heroin abuse and
then crime, what were the effects of incarceration on an already-
abused woman, and what did it take for her to fully recover from all
these experiences? How did Tammy short-circuit the self-fulfilling
prophecy to become a leader, to become someone with so much to
give—and a woman with the ability to win release from the literal and
figurative prisons of abuse, addiction, crime, fear, and hopelessness?

My trilogy explores how violence makes and keeps women poor by
trapping them in trauma and causing them to rely on drugs to cope;
ending women's poverty will require paying greater attention to violence against women and girls. In Saving Bernice: Battered Women, Welfare,
and Poverty, I show how, leaving a home marked by alcoholism and domestic violence and moving into the arms of an abuser of her own,
Bernice Hampton became trapped on welfare as a teen.[3] Her partner,
underemployed and threatened by her attempts at education, training,
and work, sabotaged her efforts, keeping her poor at home, battered,
and on cocaine. Listening to Olivia: Violence, Poverty, and Prostitution relates the
story of Olivia Howard, another teen who left a similar home early but
took a different path—into a Chicago stripclub—that led to drug addiction, which trapped her in prostitution, violence, and poverty.[4]
Now I wanted to explore just how childhood sexual assault and domestic violence could lead to drug addiction resulting in crime and
incarceration.

Bernice Hampton and Olivia Howard were already in my life when
I decided to write their stories. In the current instance, I knew no formerly incarcerated woman who wanted her biography written. This
state of affairs led me into all kinds of trouble.

As a prelude, I read much of the voluminous research literature on
women's incarceration. Then, during the summer of 2004, I began to

look for an ex-felon to interview whom I had seen described there. I wanted someone addicted to drugs, who had been the victim of child-hood sexual assault and domestic violence. A downtrodden, self-medicating, drug-taking victim who committed minor crimes to obtain money to buy her drugs, was caught, and then sent to prison—this was the image embedded in my mind.

To make a long story short, I couldn't find such a person. First of all, the women I met weren't meek at all, but feisty, even aggressive. And they weren't likely to have been incarcerated for stealing a box of pampers or for buying or selling drugs, but were more apt to have been involved in an armed robbery with their intimate partner, or a com-plicated check-kiting scheme. Their stories were filled with incident; the eyes glazed over at the sheer number of self-destructive adventures and antisocial acts. I began to understand what Alexander Masters experienced when he was writing the biography of Stuart Shorter, a seriously disturbed homeless person in Cambridge, England, with a his-tory of childhood sexual assault, drug addiction, and incarceration.

> The perennial problem of the chaotic has crept in: this is
> a life with too much intensity. The wildness is fascinating
> in hints, but the days are over-concentrated and piled
> high with outrage for extended listening. Such people
> might be rich for novelists, but they are a downright
> liability for a biographer.[5]

When Tammy Johnson, recommended to me late that summer, related the outlines of her story, it took a mind-numbing three hours. But by this time I knew that all the comings and goings, the many different men in her life, and the crime were typical and it was high time to end my needle-in-the haystack search for the "perfect victim." And by shucking off my preconceptions and listening to Tammy and the things that were important to her, I was able to establish a collaboration that enabled Tammy, like Bernice and Olivia, to lay out the major themes of her story and not just those validating my preexisting feminist ideas or theories.

Although Bernice and Olivia came from poor households they fled as teens, Tammy's family was solidly middle class. She too left home early, because, for reasons she did not understand at the time, she was unable to meet her parents' expectations. Tammy's story graphically demonstrates how childhood sexual assault and domestic violence can *make* women poor, and, through dysfunctional coping strategies such as drug usage, *keep* them poor. Her experiences are a reminder that violence against women and girls in fact impoverishes women economically by trapping them in addictions leading to crime and other self-destructive activities.

Novelist B. J. Johnson has written:

> Life does not tell stories. Life is chaotic, fluid, random; it leaves myriads of ends untied, untidily. Writers can extract a story from life only by strict, close selection, and this must mean falsification.[6]

I have tried to order and make sense of Tammy's life without destroying its complexity; I hope in this way I am able to make some contribution to a better understanding of the linkages between childhood sexual assault and domestic violence with women's drug addiction and crime. I tell the story backwards, from the most recent events to the earliest, because that is the way Tammy chose to reveal it and how her repressed memories surfaced.

A recent search at amazon.com under "women prisoners" revealed 573 titles in print, and in only one month (October 2005), five new books appeared. Measured by the large number of works published on incarcerated women and their children, one would think that the huge increase in women prisoners was a matter of considerable societal concern. It isn't. Most people, I suspect, seem to think women prisoners are bad mothers who get the harsh punishment they deserve; there isn't a big audience out there wanting to delve into the sad and often violent details of these women's lives. Ultimately, many books on women prisoners probably end up gathering dust on the shelves of academic libraries, only read in college classes on gender, criminology, or social problems.

Researcher Joane Martel's experiences with the Canadian media demonstrate the total lack of interest in women prisoners. When she issued a report on horrific conditions for women in prison segregation in Canada, only three media outlets attended the press conference, resulting in two small newspaper articles, one of which satirized the

6   research report with this lead: "The Elizabeth Fry Society has spent $13,000 of taxpayer money to discover that women in solitary confinement are lonely." On that same day, however, two local television stations headlined the release of another research report, recommending the immediate improvement of living areas for caged animals in all the provincial zoos as well as the closure of several due to substandard conditions.[7]

As a topic of investigation, the incarceration of women has attracted some journalists and academics, most seeking to call sympathetic attention to the plight of these mothers who have been labeled misfits or deviants.[8] But despite such good intentions the women in prison stubbornly remain the studied "others." Indeed, one could argue that these often-superficial books make sympathy more difficult, confirming the strangeness of the women who continue to use drugs when they are mothers.

One new journalistic effort profiles a handful of women in a Massachusetts prison facility, but the author fails to adequately explore the early lives of the women and their crimes remain hazy.[9] Clearly, the women have been through a great deal, but without an understanding of how the trauma from violence and drug addiction has affected them, as well as the coping mechanisms they employ to survive prison, they appear kooky, aggressive, sex-crazed—slightly off. Lack of knowledge or understanding of post–traumatic stress disorder—the aftermath of violent trauma causing disassociation, emotional numbness, or hypervigilance—is apparent in this passage:

> Almost all the women I've met at Framingham have become exaggerated versions of themselves in one way or another. It is as if, lacking different experiences to reshape themselves, they repeat the same responses to the same stimuli over and over, until only those components of their character evolve.[10]

Her book, the end product of a multiyear battle to gain entrance to the prison, culminating in two lawsuits, describes the facility "like high school," doing little to advance our understanding of contemporary women's prison experiences.[11]

New works focusing on the offspring of mothers in prisons, although rich with poignant understanding of the plight of these families, fail to adequately address and explain the mothers' drug use.[12] When seen through the eyes of the children, who feel abandoned by that addiction, their parents' continued use of narcotics appears perverse. The unbearable loneliness and lack of self-worth of the children, which the authors so ably capture, make the women's acts seem even more inexplicable, inadvertently painting them as monsters.

Freeing Tammy, on the other hand, fully explores women's abuse-drugs-crime links. Although the connections are complex and varied, the pathways have one important feature in common—a quest for power and control, which sexual assault and violence have erased. Often, that journey toward empowerment leads to drug addiction, for reasons I shall thoroughly explore. Sadly, drug use can cause victims to victimize others. As the drugs are serving a real purpose, it is difficult for the women to stop using them; when they do, the pain of the past floods in, as does the guilt and shame for the addicts' lives and the abandonment of their children. And, lastly, the humiliation, shame, and stigmatization—the pure pain—the women experienced daily in prison interfere with necessary recovery tasks once they are out. In this account, Tammy has much to say that is startling and thought-provoking about how the judge's and correctional officials' humiliation of her set her back in all these postprison activities.

Tammy herself used the collaboration this book represents to explore what had occurred and why. Sympathizing "with those who have no one to talk to or no book to help them understand what has happened," she found the experience "invaluable." But Tammy does not regard herself as a heroine. She has learned, however, that she could not recover and build a drug- and crime-free life until she had constructed a true narrative of her trauma, harm, loss, and damage, put it out in the open, and confronted the pain she spent so many years burying with aggression and disassociation through drugs. Thousands of women, Tammy knows, urgently need to take this path to self-understanding and responsibility.

With this narrative Tammy hides nothing and minces no words, although the effort caused her many times to reenact the trauma. Her motivation echoes late poet and essayist Audre Lorde: "If one Black woman I do not know gains hope and strength from my story, then it has been worth the difficulty of telling."[13]

Betrayal

History and popular culture, as well as our personal lives,
are filled of tales of Black women who had "compassion
for misguided black men." Our scarred, broken, battered
and dead daughters and sisters are a mute testament to
that reality. We need to learn to have care and compassion for ourselves, also.

— AUDRE LORDE

April 4, 1997. Tammy was pleased with her progress. After many tries,
she had been off heroin now for about twelve months. It had been a
nineteen-year habit. Her college classes were going well; she was only
a year away from graduation. Making up for all that lost time felt good.
Yes, finally she had pulled her life together.

The only problem was her husband, Maurice. And "problem" was
an understatement. He just couldn't stay clean, and now it was to the
point that he had stolen and pawned one of Tammy's rings to buy his
drugs. She had kicked him out of the house at least seven different
times. Then he would go into treatment, he was going to look for a
job, and she would take her husband back in again.

They had actually met in a hospital drug rehab program.

*It was love at first sight for both of us. He looked and felt
the same way. When you saw him, you saw this polished,
classy, articulate, intelligent, handsome man, who dressed to*

*the nines, well groomed. He was a male version of me. We
were a striking couple. All the time, Maurice had no job, no
car, no home. He was actually living in a halfway house
when I met him. I'm no different from any other woman.
I think I can change someone.*

As it turned out, in Maurice's case there was a lot to change. His
childhood—one big rejection—always made Tammy feel sorry for
him. Her husband's alcoholic mother, abandoned by his father early
on, had chosen to keep Maurice's sister and shipped the other two children to relatives. Without any parents, he had lived a great deal of his
life on the streets, developing this motto: Never put too much in one
place that you can't pack it up and leave within thirty minutes. And
pack up and leave is what Maurice did frequently. Whenever there
was an emergency—when Tammy's son, Terrence, had his first asthma
attack, or when they were moving to another place—that was when
Maurice ran.

*When a problem looks too big, too scary, or too painful,
run. Don't care whom you leave behind, just go. Always.
And that's the way our marriage was. The times he would
leave me and run away when I needed him the most he was
just acting like Maurice to me, because this was what he was
raised with and knew—you run away when it hurts, when
you don't know. You don't give anyone your life or your
commitment. That's why I guess that I kept letting him
come back because I knew he came from that background.*

Her husband was, Tammy says, used to being with women on welfare
or in prostitution, who, because of economic vulnerability, would sub-
mit to his commands. Because he never held down a job, he had to take
money and resources from Tammy. Maurice hated that too.

*Even though he allowed me to take care of him, he didn't
like me taking care of him. He wanted to say whom I could
see, whom I could be friends with, and where I could go. I
remember he would never even let me go to the grocery store
alone. He was always home and waiting for me and when he*

would go someplace he was constantly calling me. He even joined church so he could be there with me and he would go to Sunday school when he didn't really want to, just so he could be there with me.

Tammy wanted to believe her childhood was perfect, so she deeply buried troubling incidences of childhood sexual molestation, and at the age of eighteen fled her Saginaw, Michigan, family of two sisters and two brothers for Chicago. As a singularly attractive woman, Tammy was always involved with men. Her first husband was a gang leader who introduced her to what would be a nineteen-year heroin habit; the second was a handsome womanizer whose serious physical abuse she put up with for three years. Tammy's son was the result of an ensuing affair with a man who died in a motorcycle accident before the baby was born. Then another man, Edward, fell in love with Tammy. She did not develop an intimate relationship with him, but she did allow him to support her and Terrence; eventually Edward became so close to the two of them that he even adopted Terrence.

Tammy's third husband—Maurice—was also abusive. He was jealous of everyone, from the drug dealer to the mailman, and especially resented Edward, Terrence's adoptive father, who was financially supporting mother and son while Tammy was in college. Although he was unemployed for most of the marriage, Maurice urged Terrence not to accept money from his father. Often Tammy had to sneak out to take Terrence to see his dad. Continually, Maurice tore Tammy down mentally, accusing her of controlling and deceiving him. The verbal abuse was relentless, but unlike her second husband, Maurice had not yet resorted to violence to try to control his wife.

They had married six months after meeting in 1996. Neither Tammy's mother nor Terrence ever liked Maurice, although Terrence kept that fact to himself.

He was handsome and charismatic, but my mother and Terrence saw the demon underneath. He was a charmer. He was able to charm a lot of people, the people in the church, the people everywhere we went were charmed by this man. My mom was the only one, from the very beginning. She said there was something about him. And my son. My son never

did warm up to him. My son knew, but he didn't say anything and didn't show it. He later said, "I wanted you
happy, Mommy, but I never liked him or trusted him. But
you liked him." He told me later—he wouldn't tell me then.

Even Tammy had her doubts.

I remember my wedding day so vividly. It should have been
the happiest day of my life. I was so depressed when I
walked out of that room. I was not ready to marry him but
he wore me down.

Being with Maurice caused Tammy to return to injecting heroin, although not because Maurice's example encouraged her. Rather, Tammy
knew her husband was bad for her so she took drugs again to mask
the discomfort she felt about her marriage. And once she started up on
heroin again, Maurice followed suit. Tammy bought the drugs for both
of them.

Maurice's whole outlook on life was warped, it was so
warped. He didn't believe in commitment. He never did anything wrong, it was always the other person, there was never
anything wrong with Maurice, ever, ever. What you do with
that, is you start looking at yourself. I started looking at
myself and wondering why. Why did I always choose these
men, when I came from a perfect role model, my dad was
great. Once again, I was doing the opposite. It was being
harmful to me.

One day, after several more tries at drug treatment, including a stint
on methadone, Tammy quit heroin cold turkey. Because heroin loses
its potency after twenty-four hours, the addict has to spend time each
day procuring the day's supply of the drug. What had been exciting
now turned into what seemed like a trap.

I remember the day, the time, like it was yesterday. I woke
up and said, "I don't need it anymore," and I never went
back. I was so tired, I was so tired. I was tired of never
being able to go on vacation. To start my day with other

addicts. Sometimes I couldn't do things with Terrence because
the drug dealers were either not answering the phone or their
page. I'd have to wait. I realized that my life was not my
own. I was so trapped. I was tired of being trapped. I wanted
to feel free and that was what it was. It was the freedom I
didn't have. I had lost so much in that time. I was tired.

I was so tired of hiding it. I was so tired, all of a sudden
normal looked very attractive to me, very attractive. All those
people I thought were stupid, I now envied. I wondered what
it was like to pay your bills on time, I wondered what it
was like to pay the rent on time, instead of having an excuse
and paying it late. I was always on the edge.

While Tammy was beginning to enjoy her freedom from heroin, Maurice sank into serious substance abuse. His wife's money didn't buy him enough drugs, and since he didn't have any funds of his own that meant stealing from anybody he could and pawning everything he could get his hands on. It was in this way that Tammy's life started spiraling downward as a result of her husband's addiction. Not that Maurice didn't try to get off drugs.

He would say, "I want to go to treatment, I'm going to
do this," and he went to treatment so many times I got a
headache. I told him, "They just need to give you a key and
just let you come and go and make your residence there." I
would never know where he was until he would call a week
or two weeks later and say, "I've been in treatment." He
would give me the pay phone number there, so he was there.
Three times I went to visit him in treatment.

Again and again, Tammy let him come back. Her friends thought of it as "Tammy's temporary insanity." She just couldn't leave him or let him stay away. He seemed so vulnerable, and he needed so much love and support.

Yet the drugs were starting to take a toll financially. This was the cause of Tammy's major blunder. Her best friend, Brenda, was a high-level drug dealer who lost the safe house in which she kept her drugs. When the woman in whose home Brenda kept the narcotics broke into the stash, using so much of it she started bleeding from the brain, she caused grave economic hardship for Brenda. In response to her plight, Tammy agreed to let Brenda temporarily store the drugs in her home until she could find a permanent place. Brenda put them in a Sentry safe and only she had the key, as well as a key to Tammy's house. The safe, the size of a regular shoe box, was hidden in a closet.

At the time Tammy thought it a good plan. She needed the money for Maurice's drugs and Brenda would pay her for helping out. No one would suspect that Tammy had drugs in her home. She was the captain of the block club and worked closely with the police department. During her nineteen-year addiction she had never ever sold drugs. But drugs had become very normal and usual for Tammy over the years; she had quite forgotten they were illegal. If she hadn't needed the money for Maurice's drugs, she is sure she would not have done it.

> I knew I wasn't a criminal. In my mind I wasn't committing any crimes. I was still in that phase where money and material things were important to me. I was the only one with the money. I didn't want to take my money and go spend it on drugs. I could keep my money and I wouldn't see my husband suffer.

But the more drugs Maurice continued to use, the more nervous Tammy got about that safe, which Maurice soon learned was there in the house. About two months after the safe had arrived, Tammy asked Brenda to remove the drugs from her home. But Brenda needed to find someplace else; she couldn't drive around with a safe full of narcotics in her car. This back and forth went on for about a week.

As it happened, Brenda had just restocked the safe the day before Tammy came home with eleven-year-old Terrence and his fifteen-year-old cousin, Vonnie, the daughter of Tammy's youngest sister, Terri, who had just arrived from her home in Michigan for a visit. Sitting in the dining room in a dazed, crazed, semicomatose state was Maurice. His eyes were glassy and he seemed unusually aggressive. Suddenly, Tammy became afraid.

> I said, "My god, you're high." And he said, "So?" And I said, "You've got to get out, get out now! Get out of my

house!" He said, "I'm not going anywhere. I'm your husband, you can't put me out, the police can't put me out, I
have a right to be here."

And then Maurice began to choke Tammy. Terrence was in his room.
He heard the arguing, a normal occurrence, but this time something
didn't sound normal. When Terrence came out to investigate, he saw
Maurice pulling Tammy's head back by her hair. Maurice had never
gotten physical before. Tammy yelled to Terrence to run across the
street to the police station.

Terrence did as he was told. The police officers arrived one minute
later. They asked, "Is there a problem here?" Tammy never got a word
out. Maurice blurted, "Officer, she has drugs in this house."

CHAPTER TWO

Trial

> What other creature in the world besides the Black woman
> has had to build the knowledge of so much hatred into
> her survival and keep going? What other human being
> absorbs so much virulent hostility and still functions?
>
> — AUDRE LORDE

Maurice showed the officers the safe in the closet. Vonnie, Tammy's niece, was screaming, so the police officers dispatched the two youths to the hallway. Clamping Tammy's hands behind her back in cuffs, they led her past the children to the police car, despite Tammy's cries, "Don't do this in front of my son!" Soon thereafter, Maurice and the safe were deposited in the squad car, and they all were driven across the street to the police station, but not before Vonnie tried to physically attack Maurice for betraying her aunt. Apparently, the police thought the children old enough to fend for themselves, and they were left alone.

Tammy was locked in a cage the size of a small closet with two other women. Maurice was in a nearby cell.

> He yelled, "Tammy, don't say a word! Don't say a word!"
> I'm livid. He said, "Tammy, I'm so sorry, I'm so sorry,
> please." I said, "Don't talk to me," and I'm really hurt.

Worried about her son, Tammy wanted to go home. Once told that she could leave if she would talk to officers from the federal Drug

16   Enforcement Administration (DEA), Tammy readily agreed. About five hours after her arrival at the police station the DEA agents appeared.

If she told them everything and didn't lie about it, they explained, she could go home. Tammy spoke the truth, but drew the line at providing the name of Brenda, her drug-dealing friend. Then the DEA officers asked her permission to open the safe. Later, they claimed that her assent meant that she claimed ownership of it. A special key the agents had immediately sprung it open.

Next, they asked whether there were any other drug paraphernalia in the house. Since she couldn't resist the prospect of getting a peek to see how her eleven-year-old son was doing, Tammy agreed to show them.

> As soon as I opened the door, I ran into the bedroom. My
> son was sound asleep and my niece was in there asleep too.
> And I started kissing him and he woke up, and I don't think
> he could believe his eyes. He cried, "Mommy, Mommy,
> Mommy!"—it came to him that I was really there.
> I think he was dreaming that I would come.

Methodically, Tammy pulled the equipment down from a high cabinet— the baggies, the sifter, the scales, and the coffee grinders. When they returned to the police station, Tammy was let out on her own recognizance. Maurice wasn't charged. His sister picked him up at the police station and that was the last Tammy saw him for nine months.

Terrence vividly remembers the arrest. He didn't call anyone for help, but says he fell into a deep slumber. Today, he claims he slept for three days until his mother came home; that is how long it seemed to the eleven-year-old at the time. Loyal Vonnie, who stayed with Terrence when Tammy was at the police station, didn't even call her Aunt Pat, the middle Johnson sister in Chicago, to report the episode since she knew how judgmental Pat would be. Vonnie today has absolutely no recollection of the arrest and her attack on Maurice.

Now Tammy had to deal with her drug-dealer friend. Brenda's confederates interrogated Tammy for hours. They wondered how she was released without having to post bond; they thought Tammy had ratted on them. Surprisingly, Brenda herself was largely silent, but Brenda's mother believed in Tammy and asked them to leave Tammy alone. Telling her it all sounded "fishy," the dealers continued to abuse

Tammy, who found the encounter frightening and believed her life was in danger.

Two months later, the grand jury indictment arrived in the mail. Brenda's restocking the safe had resulted in a stash of 65.1 grams, the equivalent of 650 ten-dollar bags of heroin. Tammy was accused of possession with intent to deliver at least 15 grams or more of heroin.

After Tammy was indicted, Brenda began to act differently and the two became estranged. Brenda might have felt guilty and remorseful about not backing her during the interrogation, Tammy thinks, and undoubtedly regretted her own actions that got Tammy in trouble in the first place. When she was awaiting trial, Tammy didn't see Brenda much.

Maurice finally called. He had gotten an indictment too.

> He said, "I can't do it, Tammy. I've got a drug record."
> And he said, "I can't come back." And I said, "Okay, I
> understand, you just do what you have to do, and I'll deal
> with it." He completely disappeared.

Tammy's appearances in a felony drug night courtroom now began, and, as there were many continuances, they lasted a further ten months. Her public defender assured her she would receive probation; the disappearance of her husband pointed to his culpability and supposedly would be helpful to Tammy.

Life then delivered a series of devastating blows. Right before trial, Tammy's sixty-seven-year-old mother died of pneumonia, and the sudden death overwhelmed her. Then Tammy received a telephone call from an attorney, announcing that he was representing Maurice in a divorce action against her. Explaining that there was only so much she could take at one time, Tammy said she would deal with the matter only after the funeral and the criminal case.

Every single person blamed Tammy for her predicament.

> Maurice blamed me, because in his eyes I should never have
> called the police on him. Everyone blamed me because I called
> the police. They said, "How could you be so stupid to call
> the police on him? Why would you call the police on your
> husband?"

18   Hiding the drugs in her house seemed such a dumb move that some
family members simply didn't believe Tammy's story. Her sister Pat
says that since she thought that Tammy had to be involved in selling
drugs, she was totally outdone by what happened.

Coping with and enabling her abusive husband's drug addiction was
thus Tammy's main pathway to crime. And although Tammy hid the
drugs in a misguided effort to help Maurice, who later betrayed her,
she received all the blame.

> I took those drugs in because I needed money for his drugs.
> No one could have told me he would turn my life around like
> this when all I wanted the police to do was remove him. I
> needed help getting him out, and he wouldn't leave. Although
> I wasn't on drugs, I was still hanging around the culture. It
> was what I knew, it was comfortable. It meant nothing to
> me. There was no criminal intent. Would I have called the
> police to get him out because he was high on drugs if I
> thought I was committing a crime with a safe with drugs
> in my house?

Others asked why Tammy didn't just leave instead of calling the police.

> I could have done that, but my home would have been cleaned
> out. I wouldn't ever have left that drug addict in my home.
> If I had come back, I wouldn't have had anything.

※

April 1998. D-Day in night court. As usual, Terrence went with Tammy.

> My son and I were never separated. Every time I went to
> court he went with me, every time he went with me. He
> wanted to, and I didn't want to leave him with anyone. I
> didn't know that I was infuriating the judge when I was
> doing this, because there were a lot of children in court.
> Everybody brought their kids to court.

And Maurice was along for the ride too. When his attorney told him
about the death of his mother-in-law, he called his wife, and one sym-

pathetic communication led to another. The upshot was that he wanted to come back. He wanted to make it up to Tammy, be there for her. Maurice was still on the lam, but he now had a fake ID. Incredibly, Tammy let him come back home.

On the day of the trial Maurice got cold feet about going to court with his wife. Although he had a feeling of danger, he allowed Tammy's fears to overcome his usual impulse to cut and run.

While they sat until about ten at night waiting for the case to be called, Tammy could see the judge continually eying her and Maurice. Her husband had his arm around Tammy, draped on the back of the bench.

> This particular time she was looking at me through all her cases. You could see her looking with this horrible look on her face. So I am feeling really funny now, and I want to run, but I can't because they already promised me probation, so what do I have to be afraid of? I'm getting probation, it is going to be over in a minute.

Tammy's public defender never rebutted anything, never objected to anything, and never cross-examined anyone during the entire trial. Then the judge called Tammy up to the bench.

> She said, "You have been found guilty of the charge of man-ufacturing and delivering. I've never met a more ignorant woman in my life. How could you be so stupid," these were her words, "to let someone put some drugs in your home and put your son's life in jeopardy? And then you have brought him to court every time you have come." She said, "You are the worst mother I've ever seen, and I am sending you to jail. You deserve to go to jail. The amount of drugs that was found in that safe carries a sentence of thirty years. And sen-tencing will be one month away. Take her into custody."

As Tammy lay in the courthouse lockup crying her eyes out, the sher-iff's deputy came back and announced, "Your husband has left. Your son is here and your husband has left." It was now midnight. "Do you have relatives you can call to come and get your son?"

I said "No." I'm thinking that if I don't have anybody,
they'll let me go home with my son. I have this plan in
mind. If there's nobody to come get him, they would still
let me go home. I'm thinking that she is just mad at me.
I remember her saying I was despicable.

Next, shorn of her robe, the judge herself came back to inquire if there
was anyone to call to pick up Terrence.

I'm in tears, I say, "No, there's nobody. I don't know how
to reach anybody." She says, "I'm so sorry about that, we'll
see what we can do," and she walked out.

Alone and abandoned, Terrence sat in the judge's office. Pat, Tammy's
sister, spoke with him on the telephone, but he told her over and over
that Tammy would not want her to take care of him because of Pat's
earlier, less-than-supportive reaction to Tammy's arrest. At the time,
Pat and Tammy did not have a particularly good relationship; Pat found
Tammy's selfish, drug-induced behavior difficult to deal with. Tammy's
family had never seen Tammy use drugs, but they did know somehow
about her addiction, even though they had never talked with Tammy
about it. Given her difficulties in coping with Tammy's mood swings
and sudden aggression, Pat generally kept her distance from Tammy
and her son. So, although Pat says she was willing to come and get
Terrence, his refusal to go with her held her back.

A juvenile officer, summoned to the scene, drove Terrence to his
best friend, whose parents agreed to take him in. When by the next
day it appeared that Maurice was gone for good, Terrence changed his
mind and moved into his aunt's home.

Tammy says the judge's harsh words will stay with her forever.

The judge was so angry at me. She wanted to humiliate me.
She humiliated me in the worst way. I just wanted to shrivel
and die.

The criminal justice system, Tammy believes, underestimates the effects
of this level of humiliation on the human psyche.

The period from the little jail right behind the courtroom to the jail bull pen is when I went into shock. I lay on that bench and cried and cried. When I walked into Cook County Jail my hair was totally white. My whole head turned white.

CHAPTER THREE

County Jail

For to survive in the mouth of this dragon we call America, we have to learn this first and most vital lesson—that we were never meant to survive. Not as human beings.

— AUDRE LORDE

It was now the middle of the night, and Tammy sat in a small cage in the jail while the guards outside verbally abused her.

> You could hear them right outside your bull pen, laughing with their friends, eating, and making jokes. "Who's going to process her?" "I don't feel like it," "I don't feel like smelling her," "I just don't feel like this crap tonight." I heard one say, "I'm getting off in a little while, you do her." All women.

As she waited in the bull pen, Tammy continued to cry. Three hours passed before she was taken out for fingerprinting and photographing.

> The mug shots are probably the worst part for me. The number is given to you. I actually had to hold it because the chain holding the number that goes around the neck was missing. You are photographed from the front and then from the side. It was bad to me. It sealed my fate. In my mind the picture was captured for posterity, forever. There was

nothing that I could do about it. I've looked at mug shots
and the part that gets me is how anybody can smile in a
mug shot. I was still crying in mine. You have to understand, too, that when that shot is taken, you have already
spent a night elsewhere. So by the time you get to the pro-
cessing in the county jail you are disheveled and in shambles.

And if this weren't bad enough, the ensuing strip search brought home
the reality of Tammy's new status. A sheriff's deputy barked at Tammy,
"You'll stop crying right now, we don't have time for that, get up and
strip."

First of all they ask you to remove everything that you have
on, minus your underwear. Your clothes are tagged and put
into a plastic bag. Then your undergarments have to be examined. So you remove your panties and your bra. You have
to shake the panties and turn the bra cup inside out. The
guard takes them, examines them for any tears and breaks
around the cups, and if there aren't any, you are given them
back. The guards wear rubber gloves during this process.

Then the guard asked the now totally naked Tammy to squat three
times and cough. She was then required to bend over and spread her
buttocks while the guard looked inside. Next, she was asked to lift her
breasts up, turn the palms of her hands out, hold up the bottoms of
her feet while spreading her toes, open her mouth wide, take her fin-
gers and run them backwards through her hair, and undergo an ear
inspection.

It was very degrading to spread my buttocks. Lifting my
breasts and all of those things were not hard or degrading
because I looked in their eyes and I wasn't a person anyway.
It wasn't like they were invading my privacy, because they
didn't see me as a human being. And you could see it in
their eyes, that you weren't a person.

The officer gave Tammy a blue uniform that was big and baggy and
had a number stamped on it, an outfit resembling the scrubs worn by

medical operating room personnel. And upstairs she then went to the division that was to be her home for the next thirty days.

Tammy's new residence was a jail cell, a ten-by-ten-foot cinder-block room with a bunk bed set with pencil-thin mattresses. A narrow window at one end was covered by a mesh so thick that no light came through. Guards used a small slot, a three-inch-by-twelve-inch slit in the cell's steel door, to monitor the prisoners. A steel toilet, without lid or seat, and a small sink completed the cell's furnishings. Apparently at one time or other prisoners had removed seats and toilet bowl covers and used them as weapons, resulting in their current ban. To keep the mice out, everyone stuffed towels under the doors.

Detainees, Tammy soon learned, were sealed into these cells from ten in the evening until breakfast time. And whenever the shift changed during the day, which occurred twice, the women would be locked in and counted. At other times lockdowns would occur—when a fight broke out, something was missing, or drugs were found on the tier.

Tammy's claustrophobia made staying in that cell problematic. To make matters worse, getting the attention of the guards in an emergency could be difficult.

> The guards were behind a glass cage near the dayroom. If you screamed they wouldn't hear you. So do you know what you were supposed to do? You were supposed to wave your hand through that slit, or a towel, and they are supposed to see that on the TV monitors. But many of the times they may not glance at the monitors. So I saw occasions where the person had to get the help of everybody else. One person was sick, and all of us would scream, and all of us would wave our towels. You could talk if it was the person across from you or next to you. It was a chain reaction. Everyone would get a towel and wave it and hope that someone would finally see it. There was no buzzer system. That was scary to me.

She just had to escape being locked up all night. Her claustrophobia was one thing, but she also feared perishing in that cell for lack of attention: "If I died or became violently ill during the course of the night, I knew no one would find me until I was stiff and stinking the following morning."

Sleeping in the heat of the cells without any fresh air or movement of air also proved unbearable.

> The lack of ventilation did not have to be spoken about. You
> could see it in the skin of the prisoners. The dry, cracked
> heels and hands and the lack of color on the prisoners' faces
> told the story. We knew because we compared how we looked
> to the newcomers who had been out in the world and receiv-
> ing a sufficient amount of sunshine. Even the crack addicts
> coming in looked better than we did.

During warm weather prisoners were allowed to go out into the yard, a small space surrounded by buildings. Because it reminded her of just how confined she really was, Tammy found the yard depressing. Soon, however, the yard hours conflicted with her work schedule.

Constant noise in the tier also made sleeping difficult. Guards walking the shifts seemed to enjoy being deliberately loud when around the prisoners.

> Noise was just something you could not escape. You had to
> learn to live with it. I would pray for just one moment when
> everything was quiet. There was always noise. It was running
> up and down the corridors, something that was prohibited,
> but who was going to stop it? And the yelling back and forth
> to one another's cells.

Management worked overtime to ensure that the concrete cubicles remained jail cells with no attributes of home. Theoretically, prisoners could decorate, but they weren't allowed to place anything over the window or put anything on the walls, which left very little room for creativity. Two women across from Tammy decorated by hanging towels of every color from makeshift lines and placing them on the floor as rugs.

> Raids on the cells were a regular occurrence and for some rea-
> son the guards resented us making the cells livable, so they
> would confiscate anything that added beauty or comfort to
> the cells. They even confiscated all the pretty towels from the

*cell across from me, eventually. They also confiscated my
pictures that I had pasted on the concrete walls with tooth-
paste. One of them was Terrence. That was my lowest point
and that's when I felt life as I knew it was over.*

County's "color scheme," Tammy now realizes, was a deliberate com-
ponent of the "punishment scheme."

> *The drab, depressing colors seemed to be a prerequisite that
> correlated with the way the guards made me feel. I truly
> believe that the lack of color, the peeling paint, the dirt left
> in the corners, and the absence of any reminders of home
> contributed to the fights that occurred among the prisoners.*

As Shelley Williams, a prisoner in Division 4 of the Cook County Jail,
sums it all up in part of her poem:

> Nasty, dirty people surround you all day.
> Small rooms, steel toilets and hard bunk beds.
> Roaches the size of mice and mice the size of rats.
> Cold food, sleepless nights.
> Make a phone call, yeah, right.
> You can't hear anything anyway.[1]

In the beginning, none of the other women approached Tammy or befriended her. Because Tammy was so uncomfortable, she went back to
her cell.

> *I didn't eat. I didn't eat for, it had to be five days. I didn't
> know anything, I didn't know what had happened to my son.
> I didn't know how to call. There is a phone right there in
> the tier, in the dayroom. I didn't know. I was afraid to go
> in the dayroom. I stayed in my cell most of the time. After
> awhile, I became so enmeshed in my misery that the cell
> seemed appropriate for the way I was feeling. I felt like I
> was in hell and the cell was where people in hell slept.*

And she quickly developed suicidal thoughts.

> I was already so mentally sick and so mentally whipped,
> coming off drugs, and so mentally drained, that at the mo-
> ment, in those first hours in County I was in a black pit,
> and I knew that I was going to try to die. And everything
> was just going through the motions until I could find the
> way and the opportunity to die. Because it just couldn't get
> any worse than that.

Finally one woman befriended her, explaining how she could make collect calls on the telephones in the dayroom, and at long last Tammy located and spoke with Terrence. Since Maurice had contacted sister Pat with his whereabouts, she was eventually able to speak with her husband and direct him to pay some bills.

Still, Tammy remained tearful and fearful. Mainly she was afraid of the other incarcerated women and she could not figure out the rules. She wanted to obey them but there just didn't seem to be any consistency. Every guard shift appeared to have a different approach.

The young woman who inadvertently rescued Tammy from this phase was appealing a murder conviction. It was she who passed out the lunch trays in the dayroom. One day Tammy had just begun to eat.

> She gave me my tray. We were so excited because we had
> chocolate cake that day. My tray was missing the chocolate
> cake. So I sat down and started to cry. I wanted that cake
> so badly. She looked behind her, and she said, "What's the
> matter with you?" I said, "I don't have any cake," and she
> said, "What, you stupid bitch," and she pulled another tray
> out and gave me a piece of cake, and then another, "Here's
> another one, here's another one." I don't know why that
> piece of chocolate cake was so important. I know that it
> changed my life, because after that I said, No more, I'm
> pitiful here, something's gotta change, I am really
> pitiful. So I picked myself off the floor and decided to see
> what was going on with my life. I've got to be here,
> so I'm going to make the most of it. So let's start
> talking to people and see what's going on.

First, Tammy had to find a way to deal with her fear of enclosed places.

*I am so extremely claustrophobic, I am the screaming,
pulling-my-hair-out kind of claustrophobic. So I knew I was
in jail and I had to transcend myself, go someplace else, and
that is how I made it through. That to me was horrible.*
*I used the same technique that battered women and sexually
abused children use, that same mechanism. Disassociation.*
*I had to use that. I would put myself back home, and that
is how I made it through.*

Her other step was to secure a job on the late shift, from eleven at
night to seven in the morning, the hours when she would have been
locked up in that small cement cell where the lack of air conditioning
or ventilation made it seem like a concrete tomb. Prisoners were not
required to work at the jail, but Tammy grabbed at the opportunity for
employment (at one dollar a day) in food service, a night job preparing the next day's food.

Several other advantages to Tammy's job accrued. Those who worked
in food service could eat their meals in the kitchens where the food
was still hot; by the time it reached the tiers it was stone cold. To deal
with the cold food, the women developed creative strategies. They
wrapped the baloney and cheese sandwich in paper towels and tied it
to the back of the large industrial fan in the dayroom so that the heat
from the back of the fan would melt the cheese. Running hot water
over the cup, covered by another cup, for fifteen minutes warmed up
cold soup.

Another bonus was that at the end of the night's shift Tammy's boss
would give each incarcerated woman a filtered cigarette.

*That was gold. She would take us outside, right outside the
gate at the end, and we would sit out there and dream that
we were on the outside and we would smoke a cigarette. I
used to look up at the stars and pretend not to see the brick
walls that surrounded me, and I would dream that I was
wearing high heels and a pretty suit instead of the ill-fitting
blue uniform and the ugly, flat, blue gym shoes. It was like
escaping to a paradise and the smell of that one cigarette was
the most pleasant aroma as I inhaled it deep into my lungs
as if it would be the last thing I did. It was heaven. We*

*worked like dogs for the end of that night to smoke that cig-
arette and to sit out in the free air.*

Amazingly, prisoners who worked the night shift were not allowed to
have any special sleep time. Despite repeated requests, they were always required to go immediately out into the yard after their work
shift ended in the morning. Finally, when the social worker went to
bat for the night workers they were able to return to their cells to get
some sleep, but the noise on the tier frequently interrupted proper rest.

One night Tammy came within a hair's breath of losing the assignment that took her out of that locked cell. To save her job she had to
endure a major humiliation, the memory of which causes trauma to
this very day. While they were on the elevator going to the kitchens,
Tammy and her coworkers were discussing some new and irrational
rule or order. Protesting the change and complaining about the deputy
who had instigated it, Tammy talked on and on. A guard got on the
elevator and overheard. The next thing she knew, the officer on the elevator, accompanied by the woman deputy who had made the change,
confronted Tammy at her place of work.

> She said, "You, the lowest of the low scum. How dare you
> say anything? You have nothing to say. I'll take your job
> from you right now. Tell me you're sorry." I thought about
> it. I thought, A dollar a day, I'm fighting this for a
> dollar a day. I haven't done anything wrong. She
> said, "You'll get locked up right now and I'll keep your cell
> locked up and I'll tell the next guard to come on and keep
> you on a three-day lockdown." And I thought about it. And
> I said, I have to do this. I apologized for talking to
> someone else. She humiliated me. I had to literally beg her
> not to take my job from me, beg her not to. And I think
> that was pretty awful.

Adding to the stress of Tammy's days was the verbal abuse from many
of the deputies. Some would feel the need to remind her, "You're a
number now, you're the property of Cook County." And they would
talk loudly among themselves when prisoners were nearby: "She's just
a ho," or a "dope fiend," or a "bitch."

30   The female guards were the most unsympathetic.

> I think they thought we were a disgrace to our race. They
> think we should have had the strength to say "no" to a man.
> They look down on us as weak. They thought we were the
> weakest women in the world. They couldn't conceive of
> killing your husband because he beat you day and night for
> seven years, they couldn't conceive of prostitution, drugs,
> they thought we were weak women.
>
> The verbal abuse would be if they gave us an order and
> we didn't jump fast enough. We would be verbally abused
> if we looked the wrong way. If we muttered something under
> our breath. The whole tier collectively would be verbally
> abused if the floor wasn't mopped right.
>
> I'm crying and I'm lost and you tell me to shut up and
> move, or you make me sit here while you're laughing and
> talking about the dates you have or the house you bought,
> and I have lost everything that I know is near and dear to
> me. I'm already drowning and you throw me a lead pipe.

Tammy remembers thinking she was equal to the officers, and was
angry because they did not know it.

> I wanted to pound it into their heads that I wasn't this ter-
> rible person and I wanted them to understand and feel some
> measure of empathy for me. I knew there were so many
> women that were there that did not deserve to be there. I
> heard their pains and sorrows. I felt their hopelessness and
> defeat. It was real. I heard their stories and knew that they
> were there for one bad choice, not a lifestyle. But the jail
> did not differentiate. We were all felons and criminals.

After awhile, Tammy actually began to believe she was worthless and
it is not easy for her, even today, to remember that she is not. She believes that the effects of the verbal abuse will remain with her forever.

> It will never go away. The humiliation and the helplessness
> and the hopelessness. No matter what is said, and even if it

is a lie, and even if you know it's not true, you can't verbally defend yourself for fear of further retribution. You suck
it in, and after awhile you've got this whole thing inside
with all this negative stuff that you have sucked in and
sucked in, and you have a cancer sore that's grown and
grown and wipes away all your self-esteem.

From the time of admission, explains Tammy, the jail culture is deliberately designed to humiliate the detainees.

You are overwhelmed by the chains on your legs, or the glass
between the visitors, or the strip searches. They want you to
be overwhelmed. We're like cattle, we're not people anymore.
We're not worthy of any privacy. The mentality is, that
when you become a property and get a number, all your
rights are stripped away, you have no privacy, you have no
rights. Sadistic. And guess who they blame for recidivism?
Us. And they share no responsibility for the revolving door.

And the mortifying strip searches continued. In thirty days, Tammy endured at least fifteen of them. During the procedure, the guards carried on conversations among themselves as if the women weren't even
there. Because they usually took place in groups, the searches were
even more dehumanizing. "We tried not to look at one another because the pain was so great, but you could cut the air with a knife,"
says Tammy. She never got used to the strip searching.

It reminded me where I was. I felt like a number, like an
object—it stripped away the human part of me. I felt like a
criminal, like I wasn't a person anymore. The strip searches
and the invasion into my body and my private parts were
probably the main factors that let me know that I had lost
all rights as a human being.

Pat brought Terrence to see Tammy a few times in the jail. During
visits the parties were only able to view each other through a large sheet
of glass. Tammy was all skin and bones and white-haired, and did not
want her son to see her like that. Pat found the jail visiting a horror too.

You have the glass, and then you have this little hole that
you are talking through, but you can hardly hear. People
are right next to you, there is no privacy, and you're
shouting, trying to hear, and everyone else is shouting.
It is really cramped and it's not even clean.

Maurice, though, came faithfully every week. He would bring the mail
and the bills, receiving instructions from Tammy about how to handle
everything.

Terror was Tammy's main emotion while in jail. She was afraid of
the guards, fearful of not doing the right thing, and worried about
whom she might upset. The ever-changing rules and regulations continued to strike fear into her.

A large majority of the women in the jail were involved with drugs
on the outside, had charges that involved selling, and had been dealing to support their habit; at the end of the day they received a small
amount of money and their drugs from the dealer. Most of the women
wouldn't have been out dealing if they weren't using illegal substances
themselves. Tammy realized that there were a few women not using
narcotics who had been involved in the drug trade. Selling drugs is a
source of quick and easy money, but power is the job's major attraction. By virtue of the reflected power and glory of the boss, the large
dealer, people tend to leave you alone and you will never be robbed.
But more importantly a dealer, no matter how small, always has power
over the addict, who desperately needs him or her on a daily basis.

From her jail conversations, Tammy learned that drugs were also
involved in other charges as well. In most of the assaults, the prisoner
had been high at the time; all the frauds were perpetrated by addicts
too. And there were always a few cases in which men had deliberately
placed their women in harm's way. One rather plain young girl had
fallen in love with a handsome and popular drug dealer, who obviously manipulated and took advantage of her infatuation. Numerous
times she unwittingly served as a courier for him, delivering packages
and envelopes. A long sentence was her fate.

For the most part the other detainees were kind to Tammy, whom
they knew was scared, confused, and weepy. But the many fights among
the women and the behavior of some constituted traps that were important to avoid. Undoubtedly, the aggression reflected a need to seek

and exercise power in an atmosphere of total disempowerment, and other actions could be attributed to a necessary release of anger. Understanding and having compassion for the prisoners, however, did not necessarily make them any easier to deal with.

Most of the fights involved cigarettes. Unless they were in the boot camp tier, prisoners at County were not allowed to have tobacco. One especially brutal row occurred when the system erroneously delivered several packs of roll-ups (tobacco used to make homemade cigarettes) to a particularly timid woman on Tammy's tier, who suddenly became a celebrity. Two tough-looking women began a pitched physical battle over who was going to become the celebrity person's "agent," who would protect the prisoner from having her booty ripped off, while taking a cut of it for herself. As a result of the violence, both combatants were escorted to solitary confinement.

> I never saw solitary in County, but I heard enough about it
> to make me even more of a shy mouse than they had turned
> me into. I also knew not to be anywhere near a fight because
> it would be so easy for me to become involved by accident.

And it was over a cigarette that Tammy came close to her own fight. Usually she tried to mind her own business and just cried a lot, but sometimes things would get to her and the bottled-up anger needed release. One night the regular guard who supervised the kitchen workers was ill and a substitute took over. Having been advised of the cigarette treat bestowed at the end of the night's work, the substitute brought out an entire pack of tobacco. Stating that it was up to the women to get it back to the tier, he put it in the hands of one prisoner to divide among all the workers.

> She did not divide it but kept it all to herself. If that wasn't
> bad enough, she further humiliated us by asking us to do
> horrible, immoral acts on the promise that she would give us
> our tobacco if we conformed to her wishes. I did not want to
> perform to get what was given to me, and for the first time
> while I was there I wanted to fight. Instead I prayed that
> God would remove me from this hell, or at least remove the
> desire to smoke. I finally realized that my existence in this
> place would go smoother if I did not have any vices.

34 Tammy says the most difficult thing was this: to survive she needed to
fit in with the other prisoners, but she did not want to fit in. That was
because so many of the women, having been in jail or prison before,
seemed resigned to their fate, complacent somehow. Not that Tammy
felt superior to them, but she did not want to believe that being in jail
defined her true self. And so many of the women were so angry all
the time.

> I did not want to be angry anymore. It took too much
> energy. I wasn't so confused that I did not know that just
> one slip and I would lose my identity, who I was, what I
> believed, and the heart that I had. I was not willing to give
> that up. When I saw myself slipping deeper and deeper is
> when I made a pact with myself that I would not become
> one of them.

Some openly lesbian prisoners importuned Tammy for a sexual relationship. They told her she was gay but didn't know it. Dealing with
this issue also caused confusion.

> I'm lost, I'm in jail, I need someone to hold me and someone
> to say it's all right. On some level I want this person who is
> constantly hitting on me to do it, but I am confused and I'm
> scared. I'm straight. I'm not making myself be straight, I
> am straight.

Whenever Tammy dwells on her incarceration at County, she relives
the trauma which time has not, and may never, heal. The only way to
eliminate the effects of the ordeal from her daily life today, she says,
is not to think about it.

> It really hurts to remember. The thought of it really happen-
> ing to me is a little more than I can bear right now. I won-
> der if people really know how much incarceration traumatizes
> anyone. We have to find a different, more humane way to
> punish.
>   I believe that when a guard fills out an initial employ-

ment application, there is a question on there that asks if he or she has compassion, and if the answer is "yes," he or she is not hired. The first two weeks of my incarceration, I cried all the time. I would sit directly in front of the guards' booth where they could see me, and I cried.

Why did Tammy do this?

I just wanted someone to look at me and see me. I didn't want anything but someone to see a person, in tears. I knew they couldn't release me, fix the problem, or help. I just wanted to see compassion or empathy in one person's eyes.

I was an animal in a cage, with so many other animals. I lost my first name because everyone was called by their last name or number only. I lost my identity, my respect, my soul, and I could feel the loving heart that I had all my life slipping away. My heart was the one thing I wanted to keep.

I would look in the faces of these guards and wonder if they were even human. I wondered what kind of person could have a job like this. I wondered if the politicians knew what we were going through. I wondered why we had to suffer so horribly because of a mistake, and why we could not have a little color on the walls to lift our spirits. I wondered why we could not have pictures of our families on the walls. I wondered if anyone knew how lost I was, if they knew I was slowly losing my mind. And I wondered if the guards ever thought about us once they left the jail.

*

Tammy didn't know it then, but this was her first encounter with the new penology, America's current retreat from rehabilitation to the deliberate infliction of prison pain, intended to punish wrongdoers. Journalist Steve Bogira observed the same verbal brutalization of incoming detainees at the Cook County Jail that Tammy experienced, and confirmed through interviews that it is intentional, a standard operating practice for both men and women prisoners. Its main purpose, he found, was control. The deputies could not be armed, lest a detainee seize a weapon.

There's a method to the deputies' malice, Sergeant Thomas says later: it's to let the prisoners know immediately who's in charge in the courthouse.

"Control is something we cannot relinquish," the sergeant says. "If we did that, we'd be fucked up right away. Extremely. . . . We're armed with gloves, handcuffs, and attitude."[2]

And that attitude, as Tammy also experienced, is extreme in its viciousness. To the snickers of other deputies, one officer mocks a trembling detainee with MS as having PMS.[3] Bogira continues:

> A different deputy gives the welcoming speech to the second bedraggled collection, reminding these men "what a fucked-up bunch of smelly motherfuckers" they are. There's never a lack of volunteers among the deputies for the honor of delivering the welcoming talk, with each succeeding speaker trying to outbadass the last one. "Some of 'em get off on it more than others," Sergeant Thomas says.[4]

Later, a female officer informs Bogira that the other guards will brand those who treat prisoners with dignity as "sissies." She agrees that most of the jail deputies, as Tammy noticed, genuinely appear to hold the prisoners in contempt as worthless scum.[5] One lieutenant informs Bogira, "We get the dregs of humanity here. If these people moved in next door to you, your lawn would die."[6]

Although there has been a definite retreat from ideas of rehabilitation, experts like psychologist Craig Haney believe that facility overcrowding has caused most of the harsh prison regimes we see today; the large increase in incarceration without accompanying budget rises for operating expenses means that authorities spend most of their time identifying, classifying, and managing groups sorted by dangerousness.[7] "The task is managerial, not transformative," explain two academics who have long studied the U.S. system.[8]

And the rise in the incarceration rate in the United States, which began in the mid-1970s, has been dramatic. By the end of 2004, there were 2,267,787 persons incarcerated in U.S. federal or state adult prisons, local jails, and juvenile facilities.[9] Currently, the rate of female incarceration is increasing at double that of the yearly increase for men, reflecting both lower base numbers for women and the way this population is catching up.[10] The 104,848 women locked up at the end of 2004 represent a 740 percent expansion since 1980. It's a startling fact: for most of the years of the twentieth century, we imprisoned 5,000 to 10,000 women; the tenfold increase occurred in the final two decades of the century.[11]

Many more women are under the supervision of probation and parole officers, and these numbers have grown exponentially as well and at higher rates than the equivalent numbers for men. At the end of 2004, the Department of Justice reported that the number of women on probation was 957,600, representing 23 percent of the adults on probation, up from 21 percent in 1995.[12] Many, unable to meet the conditions of probation due to continued drug use, will eventually be incarcerated. As would be expected, the overwhelming majority of probationers nationally were convicted of nonviolent crimes.[13] When the number of women on parole is figured in (94,400),[14] there were a total of 1,156,848 women under the supervision of the criminal justice system at the end of 2004.

Women's incarceration obviously affects their families. Approximately 70 percent of the women under correctional supervision in 1998 had children under the age of eighteen, a total of almost four million children.[15] In that year, 65 percent of women in state prisons and 59 percent in federal facilities had minor children—a quarter of a million children who had been deprived of their primary caretaker.[16]

Women of color are hugely overrepresented in state and federal prisons and jails. At the end of 2004, almost half the females incarcerated were women of color; 33 percent of the women were Black (16 percent were Hispanic),[17] when Black women represented only 10 percent of the female population eighteen and over, according to the 2000 census.[18] Black females were more than four times as likely as white women to be incarcerated on December 31, 2004.[19] Female prisoners also have fewer economic resources than males who are locked up; in 1998, 40 percent of the women, as compared to 60 percent of the men, said they had been employed full time prior to their arrest, and 37 percent of women (compared to 28 percent of men)

38   had incomes less than $600 per month before arrest. About 30 percent of incarcerated women were receiving welfare prior to their arrest.[20]

Drugs account for the bulk of the increase in the prison population. Arrests on drug charges in the United States tripled between 1980 and 2001, with the number of persons imprisoned for a drug crime increasing by 1,195 percent during this same period.[21] Recently, researchers have found that this rise in the rate of state incarceration can be attributed to police practices as well as to state sentencing approaches.[22]

And in Illinois, Tammy's state, the number of arrests for drug crimes nearly quadrupled between 1980 and 1999, with the Chicago metropolitan area—43 percent of the state's population—accounting for almost two-thirds of all drug charges in the state. Seventy-two percent of all persons arrested for three years during the late 1990s in Illinois were African Americans.[23]

A greater willingness than in the past to apprehend women for drug crime is certainly fueling the increase in female imprisonment. Forty percent of women prisoners in state and federal facilities in 1998 said they had been under the influence of drugs when the crime for which they were incarcerated occurred, compared to 32 percent of males; when alcohol is added to the mix, the figure rose to 50 percent.[24] Sixty percent reported they had used drugs the month before the crime.[25] In 2003, 68 percent of adult female detainees, included in the Arrestee Drug Abuse Monitoring (ADAM) Program at twenty-five U.S. sites, tested positive for one of five different illicit drugs, and 24 percent were positive for more than one.[26] Only 20 percent of women in state prison, 12 percent in jails, and 7 percent in federal prison in 2004 had committed violent offenses, with property, drug, and public order crimes making up the rest.[27] Drug crimes accounted for half the rise in the number of women held in state facilities from 1986 to 1996, according to the Sentencing Project's analysis of women's imprisonment.[28]

✳

Tammy's jail ordeal was nearing its end. Thirty long days had passed, and it was time for her to return to court for sentencing. In Chicago, the felony courthouse is attached to the jail complex. This short transfer from jail to court always involved humiliation of the worst kind and treatment that even zoo animals do not receive. All the prisoners go to court in the prison scrubs, which undoubtedly prejudices their case before judge or jury, and they travel in handcuffs and shackles. They are deposited in the bull pen behind the courtrooms at five o'clock in the morning, even though their cases may not be scheduled until night court.[29] About thirty women are jammed into one small cell with some benches, an open steel toilet without seat or cover, and a small, rusted sink. Due to the lack of seats, most women have to sit on the floor, wedged in like sardines. When she used the open toilet in front of everyone without a thought, Tammy realized how much she had become inured to her dehumanization within the last month.

After being in the bull pen all day and most of the evening, Tammy entered the courtroom late that night to find her pastor and the assistant pastor. Her minister had arrived when court was to start at 4:00 p.m. and had sat there for eight hours without moving.

> They called me out in these blues. I had lost so much weight.
> My hair was white, I was a wreck. I stood before the judge.
> She said, "Do you have anything to say before the sentenc-
> ing? Put your arms down at your side." I had them in the
> back of me, I don't know why.

Trying to speak on her behalf, Tammy's pastor offered to take Tammy in and be responsible for her during house arrest. In response, the judge told him that he seemed a nice man, she appreciated his coming, and was sorry he was here so late, but Tammy was going to prison.

Then the judge addressed Tammy. She told her that her son's school had reported that Terrence had said there was drug usage in her home. From her remarks it was obvious to Tammy that earlier the judge had believed her story, but had changed her mind during the trial, with the presentencing investigations confirming her suspicions that Tammy herself was a user and a dealer. "You are nothing but a drug addict, a dressed-up drug addict," she remembers the judge saying, "and a ter-rible mother who doesn't care about her son or herself." Tammy was deeply embarrassed that her pastors had to hear this. But finally she heard her fate: five years to be served at a downstate women's prison.

At this deeply humiliating moment, Tammy got weak in the knees. A private attorney, whom Brenda had retained for the sentencing, had to grab her to prevent her from falling to the floor. When Tammy asked

40   the attorney to find out if the judge would let her go home to straighten out her affairs and close up her house before going to prison, the judge lost her temper.

> She's not going anywhere. She's been wearing this mask
> like she's an upstanding citizen and all the time she's a
> drug dealer and selling drugs and putting her life in jeop-
> ardy. People say she stole from them to buy her drugs.

Ironically, what should have been the worst moment of Tammy's life was not. Finally she had closure. Tammy no longer had to wonder how long she would get, and she actually felt relief. A five-year sentence required only two years of actual time to be served, the attorney said, but Tammy did not believe her. "She could have given you thirty years," she exclaimed. "Consider that a gift."

※

Tammy's abrupt and shocking removal to Cook County Jail, which left her son totally abandoned, rested on the judge's belief that Tammy, as a drug dealer, was the quintessential bad mother whom the community needed to punish. Now consider the recent case of Atlanta Braves shortstop Rafael Furcal. On probation for a drunk driving conviction, he violated the terms of his supervision with his second arrest for driving under the influence. Just before game one of the play-off series against Houston in October 2004, Furcal was sentenced to a mere twenty-one days in jail and twenty-eight days in a treatment center. And in a development even more striking than this lenient sentence, the sports star was permitted to continue playing in the baseball series and begin his sentence in the Cobb County Adult Detention Center in Marietta, Georgia, at the end of the postseason.[30] Given Furcal's standing in the community, three weeks in jail was considered shock enough. For Tammy, an unemployed Black mother and former heroin addict, a two-year prison sentence was required. What is going on here?

Police, prosecutors, and judges now feel increasingly more comfortable arresting and incarcerating women for drug crimes. Indeed, the War on Drugs, an endeavor bent on removing drug users from city neighborhoods, seems to have especially targeted drug-using mothers. Based on her evaluation of Tammy as a bad and irresponsible mother, the judge's harsh sentence seems to reflect society's general beliefs.

For one thing, the woman drug addict is adjudged a more-hard-core criminal than a male. Women in our society are burdened with the responsibility of transmitting moral values and attitudes thought to immunize against drug abuse. When they become addicts themselves, the crime is thus considered more serious.[31]

As persons who bear children, women who are on drugs are seen as abusing that particularly important social responsibility; the woman addict is the very embodiment of a female who rejects her female role.

> If women are seen to "abuse" in any way their already-
> abused bodies, they are seen to be worse than their male
> counterparts. This is because these women are seen to
> defile and indeed to desecrate the sacred symbol of their
> sexual essence: their bodies, which house their wombs
> or reproductive power. While the female body is the
> embodiment of women's reproductive nature, sub-
> stance abuse is seen as an attack on women's nature.
> A substance-abusing woman is the quintessence of
> a wicked woman defiling her body with harmful
> substances.[32]

Jill McCorkel undertook recent extensive research in a medium security prison on the East Coast of the United States. During an interview the warden was not reticent about expressing a sense of the weirdness of her female charges:

> Poor men stick somebody up or sell drugs. To me, as
> strange as this may sound coming from a warden, that
> is understandable. I can see how you would make that
> choice. Women degrade themselves. Selling themselves—
> you should hear some of the stuff they do. There is no
> sense of self-respect, of dignity. . . . There is something
> wrong on the inside that makes an individual take up
> those kind of behaviors and choices.[33]

And a correctional officer who had worked at the same prison for four years commented on the women's lack of the maternal instinct:

I'm a mother of two and I know what that impulse,
that instinct, that mothering instinct feels like. It just
takes over, you would never put your kids in harm's
way. . . . Women in here lack that. Something in their
nature is not right, you know? They run out and leave
their kids alone, babies, while they score drugs or go over
to their boyfriend's house, you know? . . . That's a sign
something is wrong, some kind of psychological problem
or something.[34]

Thus women drug addicts appear to reject core womanly values; they
are seen as defiant and stigmatized as impure and despicable. Not only
have they abandoned their role as guardians of moral standards, they
are also bad mothers and wives, out of control—in short, polluted
women. Like Tammy, ex-prisoner Margaret Pereira believes the presence
of the twelve-year-old son in her life at the time of her sentencing on
a drug charge was a large factor in the harshness of the sentence for
cannabis possession.

I feel that my son was only taken into account as a reason
to despise me for not adhering to an expected, stereo-
typical female role, and to justify giving me a longer sentence. There was no consideration given to my personal
circumstances or thought given to whether prison was an
appropriate response to my individual situation or to the
12-year-old who would become the ultimate victim of
my incarceration.[35]

Carlen and Worrall point out that because relatively few women go to
prison, the public erroneously believes that those who do must have
committed very serious crimes, and upon release women serve a double
stigma:

This is primarily because a male convict is seen only as
being a bad citizen whereas, because women criminals
have traditionally been seen to be "unnatural" women, a
woman prisoner is likely to be seen as being both a bad

citizen and an unnatural woman. Not only has she offended against the state; she has also offended against her
femininity.[36]

Hard and punitive prison conditions for women may result from this
view of the toughness and immorality of women drug users. To make
an impression on these "irresponsible mothers," the atmosphere must
be harsh, it is reasoned, and furthermore, these austere settings will
not harm them. As Angela Harris has written, "You don't pamper a vicious beast; the only language it understands is force."[37] Our concern
about Tammy is seen as misplaced, a weak and liberal response to a
serious problem.

Furthermore, over the past decade a striking consistency in the language of welfare reform and criminal justice in the United States
involving "personal responsibility" has developed. Indeed, "personal
responsibility" has been the theme of U.S. approaches to antipoverty
policy for women since the 1980s. Welfare dependency has been seen
as a personal failing, the result of poor decisions in women's domestic and work lives. Because those on welfare are generally seen as irresponsible, they are now required to seek work and are subject to
sanctions for all kinds of omissions, from not seeking paternity testing
to failing to immunize their children.[38] It's a harsh response that assumes that welfare recipients must be forced to "take responsibility"
for better life choices that break their dependency on state support and
improve their mothering skills.

This concept of dependency and personal responsibility has now
permeated into the criminal justice system, where women's crime is
viewed as the result of dysfunctional, dependent relationships with
men or illegal substances, or both. Those relying on such relationships
are seen as abnormal and equated with welfare queens or even slaves.
Although the dependency framework acknowledges the role violent
relationships and drugs play in women's crime, it places the blame
solely on the women for being "criminally dependent" on their abusers.
It is for the women to take responsibility for this dependency and
transform their attitudes and actions.[39]

Prison officials, say researchers, now justify harsh punishment for
women within their facilities with the need to teach individual responsibility and independence.[40] A senior prison counselor in a women's

44   prison explained to researcher Jill McCorkel why this type of punishment is now important.

> Punishment, but I prefer to say "accountability," teaches
> people that there are consequences for their actions. This
> works for rational thinkers who weigh the costs and
> benefits before doing a crime but it also works for those
> who've spent their lives dependent on others telling
> them what to do. It's possible for someone to be *criminally
> dependent.* . . . most of them in here are. They need to un-
> derstand that they are responsible for their actions and
> that their actions, and their actions alone, will determine
> what happens to them. It's really a basic empowerment
> principle.[41]

Stereotypes about Black women disseminated by politicians and the media in the 1980s and '90s may have also encouraged police and the courts to make women of color targets in the War on Drugs. Demonizing women of color began with the campaign against the non-working "welfare queens" during the Reagan administration, gained momentum with the opprobrium directed at crack mothers later on in that decade, and continued with the outrage about promiscuous, school-dropout, minority teen mothers in the 1990s. A racialized and gendered image of drug users in our communities emerged from the media frenzy over crack babies.[42] More recently, poor women of color have been associated with international couriers in the drug trade, stereotypes that make them special targets of law enforcement at borders and in airports.[43]

Not only are the women seen as harming themselves and their families, but they are also thought to be undercutting the very fabric of society, leading to a series of policy initiatives that continue to this day to dismantle income security programs and other social safety nets.[44] And the face of each of these social parasites is always Black. Wahneema Lubiano reminds us that the Black welfare mother was considered to be the cause of all the dysfunctions in the Black community:

> She is the agent of destruction, the creator of the patho-
> logical, black, urban, poor family from which all ills flow;

a monster creating crack dealers, addicts, muggers, and
rapists—men who become those things because of being
immersed in her culture of poverty.[45]

In the last decade, legal changes have also enabled more women to be
charged and convicted of drug crimes primarily organized by their hus-
bands or boyfriends. For example, in 1988 Congress added conspiracy
to commit a drug offense to the list of crimes requiring mandatory
minimum penalties, which has caused many a girlfriend of a drug dealer
to be held liable for all his acts.[46] Accomplice liability is another means
to involve a girlfriend in criminal charges, as is the theory of constructive possession, which presumes possession of contraband based on
proximity and degree of control, making women vulnerable to charges
of possession of drugs placed in their home by a family member, partner, or friend.[47] Some experts believe that low-level dealers like women
receive the statutorily required sentence while their partners can bar-
gain for lower charges because, unlike the women, they have information that can finger others.[48]

These uncompromising approaches in the War on Drugs punish
women like Tammy who remain with a boyfriend or husband engaged
in drug activity. And some of the time, the women's partners are
abusers who physically coerce them to help out. In 1993 Sally Smith
was sentenced to life without parole in Michigan after being convicted
of conspiracy with intent to deliver over 650 grams of cocaine, based
on two telephone calls she made to collect money for her boyfriend
and two receipts she signed. Unfortunately the judge would not consider the fact that Sally's partner had brutally beaten and threatened to
kill her and one of her family members if she left him, and, in fact,
refused to admit any evidence of the domestic violence or the testimony of expert witnesses that Smith's long history of abuse left her
incapable of exercising free will.[49]

Evidentiary rulings in this case and the disproportionate sentence reflect a remarkable harshness toward women involved with drugs, but
also illustrate the court's refusal to incorporate the reality of domestic
violence in the lives of women. Although President Bill Clinton's last
minute pardons caused controversy in 2001, the clemency he granted
to two battered women, Kimba Smith and Dorothy Gaines, both serving long sentences for accomplice or conspiracy drug crime, was not

widely reported. Gaines's boyfriend was involved in a drug cartel, whose other members implicated her in order to reduce the length of their own sentences. No drugs or drug paraphernalia were found in her home or among her possessions. Based on this testimony, despite her and her partner's denial of Gaines's involvement, she received a nineteen-year sentence for conspiracy to distribute crack cocaine.[50]

In 1999 Tammy's judge had the power to provide an individualized sentence, but several years later the Illinois legislature cut off the ability to craft a more rehabilitative or therapeutic response, in lieu of incarceration, to persons like Tammy convicted of drug possession. In 2002 lawmakers approved a mandatory minimum four-year prison sentence for Tammy's crime—85 percent of which actually had to be served—resulting in a sentence a year and four months longer than Tammy was incarcerated for in 1999.[51] Thus the new law represents an approval of the approach the judge took in Tammy's case.

✳

Because everybody told her the prison was a much easier place than Cook County Jail, Tammy couldn't wait for her transfer. But she was dealt a big blow the day of her shipment. The women weren't given advance notice of their transfer, but on the day she learned she was to leave she did manage to telephone Maurice. That was when she first found out that he was in the process of selling all her possessions, closing the house, and taking off again. He would no longer continue to be there for her, even sporadically.

Tammy felt she was close to breakdown.

> I remember thinking, "If I think about this, I'm not going
> to make it, and I can't do this time if I wonder what is
> going to happen to all my stuff." That stuff is extremely
> important to me. It was who I was, it defined everything.
> I had things my mom had given me, and she had died the
> year before. All my son's baby pictures and records.

Only later did Tammy learn that Maurice had stashed some of these personal items into a rental locker. But he disposed of everything that could be sold, including the camera and her jewelry.

Before she entered the white prison bus, deputies strip-searched

Tammy. Altogether there were ten women in the vehicle, all happy to be leaving hell for a better location, even though it was seventy-three miles further away from their families. After the bus entered the largest gates Tammy had ever seen, guards inspected it to make certain that there was no jail escapee on it. Then, upon arrival, another strip search occurred. This one was to make certain that a woman wasn't bringing anything in, like letters or pictures. You can bring only yourself to prison.

> Most prisoners try to smuggle in pictures of family or their children. I had a picture of my son that I actually had to tear up and throw away. Rather than it falling in other hands, I tore it up.

CHAPTER FOUR

Prison

> And most of all, how do I fight the despair born of fear
> and anger and powerlessness which is my greatest internal
> enemy?
>
> — AUDRE LORDE

The postage-stamp size of the two-person cell to which Tammy was assigned in the maximum security unit made the county cells seem like suites in comparison. When Tammy lay on the top bunk she could touch the ceiling of the cell, and if she leaned a little bit, she could touch the wall across from her.

> Put it this way. You and your roommate cannot come in and
> out at the same time. Actually, the only way that you and
> your roommate can be in the cell at the same time is if one
> is on the bed.

Situated just eight inches away from the bottom bunk was the worst part, the toilet—just a steel hole. No matter what you had to do, you had to do it in the face of your roommate. As in County, the guards centrally locked the doors and turned off the electricity when "lights out" hit each evening. For Tammy, the cells were the most dehumanizing aspect of prison. She couldn't stand being sealed into such a small space; although there was an emergency buzzer, Tammy continued to fear dying in that cell for lack of attention.

In fact, she did see a woman nearly expire in a nearby cell. Although for days Tammy and others demanded attention for a sick woman who was rolled up in a ball on her bed, the prisoner was only rushed to the hospital after she went into a coma; she died soon afterwards. Buried in a pauper's grave on the prison property, the woman had no family on the outside and never received any mail or visitors. That death was the worst thing Tammy ever saw while incarcerated: "As long as I live that will be etched on my brain."

For the first few days, Tammy stayed in her cell because she was frightened and did not know how to act. When she finally emerged into the dayroom to sit on the couch, another prisoner about her own age named Doreen befriended her. Several days later, another woman confronted Tammy, saying she was in her seat. Doreen came out of her cell and said, "Don't talk to my woman like that." The other woman replied, "I didn't know she was your woman."

> And I said to myself, "How am I going to get out of this mess?" I finally got the nerve to tell her "I've never done this, and I don't want to do this." She said, "Don't worry, we're not going to do anything." As the days went by Doreen said it more and more frequently and I had to find a way to cut it off completely. She was trying to impress everyone else. She was using me. She had so little.

Tammy soon got used to being claimed as someone else's woman and to others wanting to be her friend because, thanks to her family, she always had the maximum amount of money allowed in her inmate bank account, and would come back from the commissary loaded down with provisions. These commissary purchases drew a great deal of unwanted attention. Everyone wanted to be her pal, and those with whom Tammy wouldn't be friends would then intimidate her or threaten her with bodily harm.

One time Tammy spent five days in segregation because another prisoner deliberately got her in trouble by coming into her cell and comforting the crying Tammy by kissing her on the lips just when one of the meanest officers in the prison was walking down the hallway.

Initially, Tammy was surprised the women weren't more tender and supportive of one another.

When I cried, I thought that someone would be there to say,
"It is going to be all right," or that somebody would hold
me. The other prisoners ridiculed the crying. They were
angry that I was crying. Even when they intervened or
came to my rescue, they did it in a harsh way.

Tammy had to avoid this difficult minefield. One way was to keep clear of the other prisoners as much as possible. Everyone had to be employed, so Tammy secured three jobs. She worked in the snack bar once a week at night, in the counselors' office all day five days a week, and at the campsite for prisoners and their children on weekends. The campsite job required a daily trip to feed the animals and clean the cages and weekend employment at the site during the parent-child contact visits. She had a note from the assistant warden giving her permission to leave the tier and attend to the site at whatever time she wanted. From all this work Tammy earned twenty-one dollars a month.

If relations with other incarcerated women were complicated and fraught with the potential for violence, those with the guards were even more difficult. You would assume that a prisoner would have no problems getting along with the facility's authorities if she tried to play the game properly—if she accepted her incarceration, repressed her anger, never talked back, obeyed the rules, and followed all instructions—although there might be trade-offs in terms of erosion of self-determination, sense of responsibility and self-esteem. And you would expect that rewards and special privileges would flow to such a model prisoner. But you would be wrong.

Management's goal, Tammy soon learned, was not the creation of model prisoners, because the system made sure that the women could not become them even if they wanted to. Instead, as in a concentration camp, the aim seemed to be to humiliate and degrade the women, to break and punish them on a daily basis.

How could you obey the rules if they constantly changed? This tactic, Tammy soon realized, keeps incarcerated women continually confused and always afraid.

Punishing all prisoners for the act of one also prevents a detainee from escaping punitive action no matter how hard she tries.

Arbitrary actions, such as denying privileges, cutting off the telephones, or canceling regularly scheduled recreational opportunities for no reason, reinforce the absolute power of the authorities and the complete powerlessness of the incarcerated women, keeping the prisoners in a state of continual uncertainty and humiliation.

Many of the guards, Tammy observed, acted arbitrarily not only to reinforce the power dynamic but also to play with the women to break their spirits. And the prisoner could not do anything about it. Were she to complain, the officer and his coworkers would make life even more miserable for her, telling her over and over again that it was her crime that put her there in the first place—yet another way for the authorities to reinforce the worthlessness of the incarcerated woman.

Another tactic is not to believe anything a woman says.

> Anything that comes out of the prisoner's mouth is a lie. If
> you are sick, you are lying. If your child is sick at home or
> in trouble, you're lying. If you say your mom or dad died,
> you're lying. The dog died, you're lying. Someone stole some-
> thing from you, you're lying. When two people had an alter-
> cation, they are both lying, so you punish them both. You
> have to almost cause a riot to get someone to believe you.
> The prisoner is never believable, ever.

This failure to believe the prisoners causes them to feel particularly helpless and hopeless. Years later, experiences in which her truthfulness was challenged continued to give Tammy flashbacks to prison. For example, once out of prison on her job in the drug program, whenever a coworker lied about Tammy, which she did about twice a week, Tammy would burst out crying and run out the door, much to the astonishment of Tammy's supervisor.

Tammy soon noted how all these strategies break down the prisoner.

> They degrade you and put you in a position to feel helpless
> and hopeless. They are the ones that actively turn you into
> an animal.

Aggression, Tammy recognized, would be the result of all this unresolved anger.

> You destroy your room, you destroy your clothing. I've seen
> rooms set on fire and a lot of fights among prisoners come
> from what a guard has said or done.

52   Tammy tried her best to act the model prisoner. She saw no advantage
to giving way to anger or aggression. But if she was too good and
sucked everything up with a smile, she would have created a target that
had to be taken down.

> If they don't break you, you are still the enemy, you are
> more so the enemy. They don't want you to be in control
> of your emotions. They know somewhere in the pits of your
> being there is anger, there is an angry person who will act
> out, and they try to pull the person out. And they can go
> back and say, "I told you, it was an act, I told you she's
> not this goody two-shoes."

Perhaps this is why Tammy, who still aspired to model prisoner status,
was the subject of so much direct sabotage from the guards. She tried
to remain inconspicuous, but that strategy did not always work. Once
she found herself assigned to a room with a woman who had killed
her girlfriend and slept in the bed with the dead body for two weeks.
This particular person was not supposed to have a roommate. Tammy
asked, "My god, whom did I anger now?"

On one occasion when an officer stole Tammy's permission slip from
her cell during a room shakedown, she was unable to feed the animals
and clean the cages at her campsite job. Later he claimed that Tammy
had never asked to leave to go to work. Another time, a guard visited
the campsite after Tammy had finished, let the animals out, trashed the
place, and then informed the assistant warden that Tammy had not
done her job properly. Avoiding the trap, Tammy did not respond by
accusing the officer of lying. "Have someone check the site after every
cleanup," the warden directed Tammy.

Further retaliation was on the way, Tammy knew, and she didn't
have to wait long to find out what it was going to be. It lasted about
a week. In the morning the officers unlocked the women's cell doors
all at the same time by hitting a button. Only Tammy's door remained
locked, causing her to be late for work every day.

Had it not been for the supportive assistant warden and some of the
counselors for whom she worked, Tammy believes she might not have
survived.

I wouldn't have made it. I know I wouldn't. I would have
made it, but I wouldn't have been who I am now. I would
have been a criminal and I would have gone back with a
much more serious charge.

Anger, says Tammy, is so dangerous that it has to be avoided at all cost.

The prisoners feel, "Nothing is going to happen, nothing is
going to change, so I'm going to stay the way I am." Actually, they may not even have been that way in the first
place, but they changed while locked up, while behind prison
bars. You are transformed into an animal, you become the
most devious, methodical criminal there is as a result of the
incarceration. The prisoners are already in the quicksand and
the guards are just throwing them a log to help them sink
further.

If the guards were nice, if there was positive feedback, if
a person was made to feel human, if a person received any
kind of affirmation that she just made a mistake and could
turn her life around, what a difference that would make.
Instead you are made to feel inhuman.

For incarcerated women, most of whom have been abused in the past,
Tammy thinks the degradation in prison has profound effects.

I've been belittled by a man, I've been belittled by the drug
dealer, I've been belittled by my children that I left behind
(because they can really be cruel, the children of incarcerated
mothers), and then you go in the system, and the system be-
littles you too.

Of course, the end result of the guards' approach is that the prisoners
are made to feel inhuman.

You committed the crime and you are not empowered in any
way to want to do better. They want you to do worse. What
does it feel like to become an animal? Just like an animal

behind a cage and people looking at you. Either they were
laughing at you, afraid of you, or despised you and thought
you were filthy.

Eventually Tammy realized that she had to prevent herself from drown-
ing in anger and bitterness.

I felt like I was on a little island surrounded by water, and
if I took one step, I was going to be gone forever and ever.
With the bitterness I came in with, and the bitterness and
anger that my husband had, coupled with the anger and bitterness because of the guards and the other prisoners, you
have a ticking bomb here.

Along with anger and bitterness came suicidal thoughts, and these
ideas lasted for a good half of Tammy's time in prison. She had never
been away from her son for even one night. When Tammy called him
at her sister's house, she could see how hard he was working to be
bubbly and jovial, but she knew how Terrence was struggling and how
much he was hurting, all due to her actions. Thoughts of suicide began
to occupy her. Tammy started to buy and hoard medication from other
incarcerated women.

I knew that I had money in my inmate account and that I
could buy anything that I wanted. And I wanted to buy.
I didn't want to live without my son. I didn't want to live
here, in that prison. When I was talking to Terrence and
I knew how sad he was, it was more than I could bear. It
was more that I could take on, it was so horrible for me.

Countering her suicidal feelings were Tammy's anger and bitterness
toward Maurice. A few weeks after Tammy arrived in prison, her husband sent her a packet of letters, a kind of running diary written before and after the sentencing. Although Maurice said in the letters that
he was high during the arrest incident and knew what he had done was
wrong, he continued to blame Tammy for her own plight because she
had called the police on him. Five days before the sentencing, he wrote
again that Tammy's getting locked up was due to both their anger, but

that none of this would have happened if she hadn't called in the police. He begged her to pray to God for forgiveness for the wrongs she had done.

A day after the sentencing, Maurice lamented that he did not see how he was to live without Tammy. He had, he said, based his whole existence around her and now she was gone. Then, twelve days after sentencing, near the end of May, he let Tammy know in a letter, sent along with the earlier ones, that he was going to disappear from her life, and he hoped that during the time she was locked up she would come to grips with what she had done to him and their marriage. These letters were the last communication Tammy was to have from Maurice for some years. (When she returned home from prison he telephoned her, wanting to get back together, but Tammy had no trouble turning down his request.)

At the time, Tammy's reaction to Maurice's letters was rage, an intense anger that had no focus because Maurice had disappeared and she had no way to defend herself. It was so hurtful to have a partner who, when you needed his support the most, deliberately withheld it and blamed you for abandoning him. But Tammy's fury turned out to be useful.

> That is what kept me going. I was angry. I turned the anger inward. Most prisoners turn it outward. I didn't get really aggressive, into fights, into solitary. I turned it inside. I fantasized about being a model prisoner, getting out, and finding him and killing him. When I read it, [Maurice's letter], it was a good thing. I was feeling very, very defeated and it made me, it gave me strength. No matter what, I had to get out of there.
>
> I didn't get really angry at Maurice until I got those letters. Before that, if he had come to the prison, I would have forgiven him, I wouldn't have had the bitterness in my heart. The bitterness against him and my sister stayed a long time. It was like a knot, and the knot was making me sick. I couldn't push on because of that.

Recently Tammy searched for and found Maurice's letters in an old trunk. Reading them brought back all the emotions of prison, the

56 sorrow, the anger, and the helplessness—all the pain of the incarceration. But with the passage of time Tammy could feel more sympathy;
Maurice's damaged psyche was so evident. To this author, the letters
seem to be one long cry of anguish about Tammy's abandonment of
Maurice. He saw her calling the police as an act of distrust, and a de-
sertion of both him and their marriage. And, rather than be repudiated,
Maurice would turn the tables and be the one to do the rejecting.

Depression, suicidal ideation, anger. What next? Eventually, Tammy
realized that for her to commit suicide would make life far worse
for her son, who would be dealt another cruel blow from which he
might never recover. So to survive her time in prison, Tammy numbed
herself. She simply had to put off dealing with any feelings until she
got out.

> I had to numb myself without drugs because I was going to
> kill myself otherwise, and I knew it, I prayed to God to take
> all feelings away. I had to numb myself to the fact that my
> son was out there by himself, I had to numb myself that my
> family was acting like they were ashamed of me, I had to
> numb the fact that I was homeless now and had nowhere to
> go. I remember the day, to this day, that I did it. I was on
> the top bunk and it was like a knife in my heart and I knew
> I wouldn't make it, and I told God, "Take every feeling out
> of my body, I don't want to feel anymore, it hurts too
> much, I'm not going to live." And I got off that top bunk
> and I never felt anything after that. I postponed feeling until
> I got out.

As part of the disassociation, Tammy, although physically present, was
able to totally remove herself from the prison environment.

> I looked at everyone else as foreigners and aliens whose planet
> I didn't want to belong to. I'm visiting. I'm not going
> to become a member of your society. I'm only
> visiting.

Being numb allowed Tammy to let go of her anxieties about her possessions and whether they were sold or lost. Concern about material

goods was another weight that needed to be lifted if she was going to survive prison.

She toiled at her three jobs so that exhaustion would take over and enable her to sleep at night. And she worked overtime to keep up a connection with her son. Tammy learned to do needlepoint so that she could make Terrence a rug to mail to him, and she paid other women to make him items embroidered with his name. "I flooded him with letters and cards and I kept the communication open as much as I could and let him know that I loved him."

To do the time, Tammy had to block out the outside world and she realized that this adversely affected Terrence, her sister Pat, and even Terrence's adopted father, Edward. Her numbness, for example, meant that Tammy could not effectively help Terrence with any problems when she talked with him over the telephone. It would not be possible for her to worry obsessively about her son if she was to make it through.

> There was nothing I could do. Once I realized there was
> nothing I could do, it was so easy to do the time. To know
> I was powerless. I admitted that I was powerless, and I put
> it aside.

✳

Several months after Tammy entered prison, Ruth Wyner and John Brock were locked up for refusing to disclose to police the names of drug dealers banned from Wintercomfort, a homeless shelter that Wyner ran in Cambridge, England. Like Tammy, Wyner found that the continued disrespect from the guards in Newmarket Prison was an assault on her identity, affecting both her mental and her physical health. Unfortunately the experience, Wyner soon learned, was going to be far more than the denial of personal liberty, the certain institutional regimentation, and the time of passivity and boredom that she had expected. Instead, she found the guards, or "screws," were determined to demean the prisoners at every opportunity.

> Prison is painful. It is meant to be so. It is meant to hurt.
> And you can see it on the women's faces, feel it when you
> speak with them.[1]

As a social services professional dealing with poor people in her life on the outside, Wyner arrived with her work persona intact, assuming that if she responded to the screws politely she would be respected in return. After awhile she realized that her insistence upon being treated with dignity only irritated the officers, who would not deviate from their punishing policy of verbal brutalization.

Wyner realized she had to protect herself "so that it did not hurt so much, so that I could emerge intact and hold on to that precious soul part of me, which I needed to hide away, to keep safe from the barbarism to come."[2] Another incarcerated woman, observing Wyner's pain, gave her some important advice.

> "If you think about it, about your life outside, about the time you have to do, it'll do your head in," she said.
> "Forget about the outside. Don't think, don't think at all. That's what it's about."[3]

This recommendation seemed sensible to Wyner. She simply had to toughen up, she told herself, to stop it from hurting so much.

> The best way of doing that was to cut yourself off from your feelings, to become hard and brutalized—surely the opposite of what would have been helpful in terms of socializing and rehabilitating inmates. Prison, as I experienced it, was making people feel even more alienated than they had before.[4]

It was good advice, but Wyner, unlike Tammy, was never really able to stop thinking. Other women have documented examples of guards' sadistic infliction of prison pain, which experts have now come to believe is superfluous and gratuitous.[5] Psychiatrist James Gilligan: "It is pain that is unnecessary to inflict on [the prisoner], in as much as he has already been rendered harmless by being disarmed, confined, and removed from the public as a threat."[6] Exprisoner Erwin James echoes Tammy's observation that those locked up, already deeply ashamed and humiliated, need not be subject to this kind of humbling:

> What many people fail to understand is that convincing prisoners of their own worthlessness . . . is rarely neces-

sary. When I walked through the prison gates at the beginning of my sentence, I knew I was the proverbial scum
of the earth. At my trial I had experienced the full force
of public condemnation and disgrace for my crimes. . . .
Further castigation and degradation were unnecessary. . . .
[The guards] made it clear that the prison was their do-
main and that I was going to be tolerated at best. . . . But
I felt like one of the captured humans in *Planet of the Apes*,
fearful and wary of my captors, who thought of me as
another species entirely. . . . [I]t convinced me that if we
kick people when they are down, we should expect little
of value in return.[7]

Given the amount of hurt, the results for the incarcerated women are
predictable: "Simply put, the human psyche abhors the sensation of constant pain."[8] To cope with it, those imprisoned employ "extraordinary
adaptations" to survive, with concomitant "deeper changes in prisoner
value systems or world views."[9] Psychologist Craig Haney has surveyed
the entire universe of prison coping behaviors. Some detainees assume
a tough veneer or undertake violent victimization of others to reassert
a sense of power and status; others are hypervigilant, suppressing out-
ward signs of emotion and becoming generally distrustful of others;
still others develop diagnosable psychological disorders, from clinical
depression to paranoia and psychosis, causing Haney to argue that society must define fair and humane limits to the state infliction of pain.

> The punishment component of the prison experience
> is achieved through the loss of liberty; worse depreda-
> tions must be seen as representing gratuitous cruelty
> that can incur a panoply of social and psychological
> repercussions. . . . Exposing prisoners to the destructive
> lessons of brutal mistreatment (which for many, resonate
> to already familiar themes) and schooling them in the art
> of forceful domination instead of empathetic understand-
> ing guarantees more profoundly marginalized future lives
> than in past times. The context or situation of prison itself
> must be carefully examined and restructured in ways that
> will minimize these debilitating effects.[10]

Tammy's response—numbing herself off from thinking and feeling—is one that many incarcerated women employ. One prisoner calls it "jailface."

> Partly, jailface just happens when you been under everybody's heel too long, but after a while you learn to do it on purpose so you never let on that you're scared or feeling pain or worry or sickness. What you do is, you freeze your face so nothin' moves. . . . The real mark of jailface, though, is the eyes. They don't never look straight at nobody and they don't even focus half the time. You can't look into the eyes of somebody with jailface cuz your look bounces off a glassy surface of eyeball that's so hard it would bounce bullets.
>
> Jailface ain't necessarily a bad thing to have, cuz the minute a certain kind of screw knows you're scared or weak she's got the upper hand, and she jumps on you with both feet and don't let up 'til she's had her satisfaction, which in most cases is to see your spirit dead. But if you're walking around with jailface she can't tell if something is still stirring in there or not. Most likely she thinks by your look that you're already dead, so there's no challenge, nothin' in there to kill, see. But people ain't really dead 'til they're really dead, if you know what I mean. Maybe you've given up, maybe you're a fuckin' zombie, but just about anybody got a little life left in 'em that can spark up the minute they latch on to a little piece of hope, and if you jailface you can keep that hid from the screws so they can't stomp it out of you.[11]

Disassociation brings prisoners to a bleak point:

> Sometimes you feel so lonely and isolated and hopeless that death looks very inviting. It's the flat emotionless feeling you get when you contemplate taking your own life. I've been there on several occasions. Sometimes the loneliness is self-imposed but it's hard to relate to others when you feel so ashamed and worthless.[12]

> The strain had been too much. I had stepped over that
> line where a human being has lost more than he can
> bear, where the pain is too intense, and she knows she
> is changed forever. I was now capable of killing, coldly
> and without feeling. I was empty, as I have never, before
> or since, known emptiness. I had no connection to this
> life.[13]

Coping with being locked in a cell is reason enough to stop thinking. How grossly we underestimate the effects on humans of being so confined, especially at night, was brought home after Hurricane Katrina roared through New Orleans in 2005. Detainees in one local jail had a hellish experience.

They reported they were locked in their cells in and abandoned by guards as floodwaters rose. Dan Bright, a thirty-seven-year-old construction worker, said that the power went out in the Templeman III jail, where he was being held after being arrested the day before the storm for public drunkenness and resisting arrest.

He said that guards ordered prisoners into their cells, locked the doors, and then left the facility. After power went out on Monday afternoon, floodwaters then began to gradually fill his cell, eventually reaching up to his neck. "Just imagine, you're in your cell, the lights out and the water was rising," he said. "The deputies were nowhere to be found. They completely abandoned us."[14]

Breaking jail windows to let air in, the men set fire to blankets and sheets, hanging them out of the windows to let people know they were still in the facility, and at least a dozen prisoners jumped out of the windows. Tammy always worried about being locked in and suffering a health emergency during the night. One prisoner in the New Orleans jail was in a diabetic coma.[15]

This episode graphically reminds us that the prison has little changed over time. Craig Haney writes:

> Indeed, few if any social institutions in our society have
> retained so much of their original 19th century form.
> Thus, at the start of the 21st century, our otherwise

technologically advanced and sophisticated society still responds to crime largely by locking human beings in cages.[16]

Toward the end of Franz Kafka's novel *The Trial*, his protagonist, K., tries to defend himself. "But I am not guilty," says K.; "it's a mistake . . ." "That is true," says the priest, "but that's how all guilty men talk."[17] The totalitarian system that traps K. assumes its charges are always guilty. K. is accused of an unknown crime and executed without ever learning the nature of the charge or having a chance to defend himself; to the contrary, it seems that all efforts at defense need to occur behind the scenes by persons with influence. As K. becomes gradually enmeshed in this elaborate, clandestine legal organization with undiscovered or arbitrary rules and practices, the effect is totally hallucinatory.[18]

Today the word Tammy frequently uses to describe her experience is "surreal," and the term is apt. Indeed, the nightmarish prison atmosphere does closely resemble the phantasmal world of *The Trial*. And the ever-growing dehumanization and isolation of K. so well captures the effects on Tammy of living in such a milieu.

CHAPTER FIVE

Numbing

> To grow up metabolizing hatred like daily bread means
> that eventually every human interaction becomes tainted
> with the negative passion and intensity of its byproducts—
> anger and cruelty.
>
> — AUDRE LORDE

While Tammy was in prison, Terrence tried to conceal his difficulties
from his mother. The twelve-year-old was dealing with Tammy's incarceration in an abnormal way, but one that enabled him to cope with
her absence. Externally, he appeared angry and upset.

> I remember going to school, and my teacher would say
> the smallest thing, and I would blow up. Or somebody
> would do something and I would blow up. I remember
> getting suspended from school for three days at a time
> and not telling my aunt, and still have her drop me off at
> school. I would get to school, and they would say, "You're
> suspended, you can't be in the building," and I would
> walk around for six hours, and then walk out of the build-
> ing like I had been in school. I think I was suspended nine
> times during that year for losing my temper. The teacher
> would say, "Terrence," and I would blow up. I would ask
> to go to the bathroom, they would say, "Not right now."
> I'd say, "I'm leaving." I'd leave. I'd just blow up.

64   Tammy's collect calls, her lifeline to her son, caused continual strife. When you telephoned collect from the jail, the call registered "private" on caller-ID. Fearing bill collectors, Terrence's aunt and uncle would direct Terrence not to answer the telephone.

> That enraged me and started a mountain of arguments. By the time we would argue and I would answer the phone, I could hear her hanging up. I can remember one time when that happened I literally smacked my uncle with that phone. And I remember he picked me up and threw me into a wall. Then they would get the telephone bill from the collect calls and there would be another round of arguments and threats to disconnect the telephone or change the number.

Aunt Pat confirms that Terrence was raging out of control the year he spent with her.

> It was rough. He was rebelling. He was so unhappy, and he acted out with me because he was just so frustrated. He saw her being taken away, and that surely had to blow his mind. He loved his mom so. He couldn't handle it. He couldn't keep it inside, and he wouldn't listen to me. I have always been able to talk to him or calm him down, but he felt like he had no one. He had me, but he didn't believe that, because he was so out of it.

Terri, Tammy's youngest sister, says Terrence was suicidal when his mother was away. When she saw him he was clearly depressed and would sit writing in his journal and working on his poetry. As a child, she explains, he always tried to protect his mother and now he could not: "He loves his mom. He's always been like that."

Although Terrence can look back now and see that he was furious, he says that at the time he does not recall being angry: "I was angry but I didn't know it." He does remember coping with Tammy's absence by telling himself that she was just on an extended vacation. The fact that Tammy was incarcerated was just too big for the child to acknowledge, and he developed a fantasy that enabled him to continue on with life without blaming his mother.

> I wasn't angry for her leaving, because in my mind then, and sometimes in my mind now, it was just an extended vacation that she went on. I never looked at it that she was in prison or she left me or she abandoned me. She went somewhere. . . . The times I got angry were when people would make it seem like that. I can remember the times when I was in school and I would get into an argument with a boy. To hurt me, he would say, "Your mom is in prison, and mine's at home." Or my aunt would say, "Where's your mom right now?" Those were the times I would get angry. "She's on vacation, she's away, how dare you? She's just away."

So Terrence was effectively numbing himself too. Tammy now understands that her son could not call where she was "prison."

> It was huge, he couldn't put that in his mind. Even when we look at it now, it is surreal. If I think now that it really happened to me, I would probably have a nervous breakdown. When we look back over it now, when Terrence thinks about it now, it is like it happened to somebody else and we just read about it. It is very surreal to me. The only time I get traumatized and cry again is when I realize that it really did happen to me and it really did happen to him. That is the only time that it hurts. It is hard to remember what happened in there because it is like it didn't happen to me.

All the rules and regulations in Terrence's new life were also major adjustments. Pat lived about thirty minutes south of Terrence's public school, which had been only four blocks from his old home. She took it upon herself to drive Terrence to his school and pick him up afterwards, but she had to get to work herself. As a result, Pat had to drop Terrence off way too early and he had to wait, often in the dark, for the building to open. The after-school program supervised him at the end of the day. Terrence was used to his mother trouble-shooting and handling all his problems for him, but he found his aunt had a more laissez-faire attitude.

> My aunt would say, "You have a problem, handle it." I
> don't know how to handle it, so I would just blow up.
> My mother wouldn't let me do whatever I wanted to, but
> I wasn't always hearing the word "no." When I got "no"
> I would be outraged. "I can't go where? I can't do what?"
> and I would blow up, because I wasn't used to it. I didn't
> think of it like, "My aunt's taking care of me, so I need to
> play by her rules," I thought of it like, "My mom's on
> vacation, she's still my keeper, you can't tell me what to
> do. Even if I'm in your house, I'll ask my mother if I can
> go to a party, and if she says yes, then I'm going. This is
> your house, these are your rules, but if she tells me I can
> go, I'm going." That caused a lot of conflict between my
> aunt and her husband, because they felt, and they should
> have, that it was their house and their rules.

For her part, Pat says she knew Terrence was too angry and confused to know how to handle any problem, but he would simply not let his aunt help him. Nor was her nephew willing to go to counseling Pat had arranged at a nearby church.

> Also, the counselors at school were trying to work with
> him, but he would not have it. Too much anger was
> there, and he would not express himself. I always tried to
> reassure Terrence that I loved him and was there for him.
> I think he felt no one understood him, so he just closed
> himself off. I know it was hard for him. I'm just so sorry
> I wasn't able to get through to him how much I truly
> cared.

Terrence made only one trip to see Tammy in prison, a weekend contact visit. He says he didn't think much about it because he hadn't accepted in his mind that his mother was in prison. So when he did come he was surprised by the smell of disinfectant and by the unusual clothing Tammy was wearing. For Tammy, the visit was a episode that she didn't particularly want to have repeated.

> After that visit I didn't care because it was just too hard, it was too hard for me to adjust after that. It was too hard for me to adjust, it was too hard for me to see him go. He was my son. I wanted to hold him and be there with him. It was just really hard to let him go.

Pat and Terrence continued to hide the extent of Terrence's anger and upset.

> My sister had said she was having a lot of problems with him, but she didn't tell me the extent of it. He was tearing up my sister's house, you couldn't talk to him at any time, he screamed, he cried, he was terrible.

Later, when Tammy was finally back home, she soon saw for herself.

> He was very angry, very, very angry. Separation is hard for him. My son hides his pain very well. He hid his pain from me because he didn't want to cause me any pain. I didn't find out until later. He still does that now.

In the midst of all this turmoil, Terrence confronted the fact that he was gay and began to come out to those around him.

> I think when I was a little kid, a young teenager, I knew that I was never attracted to women. I knew that. When she left that gave me ample time. I had gotten to the point in my life when I realized that I was gay. I have no control over that, that is what it is. I came out to everyone, it was fine, everything was cool. The only person who did not know was my mother.

Not wishing to burden Tammy while she was away, Terrence never sent a letter he had written telling his mother about it. The letter sat on his dresser for about a year until one day his aunt found it and mailed it off.

68 For Terrence it seemed to be the perfect time to come out. And once he was out, there was no more hiding, no going back. It might have seemed like the perfect moment to Terrence, but the news hit Tammy like a thunderclap. She blamed herself: if she hadn't been away, had she been able to shelter him, none of this would have happened. She refused to accept the fact that her son would be cursed and stigmatized for the rest of his life because of something she had done.

As Terrence remembers it, his mother waxed hot and cold about his news. One week it was all right and the next it wasn't.

> She called me and she just said, "It's okay, I understand." At the time I said, "Oh my god, my mother's okay with this. I don't care what anybody else has to say." Little did I know she felt guilty that she was away. She was saying, "I'll be okay with it just for the moment." That's really what she was saying. She was going to fix it when she gets home.

Terrence was confused. Soon he realized that he couldn't let Tammy's attitude hold him back. He had no choice about his sexual orientation and he understood he had to lead his life the way he saw fit. This decision marked Terrence's first step away from his mother and the beginning of a corrosive anger that was to have tragic consequences when Tammy returned home for good.

> Because even though I didn't think that she abandoned me, I was at the point, "You're not around, so why are you telling me what to do, who I can be with, or who I talk to? How dare you?" That's when I really started to accept the fact that she went to prison. Because in my head, it's like "I accepted the fact that she went to prison and left me, but she can't accept this." And that is where my anger came from when she finally came home.

To make matters even worse, in a letter from a mutual acquaintance Tammy learned of her friend Brenda's death. After Tammy was locked up, Brenda, who had been off drugs for about six years, started in again, eventually taking what everyone believed was a deliberate overdose.

She couldn't live with herself. To this day I know it was
because of me. She felt guilty. I believe the guilt was so bad.
She couldn't live with herself. So she is dead. They had to
actually sedate me when I found out.

Tammy spoke with a counselor at the prison about her conviction that she was responsible for Brenda's death. The counselor's reaction was a helpful one that put things in a better perspective. "What makes you think you had that much power over another individual?" she asked.

Later, upon her release, Tammy went to see Brenda's mother. Brenda's family greeted Tammy warmly, but Tammy never asked them what they thought because she was afraid of the answer. Although they urged Tammy to continue to visit, she never went back.

At Aunt Pat's house, things continued to deteriorate, with Terrence in continuous arguments with everyone—Pat, her husband, and her husband's son. Soon Terrence began running around out late with his friends. He would leave the house at five in the afternoon, stay out all night, and go straight to school in the morning. Most of time he was downtown, walking around and visiting bars and clubs. On one occasion he and a friend were robbed at gunpoint on the subway. More and more, Terrence slept over with friends in the neighborhood, and Pat wouldn't see him for a day or two until he would return to eat or to get clothing. His grief had turned into an unmanageable aggression that had pretty well alienated everyone around him, even when they fully understood and sympathized with its cause. Terrence's grades were barely passing, he was nearly homeless, and his mother, miles away, had also walled herself off from thinking and feeling.

As an abuse survivor, Tammy was an old hat at numbing herself. Heroin had done the trick for nineteen years, and her two years of incarceration were to prolong this habit of nonthinking. If politicians or members of the public think that imprisonment is a time out, enabling prisoners to think about their lives, Tammy says they are very much mistaken. To cope with their incarceration, she explains, many women learn to disassociate. Some accomplish the task by immersion in religion, into which they lose themselves completely. Those who do not numb themselves are at risk of turning into antisocial criminals due to unchecked anger and humiliation.

Because of the mortifying strip searches after contact visits, Tammy

70   was glad that Terrence only visited once. Even worse than the search itself was the process used. The prisoners had to wait their turn for the examination.

> You sit there on a bench with the other prisoners whose visitors have gone. You may sit there for as long as an hour waiting to be searched. So you are sitting on a bench facing all the other visitors and it looks like criminals sitting on a bench in front of the public. You feel like you are on display. You can see visitors turning around and looking at you. I hated that part. It was terrible. You just want to crawl into your skin and disappear.

As the women waited, the guards called them in one by one.

> Everything comes off. If you are having your menstrual period during the search, the tampon has to come out and you have to be given another one. I felt so much empathy for the women that happened to. [After Tammy's hair turned white during her committal to the Cook County Jail, she never got a menstrual period again.]

And it didn't take long for the effects of the strip searches on the women to be seen.

> The strange thing about the strip searches was that after it was over, none of the women would talk to or look at one another. We all would talk some and others would chatter away, but after the searches we all retreated within ourselves.

Every single time she was strip-searched, Tammy had to disassociate.

> For me the strip search took away my personal power to say "no." It would be the same thing as being raped. Knowing that you have no choice but to comply with something that is so personal and so private gave me a feeling of total defeat. I had to remove my heart and soul and go to a much more pleasant place. I remember thinking, "If I don't transcend myself at this very moment, I will say 'no' and will suffer

> consequences that I cannot imagine." I went to a place that
> was pleasant as a child. It was Christmas and I was nine
> years old. I was able to mechanically remove my clothing
> only because I followed the lead of the other women and
> because I blocked out the voices of the guards as well.

Trauma from the strip searches lasted for years afterwards. Tammy felt dirty.

> It took a couple of years before the feeling completely went
> away. I know now that it was because of the strip searches.
> It's almost like someone being raped. My body was no longer
> the sacred temple that I felt it was before I went to prison.
> I no longer felt it was my own. There were so many mixed
> feelings and emotions that I remained confused for a very
> long time.

And from her first day, Tammy learned that the strip searches weren't effective anyway. To Tammy's shock and surprise, her cellmate in the assessment unit was smoking a forbidden cigarette. Blowing the smoke out the window, she explained how she had been able to smuggle in the contraband. (Cigarettes were allowed in other areas of the facility.) She ripped the matches from the book, tore off a piece of flint, stuck everything into some cellophane with the cigarettes, sealed the packet, stuck it up her vagina, and contracted her vagina during the strip search so that the small parcel would not come out.

Descriptions of isolation, fear, and helplessness experienced by prisoners as they struggle to retain and reassert individual self-worth while imprisoned abound in the literature. But the odds were stacked against the incarcerated woman from the beginning, Tammy learned, for management made certain that the prisoner was stripped of anything resembling self-esteem. It was very much like living with domestic violence. No matter what you did to comply with the wishes of your tormentor, you never knew when or from what direction the next insult or assault would come. And the years of trying to please and numbing and disassociating oneself from the abuse and violence had, before you knew it, cut into your autonomy and sense of efficacy so that your will to leave was steadily eroded.

72   Tammy is grateful to her incarceration for only one thing: it totally disrupted her relationship with Maurice. Without imprisonment, might she still be with her husband, and might she have also gone back on heroin? Who knows? But at what price was this necessary separation accomplished?

> In prison the effects of being stripped of your dignity and your self-esteem have a long-lasting effect. It has an effect that is so damaging that I don't even think that therapy can take it away. Prior to the incarceration I knew I needed help. Even though I was clean, I had made an appointment to go and see a therapist. I believe that through long-term treatment I would have become well or whole again. The prison took a person who was already sick and made her sicker.

✳

The substantial number of women prisoners who have been sexually abused means that Tammy's disassociation experiences are not unusual. In research in the mid- to late-1990s with jail, prison, and probation populations, the U.S. Department of Justice found that 57 percent of women in state prisons (compared to 16 percent of men), 40 percent in federal facilities (7 percent of men), 48 percent of women in jail (13 percent of men), and 40 percent of female probationers (9 percent of male) reported having been subject to physical or sexual abuse before incarceration.[1]

Thirty-nine percent of state women prisoners and 37 percent of female jail detainees had been sexually abused, and almost 26 percent of all female state prisoners were molested before the age of eighteen.[2] Research in specific jails and prisons has produced even higher percentages. For example, a study of new admittees to the Bedford Hills (New York) Maximum Security Correctional Facility (for Women) found that 59 percent reported some form of sexual abuse during childhood or adolescence, with 41 percent experiencing some kind of sexual penetration. And 75 percent of respondents were victims of severe physical violence at the hands of intimate partners in adulthood.[3]

Reported past abuse correlates in research with convictions for violent crime; in the U.S. Department of Justice study, 34 percent of abused women, compared with 21 percent of nonabused women, were in prison for a violent offense.[4] Abused women who were locked up also reported higher use of illegal drugs and alcohol. Eighty percent of abused women, compared to 65 percent of nonabused women, had used illegal drugs regularly.[5] And abused women prisoners were more likely than nonabused women detainees to have been using alcohol or illegal drugs at the time of the crime; 47 percent of abused women committed their current offense under the influence of illegal drugs (compared to 32 percent of nonabused women), and 33 percent while drinking (compared to 24 percent of nonabused women).[6]

Incarcerated women who are survivors of abuse are often exposed to situations reminiscent of their childhoods, calling upon them to activate their talents for disassociation. For example, women who had been locked in closets as children find being confined in a dark segregation unit to be difficult to survive with their sanity intact. Invasive searches, restraints, reading of mail, lack of privacy, arbitrary rules, capricious punishment for imaginary infractions, and the earning of privileges through "good" behavior all mimic the abusive control of intimate partners or family members that can trigger memories of earlier maltreatment. Avoiding punishment through favor-giving also copies the behavior patterns of exploitative relationships.[7]

In addition to causing the women to relive the terror of earlier mistreatment, the totalitarian prison atmosphere can undermine their ability to live abuse-free on the outside. Many women, like Tammy, are incarcerated because of excessive dependence on abusers or an inability to extricate themselves from dysfunctional thinking and behavioral patterns that develop when living and coping with violence and abuse. Certainly, the corrosive fear that most women experience in prison is not conducive to an increase in confidence or self-esteem necessary for independent living, and when they stop thinking altogether while locked up they cannot, as we shall see, begin immediately to start thinking upon release.[8]

On top of all this, the sexual aspect of the guards' abuse of incarcerated women is deeply troubling and has received little serious attention. When it was made public, the deliberate sexual humiliation of detainees in prisons in Iraq caused considerable alarm and distress, but few understood that these were common practices in U.S. facilities, where for women prisoners sexual humiliation on a daily basis frequently crosses the line into a kind of sexual assault.[9] All women, as Tammy did, find

74   the strip-search process terrifying and shaming, but the frequency of strip searching as punishment for alleged misdeeds of incarcerated women demonstrates just how often prisons use nakedness as a penalty.

In 1965 activist and writer Andrea Dworkin was arrested at an anti–Vietnam War demonstration and imprisoned in the New York City Women's House of Detention for four days before a judge released her on her own recognizance. Many of the women held in the facility were involved in prostitution.

> In the jail, all the orifices of my body, including mouth, vagina, and rectum were searched many times, by hand, by many persons. I was told the jailers were looking for heroin. My clothes were taken away. . . .
>
> I was given a flimsy robe that had no buttons or hooks—there was no way to close it. My bra, underpants, and the sash to the robe were taken away so I wouldn't kill myself. . . .
>
> To see whether I had syphilis, I was examined by two male doctors. They never did the blood test for syphilis; instead, they drew blood from my vagina. The brutal internal examination they forced on me, my first, caused me to bleed for fifteen days—when I finally decided it wasn't my period. My family doctor, a taciturn man whom I had never seen express emotion, even as he treated my mother's heart attacks, strokes, and experimental heart surgery, said he had never seen a uterus so bruised or a vagina so ripped. He cried. I was eighteen.[10]

Now, forty years later, the Women's House of Detention has been razed to make way for a community garden, but how much has changed? A few years ago, Ted Koppel in a *Nightline* interview asked the medical director of the (California) Valley State Prison for Women a question related to unnecessary gynecological exams. The guest replied, "I've heard inmates tell me that they would deliberately like to be examined. It's the only male contact they get."[11]

Writing that the practice of making people undress is a method of asserting dominance, prisoner Christy Marie Camp explains how being naked for any length of time makes prisoners physically and emotionally vulnerable.

> All 19 of us were then ordered to turn around [after their clothes were removed]. We had to stand in a circle bare naked. There was nothing to hide behind. Some of us crossed our arms over our breasts.
>
> After the first cell had been stripped, we saw two male employees pretend to be looking through our arriving files as they took glances over to where the first group was being searched. Everyone working behind the counter in the reception center had a clear view of the search procedure. . . .
>
> Once we were naked, the process went on at a slower pace. First we had to spread our fingers to insure there was no "contraband" between our fingers or under our nails. Next we lifted our breasts and/or bellies, combed through our hair with our fingers, rubbed our belly buttons, combed through our public hair with our hands, raised our arms, showed the underneath of our feet and between our toes. Of course everyone was humiliated. Finally we were told to face the wall, squat and cough three times as an officer held a vanity mirror five inches under each of our vaginas to search for "contraband." Nothing was found on any of us.[12]

Attorney Mark Merin, whose litigation on behalf of jail detainees resulted in a fifteen-million-dollar settlement a few years ago, described a typical strip search in the Sacramento, California, County Jail.

> A group of women who didn't know each other, could be 18 years old to 78, would be brought into a room, six or eight at a time, in a room that was no longer—no larger than six by eight feet with footprints painted on the floor. They were totally naked. They had been disrobed before they entered the room. Then they had to in groups bend over, expose their body cavities, spread their genitalia for visual inspection with someone with a flashlight

looking in, harassing them, ordering them at times to
jump, to dance. People—Mormons who wear a religious
garment so they can enter the temple were ordered to rip
it off, or to remove it or it would be ripped off. Women
who were menstruating without any sanitary napkins
were required to remove tampons and stand there bleeding in other people's blood. I mean, absolutely unbelievable. And it was videotaped. All of these were archived. . . .

It seems that it's very current with the Abu Ghraib dis-
closures to discover that nudity, forced nudity and group
nudity and activities in the nude is a way that the administration in these facilities oppress and dehumanize the jail
population. . . . I realized that the people who were sent
over there from the United States to run those prisons
were just extending the experience that they had here
in our prison system. It seems that it was just a further
step that they were taking to use nudity to control and
dehumanize and humiliate.[13]

Arrested in 2003 during a political rally, Judy Haney was forced to strip
in the Miami-Dade County Pre-Trial Detention Center. None of the
males held for minor offenses, she later learned, were stripped prior
to first arraignment. Making clear that the process was about humiliation and control, not about safety, she described her experience in testimony to the Commission on Safety and Abuse in America's Prisons
two years later.

When it came my turn to be strip searched, the guard led
me into the same small room the others had been in; it
was approximately 6' by 8' and had a bench along one
wall. The guard stood in the doorway and ordered me
to stand facing her and to remove my clothing piece by
piece. . . . I proceeded to remove each piece of clothing
and drop each piece on the bench. While I was removing
my clothes, the guard continued to stand at the door and
watched as another guard stood behind her in the hall-
ways, also watching me. . . .

> After I removed all my clothes, the guard told me to
> turn around, bend all the way over, and spread my
> cheeks. I'm not sure that I can really convey the emo-
> tional and physical complexity of the situation. Bending
> over and "spreading my cheeks" exposed my genitalia
> and anus to a complete stranger, who had physical au-
> thority over me, so that she could visually inspect my
> body cavities. The only way I could cope with this was
> to stay very focused in my head and just separate from
> my body. The feeling was sort of like floating while also
> feeling like a big lump.
>
> The guard's next set of instructions were to squat—
> and then—to hop like a bunny. Remember, I'm still
> "spreading my cheeks." So I can't use my arms to balance
> or assist me in the hopping process. . . . I stood, bent
> over, and hopped naked under orders and in view of
> at least two guards in a small room with a door open
> to a hallway that passersby could see in for about 10 to
> 15 minutes. My genitalia and anus were exposed and
> viewable to anyone passing through the hallway for over
> 5 minutes.[14]

To be sure, men in jails and prisons are not exempt from humiliating practices also centered on their genitals. Detainees in the Cook County Jail (Chicago) brought a lawsuit in 2005 to end the mandatory inva-sive sexual disease check involving the insertion of a metal rod with a swab on the end into the penis. Although the jail maintains the test is voluntary, the plaintiff asserts that a doctor ordered him to unzip, warning him and the other pretrial detainees, "You don't want to piss off the d——doctor."[15] And former baseball star Pete Rose, incarcer-ated for federal tax evasion, describes six body searches a day to and from his job and lunch.

> The whole prison process was intended to humiliate, not
> inspire. The body searches . . . the prison doctor sticking
> his fingers up your ass. That's what prison is all about:
> humiliation and control.[16]

Clearly, however, the societal nudity taboo is more powerful for women, who in general are unused to baring their bodies to others, except intimate partners.[17] Forced nudity is also reminiscent of sexual assault and abuse, a strong reminder to the women of their vulnerability and powerlessness, an especially damaging experience for women abuse victims.

Prisons find many other ways to degrade prisoners based on female bodily functions. One recent study in Canada found women in segregation denied underwear and toilet paper, made to shower with male staff looking on, and being refused a sufficient quantity of sanitary pads, forcing them into frequent and degrading requests for more.[18] Another practice is the use of leg shackles for pregnant prisoners during labor, and denying them anesthesia or other drugs. Only two states, California and Illinois, have laws forbidding use of restraints during labor; twenty-three states and the federal Bureau of Prisons have policies expressly allowing their use. The common practice in Illinois, Tammy's state, was to chain the woman to the hospital bed by one wrist and one ankle.[19]

When they refuse to strip or when they question the procedure, incarcerated women can be forcibly stripped or sent to segregation. One prisoner was a large woman, and because of her size, the guards maintained they had a difficult time figuring out if she was hiding anything. An individual interviewing the prisoner described her situation.

> They tell her to spread her buttcheeks and she does, embarrassed in front of the other two women but unwilling to take the consequences. The guards say they still can't see, tell her to bend over and spread her cheeks wider. She can't stand it and refuses. She is told that if she continues to refuse strip-searching she'll be pepper sprayed and her clothes will be cut off. . . . She finally breaks down when she tells me that the whole thing triggered her memories of all the sexual abuse she endured as a child, as a young woman. This is why the strip-searches were intolerable, why the harsh male voices demanding she remove her clothes were so traumatic. And now she has no refuge, nothing to do but sit for ten more days [in segregation] and think about these memories. She wonders why they can't understand this.[20]

When detainee Mary Bull refused to strip in the San Francisco jail, the guards forcibly removed her clothing. After pushing her to the ground, the guards pried her legs apart and up. A male officer walked into the room to watch. Bull says she was left naked in the tiny cell with a cement floor. It contained no bed or sink, and the toilet was just a hole in the floor with a grille over it. In the room was a tiny piece of cloth with Velcro, which she used to try to protect herself from the cold.[21]

Stripping is commonly used as a punishment for other infractions, as in this case from Story County, Iowa, when authorities strip-searched a woman arrested for public intoxication.

> It is not clear whether this woman was offered a paper gown, but she did not receive one. A male officer watched as she was undressed and marched naked into the cell. Some time later, there was a shift change at the jail. As the new officers came on, the woman was still shouting sporadically. So officers decided to strap her, spread-eagled and face down, on a wooden board, where she was left naked for three hours. They later testified that they did this because they were afraid she might hurt herself in the padded cell. While she was on the restraint board, a camera transmitted nude images of her to monitors in the front office, where most of the deputies on duty were men. Eventually, someone covered her buttocks with a towel.[22]

Miki Mangosing, a personal chef in San Francisco, was arrested for allegedly disturbing the peace with a friend in 2002. Her story appeared in the *San Francisco Chronicle*.

> In a holding cell at the jail, she said, she spotted her friend and shouted to her. This prompted a female deputy to snap: "Shut up, bitch," she said.
> "I said, 'What did I do?' She blew a whistle, two other women came. It was surreal. They lifted me, they threw me in a room with no bed. The toilet was like a hole. They ripped my bra and panties off. I thought they were going to rape me. My face was literally up against the floor," she said.

During the strip search, Mangosing said, she was kicked several times in the stomach and her arm was wrenched. Hours later, she said, she was given a garment to wear and asked whether she wanted water.[23]

Later, she wound up in therapy.

"I was really devastated by it," she said. "I had nightmares; I woke up in night sweats. I just kind of lay in bed for a week. I couldn't get it out of my system. I felt really dehumanized. I know it sounds stupid, but it made me feel worthless."[24]

One prisoner describes how guards punished her by forcibly tearing off her clothes because she refused to talk during an interrogation.

Somebody set fire in the cottage. I knew who set it. It wasn't me, but I wouldn't tell who did it and they knew I knew.

The guard took me to the cell and he told me to take my clothes off. I told him I wasn't gonna take shit off in front of him. . . . He snatched me and tore my clothes off. I kicked him and jumped him. I knew I wasn't gonna win 'cause he was too big, but I wasn't gonna strip in front of him. He beat the hell out of me and handcuffed me spread-eagle to the bed. The matron was out there in the corridor and she didn't do nothing. My bra and dress had been ripped off but my panties were intact. I lay spread-eagle there like that for about six hours.[25]

A prison raid in Kingston, Ontario, in 1994, fully preserved on video tape, provides a chilling example of the use of forced nudity in women's prisons to punish. In this instance, six women were in a battle with the authorities, demanding access to legal services, telephone calls, and day-to-day supplies such as blankets, sanitary napkins, and clothes. The outcome of their campaign was the women's placement in segregation cells. It was late at night and the women were sleeping. Karlene Faith observed the video of the ensuing event that the Canadian Broadcasting Corporation eventually obtained and aired.

The images televised across the nation included, first, a
silent, late-night platoon of six or seven men (the exact
number was never reported), wearing identical Darth
Vader outfits. They are unidentifiable behind helmets,
heavily padded combat suits, masks, shields, and enor-
mous boots. Part of this platoon's function is to intimidate, and they are successful. On orders of the prison
warden to conduct emergency strip-searches and cell ex-
tractions in the segregation unit, they burst into the cell
of a woman who is asleep on her cot. They rouse her by
slamming her onto the cement floor, then cut and rip off
her night clothing and underwear. They confine her with
leg irons and handcuffs. Two or three of the "team" hold
her naked body to the cement floor with their padded
knees pressed into her back. They stand her against the
cement wall, banging their batons right next to her ear.
They repeat this procedure from one cell to the next.
Some women scream, clearly terrorized. . . . After the televised scene, the women were led away, one by one, for
"body cavity" searches. Their cells were overturned; their
meager belongings were taken away; and the cots, mattresses, and bedding removed.

Following the strip-searches in the cells and the "body
cavity "searches, the women were left in shackles and leg
irons, wearing paper gowns, on the cement floors of
empty cells.[26]

Authorities found no contraband, but few would be naïve enough to
believe that the brutal raid and strip searches, which more nearly resembled rapes, were for the purpose of confiscating forbidden items.
We should not be surprised that neither the warden nor the head of
prisons found anything abhorrent about the procedure, although both
lost their jobs in the ensuing public uproar.[27] Strip searching rarely turns
up contraband. Records obtained under the Freedom of Information
Act about strip searches in Brisbane Women's Correctional Centre between 1999 and 2002 found that 15,942 full body searches turned up
drugs in only two instances.[28]

Rape, of course, takes this sexual humiliation even further. With
their absolute power over infractions and penalties, guards have many

opportunities for developing exploitative relationships that hinge on sexual favor-giving to avoid punishment. Women in prison fulfill the common male fantasy of available, powerless females. Investigations of reported incidents reveal the many instances of guards pressuring, coercing, and intimidating the women.[29] Tammy says there were many rumors in prison about guards having sex with prisoners. Although she doesn't know whether or not they were accurate, she did see some women get to do things they shouldn't have; as a result, she thinks the rumors were probably true. One incarcerated woman describes the dynamic, which is undoubtedly typical:

> I got caught up in this ring that one of the guards had
> going. At first, I had no idea what it was about. Then,
> one day this guard asked if I would like to earn some
> extra cigarettes. He knew that I smoked and that was his
> way of getting me in. He told me that I was going to
> have to give oral sex to one of the guards. At first, I ob-
> jected, but then I figured that if I didn't do it I would get
> in trouble or get beat. So I gave the guard oral sex. Before
> I knew it I was doing other things too. After a while it
> wasn't a big deal. I learned to block out the experience.[30]

Signed into law in 2003, the federal Prison Rape Elimination Act mandates what will be the first-ever survey of prisoners in jail and prisons concerning sexual violence they have experienced.[31] In the interim, the Bureau of Justice Statistics has provided data, as required by the act, on the number of reports made by prisoners to facility authorities in 2004. Because most victims do not report incidents due to fears of retaliation, the bureau cautioned that these data are not reliable estimates of the extent of sexual abuse. Even so, the numbers were not minimal: of a total of 8,210 reports, 42 percent involved staff-on-prisoner sexual abuse and an additional 11 percent, sexual harassment by staff. Over half the allegations could not be substantiated.[32]

Maricopa County (Phoenix, Arizona) Sheriff Joe Arpaio, the first penal manager in the U.S. to introduce women's chain gangs, inaugurated another cutting-edge practice in July 2000: "Jail Cam" fed images captured on four cameras in the jail to the Internet, where interested viewers worldwide could watch the booking process and life in the holding cells. Jail Cam—which, said the sheriff, served as a deterrent to the general public as well as a means of preventing abuse by guards—received two to three million hits daily. Due to a "misalignment," in spring 2001 views of the women's toilet area began broadcasting and ended up being linked to several Internet pornography sites. That camera was finally disconnected, but not until April 2002. Arpaio has been returned to office three times with high approval ratings.[33]

Jail Cam's bathroom reality TV show is a potent symbol of and reminder that officials use women's bodies in jails and prisons as instruments of punishment, humiliation, and shame. Tammy has said that she no longer felt her body was her own. Apparently the women's bodies not only belong to the guards, but they also belong to the public. We have come full circle: from Andrea Dworkin's prison rape to Sheriff Joe Arpaio's Jail Cam, a high-tech sexual exploitation.

CHAPTER SIX

Minimum Security

Without community, there is no liberation.

— AUDRE LORDE

Tammy's transfer to a minimum security facility for women six months after her arrival at prison should have made life more bearable, but it didn't. For one thing, in her new setting she found the other incarcerated women cruel.

> They would give you wrong advice, wrong information, de-
> liberately. I was filling out my commissary card, they told
> me to "put them in this way." It was the wrong day and
> I didn't get any food.

And, ironically, her things kept coming up missing, when the women in maximum security never stole from one another. One prisoner threatened Tammy with bodily harm because her girlfriend kept staring at Tammy. Her blood pressure having shot up to stroke level, Tammy was rushed back to the medical center at the prison. There the doctor, hearing that she feared for her life, wrote, to Tammy's great delight, "Do not ship back. Must remain here." She had been away three weeks.

Eventually, however, the authorities insisted on transferring Tammy to another minimum security facility. With four women to a room and your own key to the front door, the cottage should have been heaven, but it more nearly resembled hell. In the maximum security tier, Tammy was less free but she was safe. Here there seemed to be drugs available everywhere. Threats of violence and physical assault were constant. Making the women freer seemed to make them also freer to prey on one another. In Tammy's cottage, some prisoners gang-raped a woman and sodomized her with instruments, leaving her bleeding.

One lesbian prisoner, who had also been housed in the first prison with Tammy, had used Tammy to make her girlfriend jealous. So Tammy arrived in the second institution as someone's enemy, who made threats against Tammy. Another lesbian beat Tammy up badly and tried to get her into trouble. Finally she got a girlfriend and left Tammy alone.

> It was so open, very open. I was so afraid. I was so afraid
> that I paid for a body guard. I found the roughest person and
> ordered everything she wanted on the commissary. I was that
> afraid.

Everyone knew that Tammy had applied for work release. They realized that she did not want to fight back so that she could keep her record clean. As a result, many tried to goad her into physical conflict.

Another woman prisoner told Tammy that when she went to sleep she was going to kill her.

> I believed her. She had a right to be mad. It was the first
> time I had done anything dangerous. I couldn't take any
> more of her lies. She had been trying a lie on a guard, a
> guard I loved, that would have gotten the guard fired.

When Tammy told the guard, the woman was confined to the cottage, but word got out who had "ratted." Upon receiving a letter from Tammy about her plight, Tammy's pastor's wife intervened and Tammy was allowed to live in a cottage inhabited by older women where the atmosphere was calmer.

> One day I was called to the front office and the person that
> called me is the man who delivers bad news, so when you
> get a call slip from him, there is a death in the family or

something seriously wrong. There were six people he called from various cottages. When I got up there, we were all so scared, we were holding hands we were so nervous. He calls everyone before me, and I was the last person. I was there alone and naturally my mind went berserk and I started thinking all these horrible things and I was crying uncontrollably and sobbing so horribly. When he called me into his office he looked at me and said, "What is the matter with you?" And I said, "What happened? Did my son die? What happened? I know it's bad news because you are the bad news officer." He started laughing, he said, "No, honey, you evidently know someone in high places because the state's attorney's office has told me to move you to another cottage."

Although things became more peaceful after that and Terrence actually visited her new "home" a few times, Tammy was banking on serving the remainder of her time—another full year—in a Chicago work release center. Detainees there could eventually earn the right to weekend passes to spend time away from the center with their families. Her formal application had been on file for some time, but since Tammy was incarcerated for a Class 1 felony, she was the lowest priority for work release. Still, she waged a ferocious campaign with the work release counselor who came to the facility once a week.

Eventually Tammy's persistence paid off. The very Friday that she confronted him, saying, "I deserve to go to work release, what is going on?" he replied, "Evidently they think you do too, so pack your bags. You've leaving Tuesday." It was Tammy's birthday.

✳

Author Jeffrey Archer, incarcerated in England on a perjury charge, found that, regardless of the facility in which he was housed, the prison authorities could not guarantee a safe environment for their charges. This excerpt from his prison diary expresses this horrifying bottom line, with which Tammy would heartily agree.

> I go into great detail to describe this incident simply because those casually reading this diary might be left with an impression that life at Wayland is almost bearable. It

isn't. You can never be sure from one moment to the
next if your life is in danger.[1]

Incarcerated women consistently describe the intimidation prisoners use
against those who show any weakness. One described her exploitation.

> I made the mistake of letting this one girl help me. She
> had been in for a while and she had a reputation for
> being tougher. I was new and didn't know much about
> her. I thought she was just being nice. She told me to
> stick by her and she would protect me. I was relieved. . . .
> Anyway, it started out great, we would take walks to-
> gether and I would cry about losing my daughter and
> being locked up. She would just listen and it felt good
> having someone who seemed to care. After a while she
> started having me do little things for her, and I didn't
> mind, we were friends. Then it got bigger and she knew
> my family had a little money and got me to give [money]
> to her. It got out of hand and she would be mean if I
> didn't give it to her and I was kind of scared.[2]

The abuse lasted for over two years, until the more powerful and experienced prisoner was transferred to another facility.

> Another girl came up to me and threatened me if I didn't
> give her money, but I wasn't getting into that again and I
> told her no. She bashed my head one day, I had to get six
> stitches.[3]

Many have speculated about the reasons for the strong's manipulation
of the weak in the prison system. Some assert that since so many come
from the ghetto, they bring with them streetwise strategies for survival, where violence is the means for upholding respect, regulating
encounters, and controlling territory.[4] It is for this reason, prisoner
Barbara Lane writes, that drug addicts are the most dangerous.

> Trapped in the revolving door of the justice system, the
> majority have become immune to rehabilitation and hope.

To survive, they lie, steal, betray, manipulate staff, and in-
cite chaos. Substance abusers with charismatic personali-
ties are particularly powerful. They draw others into the
excitement and anarchy and end up ruining lives.

I am more suspicious now—untrusting, disillusioned,
and bitter. My eyes are wide open and I don't like what
I see around me.[5]

During incarceration, when money and possessions cannot serve as an
indication of status, explains prisoner Christy Marie Camp, verbal or
physical violence instead will be employed to establish power.

Victimization takes on a variety of forms, only some of
them physical, but the threat of physical harm underlies
everything else. It also involves more intangible tokens of
power; who chooses the programs to be watched on the
unit's TV sets, what seats you sit in, line cutting, who has
first rights to the shower and so on. Prison life provides
the opportunity for some prisoners to "mess over" other
prisoners and to demonstrate their domination and other
prisoner's [sic] submission.[6]

However, psychiatrist James Gilligan believes that prisons themselves
stimulate violence among those incarcerated, because the punishment
itself "constitutes an imitable model of aggression."[7] As abused children develop into aggressive children, who learn by example, so do
nonviolent prisoners respond to the shame and humiliation of punishment with violence of their own.

Primo Levi would agree. Within hours of arriving at the Auschwitz
concentration camp he discovered that the aggression on the part of
prisoners he thought would be allies caused the collapse of detainees'
ability to resist. The deprivations and depredations to which the men
and women were subjected reduced them to a condition of dog-eat-
dog survival.

The harsher the oppression, the more widespread among
the oppressed is the willingness, with all its finite nuances
and motivation, to collaborate: terror, ideological seduc-

tion, servile imitation of the victor, myopic desire for any power whatsoever, even though ridiculously circumscribed in space and time, cowardice, and finally, lucid calculation aimed at eluding the imposed orders and order. . . . Alessandro Manzoni, the nineteenth century novelist and poet knew this quite well: . . . "Provocateurs, oppressors, and those who in some way injure others, are guilty, not only of the evil they commit, but also of the perversion into which they lead the spirit of the offended."[8]

Levi and political philosopher Hannah Arendt understood that concentration camps isolated and sealed individuals off as if they no longer existed. But the camps themselves created a living hell because they destroyed the bonds of human solidarity.[9]

As noted by Levi, prisoner-on-prisoner violence and abuse keeps individuals in a state of fear and unease that management condones because it makes their charges easier to control.[10] Craig Haney maintains that

> in these prisons in which there is collusion between dominant prisoners and staff to maintain the peace, sexual violence tends to be greater. . . . Violent victimization becomes a brutal strategy to facilitate their own survival by destructively elevating one's degraded sense of self above that of others, enabling them to garner a small, albeit perverse sense of status.[11]

Regardless of its causes, this violent and exploitative culture is accepted as a fact of life, an integral feature of the punishment the incarcerated person can expect, an accepted characteristic of imprisonment. Nowhere better can this be seen than in the media coverage of home-decorating guru Martha Stewart's prison sentence. Excitedly, the National Enquirer reported the horrors that Stewart could expect at the Danbury, Connecticut, federal correctional institution to which it was thought she would probably be assigned. Several federal ex-prisoners, including former "Hollywood Madam" Heidi Fleiss, told of the violent behavior that could be expected—including lesbian rape and beatings from vicious gangs, requiring Stewart to pay protection money.[12]

Stewart had hired a consultant, reported the *Christian Science Monitor*, to help prepare her for the "shock, humiliation, and isolation that often accompany a prison sentence."[13] White-collar prison consultants, themselves former federal detainees, popped up in the print media and on television advising of the terrors to be expected.[14] Surprising in this coverage was the acceptance of the correctional environment. Not one journalist sought to determine what, if anything, might be being done to remedy these horrific conditions or called any federal official to any account—or called any federal official for comment. Rather, the story was how severe the punishment from other incarcerated women was going to be for Martha Stewart.

Indeed, this press coverage makes clear that some of the media as well as members of the public endorse these aspects of the prison culture as a deterrent to crime and as appropriate state punishment. For example, California Attorney General Bill Lockyer stated publicly that he wanted to punish former Enron CEO Ken Lay for bilking the state of billions in electricity overcharges: "I would love to personally escort Lay to an 8-by-10 cell that he could share with a tattooed dude who says, 'Hi, my name is Spike, honey.'" As one reform group wryly noted, "The state's top law enforcement officer approves of nonjudicial punishment by rape."[15]

Philosopher Deirdre Golash has noted this acceptance of the culture dominated by prisoner-on-prisoner violence.

> Even more disturbingly, as the prevalence of this form of
> violence has made its way into the popular imagination, it
> has become common to hear it referred to as part of the
> punishment or as a deterrent factor. Although most jokes
> about rape are excluded from the public forum as in
> grossly bad taste, a soft drink company recently saw fit to
> make light of prison rape in a television commercial.[16]

Former prisoner Roderick Johnson sued Texas correctional officials for failing to protect him from brutal rapes and sexual slavery. Officials disputed Johnson's accounts of the assaults, believing his reports not to be credible because he did not resist the attacks: "Sometimes an inmate has to defend himself. . . . We don't expect him not to do anything."[17] The jury agreed with the Texas officials, ruling against Mr. Johnson's claims.

However, it seems clear from the newspaper account of the trial that no Texas official was prepared to deny the dangerous conditions or take responsibility for failing to ameliorate them. Assistant Warden Richard E. Wathen testified, "Prison is a violent place."[18]

✳

Work release started out badly. The living arrangements on the city's west side were dormitory style, ten to a room with a bathroom down the hall and a large cafeteria. But until you found a job you had to work on road crew. One day on road crew was enough for Tammy and reinforced her desire to find employment quickly. Road crew was more of the same old mortification. At five o'clock in the morning the prisoners donned their bright orange jumpsuits, were loaded in a truck like animals, and spent the day picking up litter in parks and on the highway.

> I was not going through any more humiliation. I was
> through. I didn't know who was going to see me on the
> highway cleaning up in this orange jumpsuit. I was finished.

Responding to a notice on the bulletin board, Tammy traveled to Republic Windows to apply for an advertised data entry job. After a positive interview, she leveled with Amy Constantino.

> I said, "Look, I have to be honest with you. I am at a work
> release center, I have just recently gotten out of prison. I have
> an ankle monitor on me. After work, I have to go back to the
> prison lockup. That is going to be my life." She said, "Well,
> I have to check and make sure we are bonded for that, but I
> want you."

Tammy gave Constantino a telephone number where she could be reached. Unfortunately, the number employers had to call was to a row of pay phones that any work release resident could answer. Tammy didn't hear anything for some days. To avoid road crew she did double duty at the center—her own chores and everybody else's. One day the counselor approached Tammy, telling her some lady was trying to find her and she should call her back. When she eventually reached her

92   potential employer, Amy told her the number she had been given was
incorrect.

> She said, "I went on a hunt, I went down to the factory,"
> and she said, "I found three of our employees from the work
> release center and that's how I found you." I said, "You did
> all that?" She said, "Yes, I wanted to give you a second
> chance in life."

Tammy turned over her $21,000 salary to the work release center,
which provided her with an allowance for transportation, lunch, and
clothing. She had to be back at the work release center by 6:30 p.m.,
which didn't give her much time because she had to take two buses
to Republic Windows.

At work Tammy mostly kept to herself, but she did make one
friend. However, when Tammy told her of her recent imprisonment,
the relationship deteriorated.

> It was the biggest mistake. She started to treat me differently,
> she started treating me very badly. She made me feel the way
> a lot of people made me feel after that, like I should be
> grateful to have her company. The things she would do for
> me before, she stopped doing. It seemed like she wanted to see
> me suffer. Amy told me that no one had to know. She was
> the best person. She was my savior.

Work release for Tammy was also surreal—being out among people
during the day and being locked up at night.

> I was still in prison in my mind. I was in the company of
> people I didn't deserve to be with. These people had homes,
> families, marriages, children. I didn't have any of these
> things. I was different. I never ever felt right at Republic
> Windows. I was the best data entry clerk there, I got a pro-
> motion there. But I was never equal. I never felt worthy. It
> was my fault.

Bridging the two worlds—employment and work release—neither of
which she really felt a part, was difficult for Tammy.

I have no identity with society at large, and I am still sepa-rated from my son. So I am not supposed to be crazy?

Until Tammy earned her right to weekend furloughs, she and Terrence met a couple of times after work at a fast food restaurant near the work release center. But it was a long and complicated journey down there for her son from the south suburbs to the west side for such a short visit. And unfortunately just at this time Terrence's own situation, never very good, took a turn for the worse. He became homeless.

CHAPTER SEVEN

Terrence Alone

I try to teach my son that I do not exist to feel for him,
that he must do that for himself in order to survive as a
human being. And that is not always easy, for him nor
for me. Because it's hard to see someone you love feel
hurt, and to know that there are some pains you cannot,
must not, protect your children from, if they are to grow
up tough and whole. It's so much easier to teach them by
order or example not to feel at all.

— AUDRE LORDE

Aunt Pat had finally had it: "I couldn't go another day." Her household
was in an uproar, and her marriage was in tatters (and would not survive). There were other issues, one involving a former girlfriend of her
husband, but the conflict with Terrence certainly didn't help matters.

When Tammy was arrested, Edward, Terrence's father, had fallen off
the wagon after seven years of sobriety. He was back to drinking, and
heavy drinking at that, living in a small room in a drug- and alcohol-
infested inner-city neighborhood. And Edward quickly became inco-
herent when drinking. So he was ruled out as the next caretaker for
Terrence.

Tammy's pastor arranged for Terrence to move in with a childless
parishioner in her late 60s. That experiment didn't make it to the two-
week mark before the woman told Terrence he had to leave. Again, the
church came through with a tiny apartment it owned in a nearby low-

income south suburb. Tammy arranged for Terrence to enroll in a
Catholic school because the public school in that neighborhood was
known to be rough and dysfunctional. Terrence went to and from
school by taxi and spent some weekends with Edward in the apartment. But the young man was thirteen years old and on his own.

Terrence had to learn to do everything for himself—grocery shop-
ping, cooking, cleaning, and laundry. He stayed close to the apartment.

> A teen's dream in a way, but I was depressed, because
> never once did I have a friend over, never once did I
> throw a party, never once was the house not clean, never
> once did I stay up all night on the telephone or watching
> TV. Never once.

It sounds like a clinical depression, and to some extent it probably was,
but perhaps Terrence instinctively knew that his own safety and the
peace of mind of his mother depended on his coming through re-
sponsibly. Tammy would call Terrence every evening at nine o'clock
from the work release center to make sure that he was okay. And Terrence knew she would be extraordinarily anxious if he wasn't there to
answer the telephone.

> I didn't go anywhere, I didn't party. I did nothing. Went
> to school, came home, watched television, waited for
> mom to call, played computer games. No writing, no
> poetry. I was in a vegetative state.

This is not to say that Terrence's life was totally devoid of excitement
and adventure. Mother and son well remember when Tammy gave
permission for Terrence to attend a live concert of his idol, Brittany
Spears. Getting to the northwest suburbs from the south suburbs involved a bus to the train station, a train, a subway, and a cab from the
last subway to the concert arena. Coming back, with only a dollar in
his pocket, Terrence learned to his dismay that the bus from the south
suburban train station ceased running after midnight. He took a taxi,
exited the cab without paying, and ran, hiding in a dark alley until the
vehicle was gone. While waiting, Terrence saw a police squad car looking for him. Terrence knew that if the police questioned him, they

96   would also discover the fact that he was living without adult supervision. Anxiously Terrence hid in the alley for what seemed like hours before he returned to the apartment.

Today Terrence is able to look at the positives from this experience. First, Maurice, whom he despised as slick and dishonest, was gone from his and his mother's lives. Most of the television and videos Terrence watched while his mother was in prison involved dancing; he became intrigued and started to dance himself. This has led to formal dancing instruction and confidence that his future vocation lies in the world of dance. Would he ever have discovered this interest had he not been alone like that?

Also, for the first time he had to take care of himself and become responsible, for which Terrence now is grateful. He admits he had been a cherished and coddled "momma's boy." Due to an irregular uterus, Tammy had been told that she would never be able to have children. So she was shocked when she became pregnant during a time when she was using a great deal of heroin on a daily basis. Terrence's natural father died in a motorcycle accident and never knew about the baby. It was his death that escalated Tammy's drug usage. She never believed she would be able to carry the baby to term.

During this time, she met a rich young woman from the northside who came to Tammy's neighborhood to buy drugs, and stayed on to get high and party with Tammy. As a result, Tammy was so high that she didn't know for the longest time that she was in labor. Although Tammy never had any prenatal care, Terrence was born without any real problems and his health remained unaffected by her drug usage.

Sobered up by the birth of this miracle baby, Tammy went back to work in data entry at a major corporation where she had been employed in the past, and found a proper place for her and her son to live. Eventually, Terrence received social security benefits on his father's account. But Tammy didn't get off heroin altogether. She simply took the infant Terrence with her to buy the drugs.

Traveling to her job on the train, she met Edward, a recovering alcoholic who worked for the railroad, and they became fast friends. One day he told Tammy he was in being evicted from his apartment because of some of the activities of his wife, who had fled, leaving Edward with his own daughter and his wife's son from another relationship. Tammy let the father and two children move into the basement of her house. She and Edward were never intimate, although certainly that would have been his wish. Unasked, Edward gave Tammy $1,500 in cash from each paycheck. Later, he became so close to Terrence that he adopted him.

Tammy thought she was a good mother. From the beginning she and Terrence were inseparable.

> Even through my addiction, I took good care of my son.
> From my point of view. Because if you are taking your child
> with you to buy drugs . . . I couldn't see that then, but to
> me, my baby went everywhere with me. I'm never without
> him. I would go to the bars, Terrence went with me to the
> bars. All the drug dealers and other addicts knew my son.
> A warped picture, isn't it?

Today she recognizes how her addiction interfered with the parenting of her child. But, on the positive side, they were always together, he was always physically safe, and a deep and loving bond developed between them.

> Let me tell you how my son got through my addiction. He
> was in the way. In order to get him out of my way, I
> showered him with every gift, every toy. I just wanted him
> to let me have my space, so he had every kind of computer
> game, everything to keep him busy except Mommy. We
> didn't sit down and do homework together. We didn't sit
> down at the dinner table together. I did all the things that
> a parent was supposed to do, but I did what I had to do in-
> between them. We went to movies, the toy store, we went
> on vacations, we did everything. But I left the tools out. I
> should have taught him some things.

After a few months on work release, Tammy began to qualify for weekend passes, which enabled her to spend Friday, Saturday, and Sunday nights with her son in the small apartment. Things were wonderful then because, for the moment, both put aside their differences over Terrence's homosexuality. Every single time Tammy had to leave, however, Terrence remembers feeling a sense of abandonment.

She would sit down and explain to me that this was a forty-eight-hour pass. "I'm only going to be here forty-eight hours." That went in this ear and right back out. Two days later, "Where are you going?" "I have to go back." Every time she had to go back it felt like she was leaving me all over again.

Concerned about her son's remaining by himself, Tammy tried to send him to a well-regarded state home for boys until the end of her work release sentence. But by deliberately sabotaging the process by telling the authorities he was gay, Terrence ensured that the application would be denied.

I wanted him to be in a stable environment until I got out of work release, and when I asked him why did he do that, he said, "Mommy, please don't send me away again. I want to be with you. Don't send me away again. Why do you keep leaving me and wanting to get rid of me?" That is when I really had to talk to him and explain to him that I was doing things for his benefit, because I loved him. He saw this as another abandonment.

It was only a matter of time before someone in the neighborhood alerted the state child protective service to this thirteen-and-a-half-year-old who appeared to be living alone, and a full-blown investigation of child abuse and neglect ensued. Although Tammy was now in the same city with Terrence, she had no power to end the neglect of her own son, and weekend passes were all that the official system had to offer. For if Tammy were released early, then every other woman prisoner would have to be let go as well.

My story is no different from anybody else's. Everyone who came to the work release center had the same story—"My child has run away," "My child is missing," "I can't find my child," "My husband has molested my child," "My daughter was raped," "My son is in jail." Everyone had a story, my story wouldn't be any different, so why would they release me?

But luckily, given Terrence's age (almost fourteen) and the support system Tammy had put in place for him, agency workers did have the goodness of heart and common sense to find the child abuse charge "unfounded," and closed the case in December 1999.

✳

Because it is easy for teenagers to slip under the radar, Terrence's being on his own is not unusual. In her book on the children of the incarcerated, Nell Bernstein found another Terrence living alone. Fifteen years of age when his mother was arrested on a drug charge, the other Terrence was on his own for some months. He washed cars and sold newspapers to earn money to buy food, but the electricity, water, and gas companies eventually cut all utilities for lack of funds. Five months passed before any kind of help was provided.

> "In my head I was like, 'I'm gonna be the man. I'm
> gonna pay the bills. I'm gonna try to do it,' Terrence said,
> 'but I just didn't know what to do. I just basically had to
> eat noodles and do what I could until my mom came
> home.'"[1]

Dorothy Gaines's son Philip was nine years old at the time his mother was sentenced for drug conspiracy; he worked hard for her release, writing the judge, and later, famously, President Clinton:

> I hope you can free my mom. I need her. Because I am
> just a little boy! I am ten years old. I need my mom very
> much. Please get her out I need her.[2]

There aren't any formal studies researching the lives of children of incarcerated parents that aren't hampered by methodological limitations of small sample size or failure to use appropriate comparison groups.[3] But from rich anecdotal evidence and what we know about child development, we can sketch out some of the obvious ways that parental imprisonment impacts children. One doesn't need a degree in psychology to understand that the loss of a parent, whether due to death, divorce, or incarceration, has extremely negative consequences for children, producing anger, depression, regression, and other antisocial behaviors, all of which divert the child from normal developmental tasks. And locking up the mother, usually the child's primary resident caregiver, punishes and harms the child more than removal of the father. Although fathers are clearly important to children, current societal expectations of mothers' roles and responsibilities add another dimension to the seriousness of the enforced absence of the child's mother.

Psychologists working in the field of women's incarceration remind us that adolescence is typically a time of heightened sensitivity and emotional reactivity. For a teen, maternal imprisonment can lead to fear, anger, confusion, shame, frustration, loneliness, sadness, depression, and loss of control. In contending with these emotions, adolescents may become attracted to illegal substances, to using anger to suppress other emotions, and to thrill seeking and sexual intimacy, or may be forced to take on adult roles prematurely—all of which may lead to crime. These coping mechanisms help them navigate painful periods, but they can impede normal adolescent development.[4] As we have seen, Terrence employed all these responses, with the exception of drug abuse.

Adolescents with incarcerated mothers, experts explain, require a safe and stable residence with appropriate adult supervision and a nurturing caregiver, along with meaningful contact with their mother. They also need counseling to break their isolation, because teens are not likely to seek assistance or share their burden with their peers. Nor are they able or likely to discuss their emotions with their own mothers because, seeking to shield them from additional upset, they often become emotional caretakers for their parents.[5]

All these sensible strategies for minimizing harm were absent in Terrence's case. Pat's own confusion and shame about Tammy's arrest, conviction, and incarceration probably made it difficult for her to provide the clear messages that her nephew needed to reduce his own anger and grief and to encourage visitation—not an untypical situation. At the time, Pat did the best she could with an intractable situation; but soon Terrence was to be without any meaningful adult supervision, let alone counseling.

Their mothers' imprisonment also severely affects younger children, who most likely will have a different caregiver and a new home. In the case of infants and toddlers, incarceration disrupts the development of the critical mother/child bond, and given their perfectly-age-appropriate narcissism, preschoolers may blame themselves for their mother's distress and absence from home. Conflicting messages—such as "Mommy loves you," when Mommy is clearly gone—are confusing, leading to sadness, anger, fear, or grief. Given their limited ability to verbalize these feelings, these young children may act out their fears or sadness, or regress emotionally and physically. Aggression or depression, leading to difficulty in concentration, threatens school success for older children.[6]

When her infant son was between the ages of seven months and two years, Joanne Archibald was imprisoned on a drug charge. Because she had always sung to her baby as she put him to bed, Joanne made a tape recording so that he could continue to hear the songs. But when she got out, the toddler no longer wanted to listen to them and he went so far as to rip up the tape. Presumably those songs were tied up with her being gone and were now too painful to listen to.

When he was nine, Joanne's son tried to commit suicide by jumping out the window, demonstrating the huge loss experienced by even the youngest children.

> He used to say, "Well, my dad left me before I was even born and then you left." The fear that I was going to leave him. And I would respond time after time, "I am not going to leave again." And him thinking that somehow it was his fault, as nonsensical as that is, he really thought it was his fault—That is what he told the psychiatrist at Children's Memorial. "Well, if I was dead, that was going to fix things." Just seeing the years that it took for him to deal with it and knowing that he didn't do anything—I did it, I made these decisions, I made the decision to be a single mother, I made the decision to carry the drugs, I put him through this—and how many years he's taken to get it together. He ended up going to counseling four days a week after that for three and a half, four years.[7]

Although not true for Joanne, we do know that many women who are drug addicts are not good mothers. Two important mitigating factors should be borne in mind. Most drug-addicted mothers, although they do not claim to be ideal, do believe they have been good parents.

Ex-prisoner Elizabeth Harris explains, "Part of the problem with substance abuse is you don't think you're doing anything wrong."[8] It was
only after she was in rehab that she realized the standards she had set
for herself were far too low.

> I thought I was doing a good job by just providing a roof
> over the head, paying the utilities. But I wasn't mentally
> and emotionally, putting his needs first.[9]

Children love even the most neglectful parents; the separation will be
experienced on a deeply emotional level, with the possibility of lifetime adverse impact. Nell Bernstein, a journalist who has studied the
issue for over five years, describes the questions she receives when she
promotes her work on radio programs. "Wouldn't the kids be better
off without these kinds of parents?" Or, "Aren't there some people who
just don't deserve to be parents?" Bernstein responds:

> But the main thing that I've learned from talking to so
> many kids, which should be so obvious, is that these are
> the parents they've got. These are the parents they love.
> And their connections to those parents are exactly as real
> and as deep as my connection to my kids. And I know
> that should go without saying, but it never does. . . .
>   We are able to lock people up in the numbers that we
> do only so long as we see them as useless—extraneous
> individuals whom our society simply does not need. But
> the majority of prisoners are mothers and fathers; they are
> needed in the most fundamental way. The parent-child
> bond, beyond its private importance to the individuals
> who share it, is a social asset that must be valued and
> preserved.[10]

Emani Davis's father was incarcerated when she was six years of age
and remains in prison today. Now twenty-six years old, Davis understands that our neglect of the children of parents in prison is sentencing the children to a social death. Children, she says, have the right to
survive and develop, and for this love is required. If they don't receive
love, they will die.

For all of us, there is somebody that we can say, "That person made a huge difference for me. That person is the reason why I got to where I am." For children it is supposed to be their parents. . . . But we have decided that they aren't worthy of that. It is one thing to sentence a parent to that, but I think that we are forgetting that we are sentencing entire families to that. We are sentencing children to that. . . . I think it is that serious. I think we are talking about the difference between life and death for kids.

For some reason people have decided [since] my father broke the law and went to prison that it is different. That I am any less proud, that I love him any less, that he is any less extraordinary and huge in my life, because he is not.

We have done a disservice by pretending that if somebody is going to prison for life, that it would be better for children to just pull them away, because of the loss. Because the truth is there isn't a loss. There is a loss of that person physically, but parents 100 percent can parent from prison. People can do it. Love cannot be contained by bars. . . . My father has been the number one man in my life, and he has been able to do that by his unbelievable commitment, not only by being there for us, but also by making himself into somebody that we would actually be proud to call "Dad."[11]

Yet a Department of Justice study found that in 1997 over half (54 percent) of mothers in state prisons never received a personal visit with their children, and only 24 percent said they had a meeting as frequently as once a month.[12] Sixty-two percent of parents in state prisons and 84 percent in federal prisons were locked up at least one hundred miles away from their last place of residence.[13]

As Terrence experienced, confiscatory rates inhibit telephone contact between incarcerated parents and their children. Only two states and the Federal Bureau of Prisons offer debit calling—telephone cards purchased by the prisoner. All other prisoners must call collect, with telephone companies charging between $1.00 and $3.00 per minute along with a fee of between $1.50 and $4.00 for placing the call. Sweetheart arrangements between the telephone companies and state correctional agencies, under which prisons receive kickbacks of forty to sixty cents on the dollar per call, providing needed money for their budgets, result in these expensive rates. The Campaign to Promote Equitable Telephone Charges has already forced some states to renegotiate contracts eliminating the kickbacks, reducing the telephone fees that the families of prisoners must bear.[14] Many households, like Terrence's Aunt Pat's, cannot afford these inflated collect telephone charges.

At an American Correctional Association convention, one telephone company representative bragged at that the collect-call system enables "criminals to support the cost of incarceration instead of taxpayers." "Isn't that the families paying for the calls?" he was asked. "Families, criminals—it's the same thing," was the vendor's reply.[15]

Nor was Terrence's and Tammy's experience with the child protective service unusual. Their mothers' imprisonment especially disadvantages children of incarcerated mothers. According to a Department of Justice study, 10 percent of incarcerated mothers have children placed in foster care, compared with 2 percent of fathers.[16] That statistic on foster care is ominous, because the Adoption and Safe Families Act (ASFA), passed by Congress in 1997, requires a state to file for a termination of parental rights proceeding when a child has been in foster care for fifteen of the most recent twenty-two months. The ASFA made no exemption for incarceration, providing only a general exception, "compelling reasons," for not terminating parental rights.[17]

Some state laws implementing the act, such as New York and Illinois, provide even more stringent tests and burdens of proof than the federal act. At least one case in New York has required women to maintain substantial and frequent contact with their children in order to avoid termination of parental rights, a difficult condition for low-income mothers incarcerated far from home.[18]

We have no hard evidence about the total number of women prisoners who have lost their children permanently due to the ASFA, but Philip Genty of Columbia University Law School made a computer search of reported cases five years after the law's enactment, finding a 250 percent rise in cases terminating rights due to parental incarceration during that time, an increase from 260 to 909 cases.[19]

Since, nationally, 65 percent of women in state prisons and 59 percent in federal prisons are parents of minors, with the majority of the children less than ten years of age, the potential impact of the ASFA is huge.[20] In New York State, more than 90 percent of all incarcerated women serve at least a year and a half—three months longer than the ASFA time limits.[21] These provisions of the ASFA can present serious barriers to mothers in prison, adding to their despair and depression and making it difficult for them to avoid drug addiction upon release. According to one expert, the possibility of reuniting with their children is "one of the most effective tools toward rehabilitation," which the ASFA eliminates.[22]

Research has shown that incarcerated mothers are less likely to have committed violent offenses and more apt to have been charged with drug crimes. In 1997, only 26 percent of female parents in state or federal prison were serving time for a violent offense, with 74 percent incarcerated for property, drug, or public order crimes, with an average sentence of forty-nine months.[23] The meaning is clear: no danger to the public would result from structuring community-based treatment alternatives that would keep mothers and their children together.[24]

Nothing, as we shall see, tears up Tammy more than what she views as her total abandonment of her son. When she got out of prison she kept a small diary for Terrence: "I thought I would not survive and I wanted Terrence to know that I did love him and I was sorry for all the trouble."

CHAPTER EIGHT

The Basement

> I moved in a fen of unexplained anger that encircled me
> and spilled out against whomever was closest that shared
> those hated selves. Of course I did not realize it at the
> time. That anger lay like a pool of acid deep inside me,
> and whenever I felt deeply, I felt it, attaching itself in the
> strangest places.
>
> — AUDRE LORDE

Finally, Tammy was home for good—with an ankle bracelet for three additional months. With the monitor she could only go to and from work and only a certain distance from the house. Once the bracelet was removed, she would be on parole supervision. From the apartment Tammy needed two trains and two buses to get to Republic Windows, her place of employment, and she began her commute at five in the morning.

Tammy and Terrence were living in two tiny rooms. She took the bedroom and Terrence slept on the floor of what was really a small storeroom. But as a result of Terrence's lack of a bed, Tammy found she couldn't sleep in the bedroom, which produced a standoff, as Tammy described in a journal she kept at the time:

> The walls are closing in on me in this tiny apartment. I still
> feel guilty because Terrence sleeps in that tiny room that's
> meant to be a closet, so I won't sleep in the bedroom. And

he feels guilty about taking the only bedroom, so he won't sleep in there either. It remains unoccupied.

Two weeks after Tammy arrived home, Edward, evicted from his apartment, joined mother and son, and broke the logjam. Tammy gave Edward the bedroom, she continued to sleep on the couch in the living room, and Terrence remained in the storage room. Clearly the cramped living conditions were not conducive to helping Terrence and Tammy make the transition back to normality.

Almost immediately relations between mother and son drastically deteriorated. Terrence did not seem amenable to being supervised or directed in any way. Having been on his own for so long, he was now unwilling to have someone else order his life. And the long-postponed but important battle around Terrence's homosexuality broke out into the open. His mother's attitude about her son's sexuality, in turn, affected Terrence's basic response to his mother's attempts to be a parent to him.

Whether it was cooking or laundry, Terrence didn't let Tammy do anything for him. Nor did he want to tell her where he was going or when he would be back, or obey any curfew. For instance, Tammy did not want to let Terrence attend parties with his friends.

> When she was gone, I didn't have parties, I didn't sneak out late, I didn't do that. So when she came home, "Momma, can I go to a party?" "No." "All this time, I did what I was supposed to do, and you tell me I can't go anywhere? How dare you?" And I said, "You know, I am going to do it anyway, I don't care."

Today Tammy understands that she had overdone it.

> *I am trying to make up for my absence and I probably tried too hard. I felt guilty and I tried to be everything to him. He had grown up in the interim, but I tried to make him my baby again.*

It was also difficult for Tammy to acknowledge that Terrence had found himself and become a better person, all without her. Undoubtedly, says Terrence, she felt excluded.

For Tammy, allowing Terrence to talk about his homosexuality in the house was out of the question. Most of the arguments started because of that. When Terrence refused to do something she wanted, Tammy would yell, "Fag!" He would respond with "Junkie!" and things might get physical after that, with the house torn up. Or Tammy would reply to an insult by blaming Terrence for telling the judge she used drugs.

In Tammy's mind, Terrence's homosexuality was bound up with her own incarceration.

> I was angry because I thought he had turned gay because I was sent to prison. If he stayed gay, the fact that I was in prison meant I messed up. It was my fault. If I hadn't gone to prison, he wouldn't have been gay. He told me he had been gay before that, but I didn't believe it.
>
> I thought of it as a lifetime curse. I refused to accept that he would be cursed for the rest of his life because of something I did. I wanted the whole incarceration trauma to be over, I wanted all that behind me, and I wanted his lifestyle behind me too. That way I'll know. It validated that I was really out and it was over. But if he continued to be gay it would haunt me for the rest of my life because it was my fault. Because it happened while I was gone. Somebody had gone and said something to him. Because I didn't shelter him any more.

At the same time, the discrimination against exprisoners Tammy was beginning to experience reinforced the wisdom of her own views about gays.

> I told him, "You are setting yourself up for so many doors to be closed, for people to look at you in a different light, for you to have a lot of misery and pain, and you are inviting this in." I said, "Why would you want to go into the world dragging this big ball and chain behind you and you are just starting your life out?" And he told me, "Mommy, I have to be who I am, what can I do?" I actually asked him, begged him, to hide it. "You can be who you want to be, but don't go around telling people."

Some openly gay friends, all going through the same thing, supported Terrence, which helped.

> "So what," I said, "she can't be with me when I go out-
> side, I don't care. I'm only at home for a few hours. If
> she doesn't like it, we just won't talk about it. She won't
> have anything to do with my life."

But of course Terrence did very much care about his mother. The home front became an increasingly ugly scene, with Edward vainly trying to act as a buffer between the two. One of Terrence's friends had given him a rainbow necklace to wear to show he was proud to be gay. Tammy took that piece of jewelry, Terrence's prized possession, and burned it. On another occasion she put Terrence's Brittany Spears CD on the stove and actually set it in flames too. Later Tammy came upon Terrence's journal and read part of it. When he found out, Terrence took to deliberately using the journal to write negative thoughts about his mother and leaving it around for her to read. Terrence called Tammy the worst person who ever lived and said he wished she was dead. Tammy fell right into the trap, further souring relations between them.

Before long, the two could not have a normal conversation.

> I thought I could come home and fix it. Terrence said there
> was nothing I could do to change him. I said, "As long as
> you are in my house, no, no." It was really bad. It got to be
> really bad. We could never even have a conversation so we
> avoided each other.

Terrence then began to hit back in other ways. He would call the police and tell them that his mother had put him out of the house.

> I don't think he really wanted me to go back, but his confu-
> sion and anger dominated, and he reacted in a way that he
> knew would hurt me. Of course the police applauded me for
> taking a stand instead of arresting me. But just seeing them
> in my home was a very low point. Then there was a time
> when we had a fight and I wouldn't take him to school so

> he took the bus to school. When he got there he told the so-
> cial worker that he had slept on the streets all night because
> I had put him out.

Three times Terrence actually ran away to a friend's home down the block. On several occasions Tammy's anger went way too far.

> At one point I was so angry that I picked up a hammer to
> hit my son on his head and that was the pivotal point when
> I knew we were both out of control. I could have killed him.

Tammy's long-imagined dream—the reunion of mother and son—turned into the worst nightmare lasting at least two years, if not longer. Now she understands that "I was lashing out at everybody who was in earshot, including my child."

Amazingly, this horrendous situation did not improve over time; it rectified itself suddenly. Terrence was participating in a support group for teens; faithfully once a week, Tammy drove him the long distance there and back. One particular evening Terrence called to say that a counselor was going to drive him home. At midnight a dazed Terrence finally walked into the apartment, where his distraught mother confronted him, without, however, gaining any useful information. The next day the youth program summoned Tammy to its premises and told her that Terrence reported a male counselor had sexually molested him the night before.

> My mother was like, "Why didn't you tell me?" "What
> was the point? You were going to think it was my fault.
> Remember, I was a fag. You weren't going to believe me."
> That was the moment everything flat lined, everything
> smoothed out. Everything was perfect. It went from un-
> bearable to perfect.

It was the turning point for Tammy. Her son clearly needed her but believed he could not talk to her about the problem. She now knew she had to be there for Terrence in every way. Terrence persevered, testifying against his abuser, who was convicted, sentenced, and fired from his job. Tammy was amazed at her son's courage.

*What happened after that was that I accepted who he was. I
wanted to know his friends, I needed to be a part of his life.
Our relationship totally changed after that and it never went
back. I was his mom again.*

Later Tammy read something that Terrence had written about this
period.

*We are closer now because we share a trauma. That is a
trauma that we both share. And I didn't realize that Terrence
would never forget it, either, until I read something that he
had written about me. He wrote that "my mom and I have
been through some of the most horrific trauma that you will
ever experience." I realized that the incarceration damaged my
son more than it damaged me.*

Terrence's worries about abandonment affect his current ability to enter
into relationships. Unfortunately, he says, if he sees his partner start to
pull away, Terrence will inevitably run first to avoid being left. More-
over, Terrence has, for the moment, decided not to have children.

I'm not going to have any kids. I will not be a father.
I just won't. If I make a mistake in my life, or if I pass
away, I will not have my child go through that. At the
time it was just hell.

Wearying of the two-and-a-half-hour commute each way to work,
Tammy decided to return to school to complete her interrupted un-
dergraduate degree. Edward's financial help would enable her to get
by, but just. All three stayed in the small apartment for about two
years, until they moved into a town house in a nearby but more af-
fluent community. Tammy installed the computer in the house's dark
basement. Then the major depression hit—a delayed depression.

She hadn't actually used her brain for years. Now, to make up for
it, in that basement bunker Tammy reflected night and day, as all the
thoughts and feelings that the drug and prison numbing had obliterated
came rushing back.

Stopping using drugs is the easy part. Everything floods back.
You have to learn to deal with these feelings. You stop grow-
ing when you use drugs. So you are talking about years and
years of not having any feelings. I couldn't deal with them.
That is what I did in the basement for two and a half years.

After taking Terrence to school in the morning, Tammy would get up
and go downstairs with her coffee. Once there in her dark cave she
would do her homework and play spider solitaire on the computer,
remaining in the basement until it was time to pick Terrence up from
school.

I knew something was wrong when I didn't have any more
homework or during summer breaks and Christmas breaks I
was still in the basement. I would wake up, get my coffee,
and I would go to the basement. And I would come up from
the basement whenever my son came home from school, and
if he didn't come home from school if he had activities, I'd
come up when it was dark. In my mind, I was still in the
dark. I was hiding so the world couldn't see me. Same thing
as being on drugs, only I didn't have the drugs. Trapped forever. It was all the same big ball of despair and degradation
and embarrassment and humiliation. I was encompassed in
that circle, and I couldn't break through that circle, so everywhere I looked I felt that humiliation, I felt the degradation,
I felt the embarrassment.

In that basement Tammy allowed her feelings, long tamped down, to
surface, and they were paralyzing.

I relived every minute of it. I relived the wasted years, the
wasted time with Terrence. I relived how much could have
happened to him because I wasn't there. I relived all the hu-
miliations, the worst of which were at Cook County. When
you are sitting there and reliving all of that, it is like a self-
fulfilling prophecy. I felt worthless. So how could I get up
and make things better when I felt worthless? Couldn't sleep.
Had insomnia so bad. I never slept—maybe an hour or two.

Her journal shows just how often Tammy's thoughts were on her son.

> Terrence deserves so much more. Last night I lay in bed re-
> membering when he had to take care of himself, had to come
> home to an empty house and cook and clean for himself.
> God, he must have been so afraid. I love him so much.

Letters in the diary indicate her overwhelming concern for her son.

> Dear Terrence,
>   I hope you realize how much I love you. There is nothing
> I want for myself anymore, I just want you to live a nor-
> mal, healthy life. I am so sorry I did not provide you with a
> father you could spend time with. I am so sorry that you
> have had to endure so much. I have never regretted having
> you my son.

And:

> I am so grateful to God for keeping Terrence safe while I was
> gone. He was in so many dangerous situations. I found out
> that he was robbed at gun point while I was away. Terrence
> tried to run and the gun man grabbed his shirt, but Terrence
> wriggled out of it. So my son was walking around bare-chested
> in downtown Chicago. He reveals these horrible things to me
> in bits and pieces, but it doesn't make things any easier.

During this time, having lost all her possessions caused Tammy a great
deal of pain as well. As her depression did not enable her to work, she
and Terrence were able only to just scrape by economically.

> My mom always said your outer appearance would always
> open doors for you. When I lost everything I owned, that
> image I had maintained was gone and my self-esteem went
> with it. I took it very personally. With all the window dress-
> ing gone, I did not know who I was, nor could I find my
> self-worth. Today, I feel rich if I can pay the bills, and the
> clothes do not matter anymore. Finding out who I am does.

The computer was in the dreariest corner of that dark and dank basement.

> When I would walk down those steps, I never felt despair.
> I felt like I am going where I should be. It would be
> tantamount to a child going to sit in the corner before some-
> one told him to. Punishing himself. When I would walk
> down those steps it was because I felt that was where I be-
> longed. I was comfortable there.

With its cinderblocks, covered-up window, and poor lighting, the basement resembled the jail: "I had replicated the prison in my own home."

> I did that because I was completely lost. I did not know what
> to do. I did not know how to pull myself out of it, I did not
> know how to get out of prison. They opened the door and let
> me out, but I was still in prison. I didn't know how to free
> myself.

From Tammy's diary:

> I pulled the shades down so that no sun light can come in. I
> should be in the dark. I wish someone could help me. I don't
> know how to help myself. I don't feel like I can help Ter-
> rence either. I have to change my attitude before he comes
> home from school. I have to stop thinking about myself and
> think about him. I wish someone would show me the way. I
> will cry alone for now.

Certainly Tammy was depressed, but perhaps it was a necessary time-
out; clearly, her body and mind needed to recuperate.

> My brain, my mind, and my heart shut down. Everything
> shut down at one time. I needed to do that. When I got out,
> I was homeless, husbandless, my son was acting crazy. It was
> a lot to deal with. It was a lot to deal with at one time.

Tammy is grateful she had the financial ability to take this time she
seemed to need. Most ex-prisoners, she realizes, must return immedi-

ately to the real world to support themselves and their families. But, says Tammy, the expectations placed on returning prisoners are unrealistic.

> I'm supposed to heal and get right back into the saddle. And
> if I don't, it's my fault, something is wrong with me. No one
> has a clue as to how long the road is really there for them.
> Even if they never get locked up again, the road is still long.

Today, Tammy understands the severity of her mental condition at the time: "I suffered in silence and I was losing all sanity."

Terrence was oblivious of Tammy's plight. Captain of the high school cheerleading squad, involved in every club there was, and dancing, dancing everywhere, Terrence had come into the light. But Tammy was still in the dark.

*

Tammy's and Terrence's experiences are not unique. Once Dorothy Gaines came home after serving six years of her nineteen-year drug conspiracy sentence after being pardoned by President Clinton in 2001, her son Philip made a (mostly symbolic) suicide attempt with a homemade noose. He wanted his mother. He had her physically, but mentally, like Tammy, she wasn't all there. Later he commented:

> She's been out for three years, but it's like she's still in-
> carcerated. Her mind is somewhere else, like she's still
> confined.[1]

As Tammy sat in the basement for two years, for the first time she confronted the choices she had made in her life, an examination from which heroin had kept her. But overwhelmed with feelings of inadequacy, Tammy lacked the critical insights needed to make sense of it all and ended up beating up on herself as she continued to hide from the outside world.

Tammy's father had only an eighth-grade education, but he made good money during his long working life at General Motors. Her mother, a college graduate, started as a school teacher and ended up the head of the local child protective agency. She was actively involved in her sorority and in the community. There were five children, three

116 girls and two boys, in a church-going family that ate dinner together every night and always took vacations together.

So why had Tammy, the oldest girl, always been the family rebel, the deviant? Since she was a child of six or seven she had refused to follow the rules and took a different path from others. As far as Tammy was concerned, there must have been something wrong with her: "There was something psychologically unbalanced in my psyche, that made me want to choose the wrong life as opposed to the right life." That choice led her to leave her small Michigan town at eighteen for the big city of Chicago and to lifestyles typical for some attractive young women on their own who lack money. The details will concern us later, but the life involved alcohol, prostitution, being a companion to a major gang leader, heroin use, and ultimately two abusive marriages.

For Tammy it remained a mystery how a young girl raised "the right way" in a two-parent, middle-class household could end up wasting her gifts for almost thirty chaotic years. And gifts they were, of heart and mind, as should be readily apparent by now. Only when Tammy and this author explored the mystery for this book was she able to put the pieces together and to understand that she was not necessarily a bad person, but one using strategies to cope with violence and abuse that ultimately proved self-destructive.

Homeless activist Alexander Masters befriended a chaotic homeless person named Stuart Shorter, an obviously brilliant man afflicted by muscular dystrophy, in Cambridge, England. In his 2005 memoir of Stuart, Masters sought to explain those circumstances in Stuart's life that led to drug abuse, violence, incarceration, and homelessness. Toward the end of the book, the reader learns that Stuart's brother and babysitter brutally sexually molested him and his sister on a regular basis when Stuart was between the ages of twelve and fifteen. But, unlike Tammy, also a victim of childhood sexual assault, Stuart never had the chance to see the book in print; a train collision, possibly suicidal, ended his life before the book was published.

Stuart read Masters's first draft and pronounced it "bullocks boring." He wanted a best seller, "something what people will read."[2] Stuart advised Masters:

> Do it the other way round. Make it more like a murder mystery. What murdered the boy I was? See? Write it backwards.[3]

As in *Stuart: A Life Backwards*, let's explore what it was that killed Tammy's healthy growth and development and led to a nineteen-year heroin addiction. Backwards is also the way Tammy chose to divulge to this author the episodes that ultimately unlocked the puzzle; as it turned out, backwards was the only way Tammy was able to disinter repressed memories.

When she was a teen, Tammy's grades were poor; she seemed to be looking for power and adventure, not academic achievement: "What was important to me was being a leader of the pack, being feared, respected, very powerful." Being the oldest girl, Tammy was put in charge of all the other children at home when her mother was out of the house. That too gave her a position of power.

At age twelve Tammy was exposed to prostitution. Auntie White, the sister of Tammy's mother's best friend, ran a small brothel that featured all-night parties and card games.

> When I would spend weeks and weekends with my god-
> mother, we would occasionally go to Auntie White's house.
> My mother knew about Auntie, what she did, where she did
> it, and with whom she did it. It was deviant, but these
> women wore pretty clothes, drove the best cars, had their
> choice of men and always had a lot of fun. I really thought
> she walked on water. I wanted to be just like her girls. I
> would never see her girls engaging in sex but knew they did.

She can't imagine that her mother was ever involved in prostitution or any illegal activity. Yet, like others in the community, her mother had friends who participated in illegal gambling as policy runners and bookmakers and in prostitution. And, although Tammy's mother worked so hard to be a good parent, she still unwittingly exposed her teen daughter to a powerful role model, a woman who seemed both to have power and to be having fun as a result of illegal sex-trade entrepreneurship.

> And when you are that young and you see this glamour and
> beautiful women it has an astounding effect on you, because
> it's all glamour and power and "I have the world by the
> balls" kind of thing. A child like me would only see that
> part. I wouldn't know about diseases and being beaten up
> and addiction.

Like Auntie White's women, Tammy ruled by means of her beauty and verve that she soon saw served to entice and control boys and men. She lost her virginity early and voluntarily, and never looked back. There was drinking but no drugs, and sex was mostly in the backseats of cars. The older men she attracted gave her money for the sex. "This made me feel powerful. Getting paid for sex makes you feel powerful," Tammy explains. She couldn't spend the money on herself without attracting attention at home, so she tossed it around in high school, treating her friends, which made her feel even more in command. Regularly, Tammy escaped out the window at night, with her siblings covering for her, and later she ran away from home more times than she could count: "I am having a ball. In high school I had a very cunning and devious personality."

After her mother died, Tammy found a filed legal petition among her mother's papers that sought to place Tammy under the care of the child protective service—that is how bad it had apparently gotten for her parents. When she finished high school, Tammy determined to leave home for good at age eighteen and traveled on her own to Chicago, packing her bag and leaving the very day she graduated.

For Tammy's mother, appearances were extremely important, which didn't help either.

> She only cared about how we looked to other people and the position that our family held within society. That was important to my mom. She spent a lot of money on material things. We had to be the first to have this, the first to have that. She watched the things that were important to her, like how we looked, how our hair was, the way we spoke.

A photograph of Tammy and her mother captures both women's beauty and sense of style. Tammy is nineteen and probably has no more than hundred and ten pounds on her willowy five-foot-five-inch frame. She is wearing a fur-trimmed stole and the shortest skirt imaginable. Think Diana Ross of the Supremes or actress Diahann Carroll at the height of her youth and beauty. And Tammy's mother, a dazzling young Ruby Dee look-alike, is wearing a fur-trimmed jacket and an elegant, velvet pants suit.

Tammy always believed she and her oldest brother were dissimilar from the rest of the family: the others were all relaxed and laid back, while she was aggressive and dramatic. "Where did she come from?" relatives would always ask. When she was fifteen, Tammy finally learned that her biological father was someone her mother met as a teen, and that the man Tammy thought of as her father was a stepfather whom her mother married when Tammy was two years old. Subconsciously, Tammy thinks now, she must have realized that something like this had happened: "I had to have known, because it manifested itself at a very early age."

As it turned out, Tammy's older brother had yet another father, and he was so different from the other children that she was frightened when she found out that he did not have the same father either; she feared she would be crazy like him too. Her brother was aloof, almost invisible, and kept his distance from his other siblings. At school, for example, he acted as if he did not know his brothers and sisters, and even though he was tall with a threatening stature, he did not protect them. Later he joined the marines and served in Vietnam. To this day, he remains detached from other family members, working odd jobs as a truck driver.

But Tammy could pry no further information from her mother about her natural father. In the only extant photograph, the man is Black and looks young. This information about her parentage sent Tammy into a tailspin, unleashing a good deal of anger and upset.

> It bothered me a lot. As a matter of fact, I became hysterical. It was a very ugly scene. I got worse after they told me that. I became very confused, because all this time I wasn't who I thought I was. Who was I? That's why I knew there was something wrong with me because I wasn't a member of that family. It seemed like the two weirdest people in the family were me and my brother, who didn't have my stepfather's genes. I started wondering what kind of man this was and because I didn't know, I didn't know how to act.

The one thing Tammy wanted but could not have was her stepfather's genes.

> I felt like we got the shaft. My brother and I were the only ones with antisocial behaviors. He and I were the oldest boy

and girl respectively, he and I were the ones with different fathers, and he and I were the only ones of our siblings who were mischievous, destructive, and strange as children and teenagers.

In truth, however, Tammy remembers being an angry child a lot earlier than that. When the family was the first to move to an all-white neighborhood, the other children at school attacked the Black newcomers. For about a year, the white children, calling her and her siblings names they didn't understand, chased them home everyday. Daily, the twelve-year-old Tammy stood and fought the attackers.

> I wasn't afraid of anything. I would stay behind because I wasn't going to run. I was going to fight. And I got beat up a lot because they ganged up on me. I had to protect everybody else because even my oldest brother, who was very tall for his age, never took up for us. So it was up to me to protect my brother and my sisters. I was always tough. The outlaw personality was developed very early.

Eventually, the anger the daily battle generated burst out inappropriately. Tammy had one white friend who regularly visited.

> She used to come, and I loved dolls and we would go into the garage and play with our dolls. We were in there and we were playing with our dolls. Something snapped in me. It snapped, because I jumped on her and pulled her hair and ripped all her clothes off her back. All the anger from what I had experienced I saw in her white face. I hurt her pretty badly. She ran home crying without a blouse on. I never saw her again. Her parents never let her come near me again. I was angry, very angry.

Finally, Tammy is ready to divulge the events she did not ever want to talk about. During tapings for this book, Tammy repeatedly denied being a victim of childhood sexual assault. But it is a fact that from the time Tammy was two until she was five, her godfather, a church minister, regularly sexually molested her in his home.

> I can see it like it was yesterday. My mother would dress me
> in these frilly dresses and he would put his hand under there
> and play with my genitals. Every time I would stand there
> and cry while he did it until he got finished. This went on
> forever, as long as I can remember, years. My godmother
> would have to go somewhere—store, meeting, church—and
> I would be left there with him. I remember when she would
> do that, me holding on to her leg and just crying and crying,
> "Let me go with you."

When her mother announced that she was going to visit her godparents, Tammy would weep in protest, but she was simply too young to tell her about it. She kept the secret until she was forty-two years old and the minister passed away. Tammy's mother was disbelieving, but the information must certainly have hit hard; from then on her mother shut the door on her daughter's sharing any other problems in her life.

It's not that Tammy forgot about the sexual molestation, but to continue to function she had to stop thinking about it. Even today, it is painful for her to dwell on it for very long.

> If I'm asked whether I'm a victim of violence, I've said "no"
> repeatedly. I haven't accepted it. That's everybody else.
> That wasn't me, I had a beautiful childhood. There
> are horrors that I completely blocked out. A therapist would
> have brought them out very early and I would have been able
> to deal with them. I never had any help.

Her godfather gave her candy afterwards.

> It would explain the voluntary teen prostitution. Grabbing
> power back. I could always be more powerful with these
> worthless men, so I would go after that crowd. I can be more
> powerful than them.

By virtue of blocking this sexual violence out for almost fifty years, Tammy lacked the tools to understand the life path she took.

> I will never use it as an excuse, but it is a contributing fac-
> tor and I am still processing it. I know I am not finished

*grieving and crying about it. As a matter of fact, I have this
picture in my mind of how I looked and the dresses I wore
when that man would put his hand up my skirt. When I
moved, I found a picture of myself at that age in one of
those dresses.*

Was the molestation a contributing cause of Tammy's anger, aggres-
siveness, and rebelliousness from age twelve on? Does it explain her
need to control men, leading her to engage in prostitution and to seek
out liaisons with weak men, who then reacted to her assertions of
power with violence and abuse?

Since conversations for this book forced Tammy to think about these
episodes of childhood sexual assault, she has been studying the effects
of this kind of abuse.

*I began reading a lot about how women victims of early sex-
ual abuse become promiscuous and turn to prostitution and
drugs. I think that if I had remembered and received counseling, my life would have been different. It amazes me how
that one thing festered in my soul and grew to such huge
proportions. It grew like a cancerous infection and I never
even knew it was there.*

Tammy also recognizes how the abuse contributed to her "choice" to
use her sexuality for what she thought was her benefit.

*But that was a double-edged sword because I used and was
used by men. It really shaped who I am today. Believe me,
I get plenty of offers today and at the same token I will not
allow men to use me. I have been celibate for a number of
years now. I just think I want to be left alone. I am still
finding myself and coming back to being the Tammy that
I like, and I don't want anyone or anything confusing the
process.*

Unfortunately, Tammy's experiences with abuse were only just beginning. In Chicago she moved in with a cousin and immediately found
a job working for a tax man who operated a ministore in the front of

his office. He had another girl employed there as well. After a few weeks of flirting, her boss locked the door to his office at lunchtime and forced Tammy to dispense sexual favors.

> *He would bend me over the desk, anyway, backwards, for-*
> *wards, however he wanted to. It started with touching me in*
> *different places and it built up. I just didn't say "no," but it*
> *wasn't consensual. He was a very big man.*

Recently, Tammy found a letter she had written to her mother fifteen years after these events. It reads, in part:

> *I don't know why he hired me, I knew nothing about taxes*
> *and even less about keeping files and papers. However, he*
> *hired me on sight. I later found out why. We'd work hard*
> *all morning going over other people's tax records, finding loop*
> *holes and phantom dependents and we'd break for lunch. I*
> *was always his lunch. I guess when I applied for the job I*
> *had a look of desperation written all over my face and he*
> *probably knew I'd do anything to have a job. He was right.*
> *So for the next months, I spent my entire lunch flat on my*
> *back on top of a desk with pens, pencils and anything else he*
> *left laying around sticking me in my back.*

Why didn't Tammy just quit?

> *I was young and I needed the job, it was what I had to do*
> *to survive. I had to have the job. It was so important for me*
> *to let my mom see that my way worked. I had been such a*
> *disappointment to her. It was so important for me not to run*
> *home again. It happened about thirty times. I would just grit*
> *my teeth.*

And instead of blaming the rapist, Tammy castigated herself. Why did he do it to her and not the other girl? What was wrong with her? Her boss's sexual assaults lasted for the three months Tammy stayed on the job.

The rapes sent Tammy into the arms of men whom she thought would protect her. However, two different men with whom she lived each ended up evicting her suddenly. Now Tammy understands that one of her big mistakes at that time was not to seek help from home. In a later college composition, she names this trait as one that trapped her in violence.

> I came from a perfect family so I had to be perfect too. As a result, I never, ever, called home or asked my parents for help since I left home at age eighteen. If I would have made that call I would not have traveled the road I did which was filled with potholes, twists, and turns. Along with striving for perfection, you also collect pride. Naturally, I was too proud to say, I am not perfect and I need help. Thinking back, I can remember hundreds, maybe thousands of times, that I have tried to be perfect and how pride prevented me from asking for help.

Thus Tammy was more than ready for her first husband, a former minister who became a gang leader involved in robberies, drug sales, and prostitution. She remembers the feeling of power and protection that being with the gang leader gave her. When he took heroin for the first time, Tammy was more than happy to go along and try it too.

> I was Ms. Disciple. I'm in love, I'm having fun, I have all this power. I wasn't afraid of anything. I have so much power. The gang was very powerful. But remember, I'm on drugs, too. My mind is like fried.

Performing the chores women married to gang members often do, Tammy carried her husband's weapons in her purse, and sometimes sat in the car as lookout. None of the robberies involved weapons, however; the guns were important for the turf wars with other gang members. While she was still in her teens, Tammy briefly participated in prostitution activities. In that arena she could easily be a superstar— she could be the most beautiful, make the most money, and put the most men under her spell.

> I wanted to be the best prostitute. I liked being important. I made more money than anybody else, I was respected by the

> pimps and all the other prostitutes. I always wanted to shine.
> You have to remember that I lost my power with these two
> other men when they threw me out. I felt powerless then.

Although Tammy wanted to be wealthy and powerful, it took a lot less effort to be commanding and important with tricks than to work in the regular economy.

> I always thought I never had to work hard for anything,
> that a knight was going to ride up on a shiny white horse
> and rescue me. I didn't think I had to do anything hard. I
> was going to stay this eighteen-year-old pretty woman that
> men were going to take care of for the rest of my life. And
> it doesn't happen. You get trapped by it.

Eventually, arrests and imprisonment of the gang broke up Tammy's power trip and her marriage. One of the members began robbing grocery stores and taverns and Tammy got caught up in a police sweep of all the gang members. She was sent to prison in 1973, when she was twenty-three years old, where she stayed two and a half years. At first, Tammy said she didn't recall much about her stay. When pressed, Tammy could, of course, remember more; she just had chosen again to bury the entire episode.

> I blocked that out so well because I was guilty of everything
> I did. It pains me to think about myself as that character.

Women's prison then was so much different than it is now. It was almost like being away at camp. Detainees lived in cottages, they could wear their own clothes, the food was good, there were few rules, Tammy made many friends, and movies were shown every night. The incarcerated women were different too. They had committed serious crimes, and drugs did not dictate their criminal behavior. Yet these particular lawbreakers were compassionate and supported one another to a degree unexperienced today in the same prison. Tammy did hate being confined, and also remembers intense searches in a gynecological chair, during which the doctor actually stuck instruments up her vagina to search for contraband.

126   After she got out of prison, Tammy went straight. She got a job at a major corporation doing data entry and, after ten years of use, stayed off heroin for awhile during a short and abusive second marriage to a handsome but alcoholic security guard. Horrific is the only way to describe the violence in Tammy's second marriage. Her husband, a dedicated womanizer, would beat Tammy so that she would flee their home, leaving the coast clear for his liaisons with other women. One time, he violently battered Tammy while she was bathing, forcing her to run naked to her neighbor's house. On another occasion he beat Tammy so badly while she was hiding in a closet that blood splattered over the walls and her eyes were closed shut, making escape difficult. Often she spent the night in the bathroom of the neighborhood gas station.

      Many times during the three-year marriage Tammy left her second husband. She would return for quite a few reasons that seem silly to her now, but are bound up with her sense of pride.

> I thought I loved him. Then, it's like having a possession
> that everybody else wants. He was such a lady's man. Every
> woman that I could think of wanted him and I was the one
> he married. It gave me this power and I was still the best.
> I have to be the best woman, because he married
> me, he didn't marry you. But being the best in that
> position was not worth it because of everything that came
> with it.

Eventually Tammy came to her senses, left with only the clothes on her back, and, incredibly, never thought about it again. Years later for a college course, Tammy was required to read and comment on two articles about domestic violence, which, for the first time, brought back her memories of the abuse. This is what she wrote then for class:

> I was in an abusive marriage and I hid it from my family
> because my mom had paid all this money for a beautiful
> wedding and I didn't want her to think she wasted her
> money. When I say this it sounds like I'm talking about
> some "air head" who doesn't have a clue. But it was me. I
> also stayed because I believed him every time he said he was

sorry and it would never happen again. It did and the beatings got worse.

It's funny but real how the mind can repress painful memories. Until I read these two articles, I had forgotten about this abuse. I didn't remember that part of my life because I didn't choose to. I try to fill my head with happy memories but I have to realize that the unhappy ones are just as important because they serve as warnings.

CHAPTER NINE

Forgetting

> And I must remember that pain is not its own reason for
> being. It is a part of living. And the only kind of pain that
> is intolerable is pain that is wasteful, pain from which we
> do not learn.
>
> — AUDRE LORDE

Few of these important insights, however, came to Tammy while she
languished in the basement. Recovery from addiction is not a one-time
occurrence, but rather a process during which long-buried events are
brought to the surface and considered. Tammy knows now that heroin
prevents this kind of thinking altogether; it stops the user from learning from the mistakes, setbacks, and sorrows of life. Alexander Masters concludes that "Stuart's life is based on forgetfulness. Is this a way
to characterize the chaotic: they are people for whom forgetting has
become more important than remembering?"[1]

Was Tammy's nineteen-year love affair with heroin mainly a means
of forgetting?

From the standpoint of the nonaddicted, who see the adverse effects
close-up, why the addict continues to take drugs remains a mystery.
For the addict's children, the drug use is an unfathomable source of
anguish. Ex-prisoner Pamela Thomas's daughter expresses it well:

> I remember thinking, "Why does she keep doing the
> same thing over and over again?" I couldn't understand,

all I knew is that she said she loved us but then she kept
hurting us. When she was clean I knew she cared, but I
thought she didn't want us, if she did it would stop.[2]

To successfully intervene with abused women addicted to drugs and
involved in crime, we must better understand abuse-drug-crime connections. Let's see what Tammy's story tells us about that nexus, and
determine its implications for crime deterrence and punishment.

Initially, Tammy viewed injecting heroin as a bold and unusual
move for a woman, associating her with the commanding crowd in
her neighborhood. Using heroin fed into the image Tammy had of
herself as unique, abnormal, and powerful. Because Tammy had buried
thoughts of her sexual molestation, all she had left was the anger and
aggression the episodes had engendered, a habit of disassociation, and
an abiding sense of powerlessness. The heroin helped calm her down,
making it possible for Tammy to continue to live without facing up
to and confronting facts from her childhood. Now Tammy knows that
the drug was a crutch: "If you don't have coping strategies, you are
going to do what makes you feel good, like drugs."

Heroin also enabled Tammy's chosen lifestyle of prostitution and
companionship with a gang-banger to continue unabated.

> The drug gives you a courage, a strength that may be there
> but you don't think you have, so you get the false courage
> from the drug. When you take the drugs, all your feelings go
> away, so you have courage all of a sudden, but only because
> you don't feel anything. Nothing is holding you back. It
> wipes away all your inhibitions. This is one of the links
> between drugs and crime.

Most of the time, Tammy used two ten-dollar bags of heroin in the
morning. A twenty-dollar hit was all she needed to stay mellow all day
and avoid being drug sick. There were only two periods during which
Tammy injected between six to nine times a day. Seeking oblivion at
these times due to external events (one was a fire that destroyed her
dog and all her possessions, another the death of Terrence's father),
Tammy says, "I didn't want to think, I didn't want to feel, I didn't want
to exist."

Providing a crucial means of forgetting—blotting out the pain of earlier abuse and damping down feelings of anger from that feeling of powerlessness—heroin also obliterates the sense of the wasted life under the narcotic's influence. One day Tammy and her mother were watching Oprah Winfrey together on television. Her mother looked over at Tammy and remarked, "That could have been you, you could have been Oprah Winfrey."

> I knew I was wasting myself. I had a lot of regrets, a lot of disappointments. But the drugs make it go away. You don't feel anymore. It masks those feelings of unworthiness. It was like a fight going on there, where the drug made me feel like I was winning over the other part that said you're really nothing, you are really the dregs of society.

The drug continued to help Tammy escape all these frustrations about how her life had turned out.

> It allowed me to stop, to let my body rest. It became the love of my life. It covered up the things that I regretted. I had a lot of regrets. A lot of disappointments.

Deep inside, Tammy knew that not only was she not developing herself, but she was also giving nothing back to society. So the longer she used heroin and the longer she continued to waste her gifts, the more Tammy needed the drug to mask her disappointment in how her life had turned out. But it was a trap: heroin allowed her to continue her current existence, but prevented her from breaking free long enough to change her life so that she would not continue to need the heroin. Even worse, the drug kept her in abusive relationships; Tammy knew that she was choosing all these men who had terrible traits and abused her, but through heroin she made herself equal to them.

> When I found out Maurice didn't even have an apartment when I met him, he was living in the halfway house, it bothered me. Something was wrong with me. He didn't even have a job. So I got high. I don't want to feel this, I don't want to think about it. I want this man, so

if I get high, I can keep this man. If I don't, I
couldn't keep him. *The drugs allowed me not to think so
I could do terrible things with no remorse or feelings.*

More and more, the drugs took over her life.

*Suddenly the job gets in the way. I didn't want to work,
I just wanted the drugs. My mind was so befuddled by my
using the drugs that, you know how the progression grows,
as you use a little bit and a little bit, then you have to use
every day, then you don't want to do anything but use drugs,
and it got to that point that I didn't want to do anything. I
would actually not go to work for a couple of weeks, then go
back to work.*

For a while there, Tammy went to twelve-step meetings. She did want
to be normal, but apparently not enough, because she continued using
drugs the whole time she was in out-patient treatment. So next she
tried an in-patient hospital program, but it was there she met Maurice
and new troubles began.

Tammy sees now that the drugs kept her problems from submerg-
ing her.

*So what women do is when they are overwhelmed by the
things that they cannot change—and we don't know how to
deal with the things we cannot change—what we do is we
block them out and in our minds they go away. The drugs
make them go away. The drugs give you a relief. When you
come down, when you become sober, the problem is there, so
that is when you become hooked, because you piled on more
drugs, so that you never feel, never think, never deal with it,
and people do this for years. That's how children become so
bitter with their parents because the parents numb themselves
for so many years that the child actually raises himself, or
the parent was unaware of the child's problems, even the
child could have been raped. The parent won't know, because
the child probably told the mother, and she piled on more
drugs and went back to that safe place that we go to. We go*

to this safe place. It is so safe up there because your mind
shuts down, and that's what we do.

If heroin is about forgetfulness, it is also about selfishness. Heroin,
Tammy believes, creates an individual who is inhuman or less than
human because of the combination of these two traits. While she was
on heroin, Tammy simply didn't need anybody else.

We used to have a saying among us who used drugs, that we
had our heroin so we didn't need a man. We didn't need our
parents, we didn't need brother, father, sisters, none of them.
I had a new best friend now that took care of everything that
I needed, met all my needs. I had no need for anyone else.
So that is where the isolation comes. You don't need anyone,
unless it is another drug addict to show you a better, easier
way to get drugs.

A user, like Tammy, is devoid of emotions and geared only to buying
and scoring drugs.

All addicts are users of other people. Why is that? An addict
absolutely positively must think only of self. You know, "I
am selfish, then why shouldn't I take your money?"

So Tammy took money from Edward and others without a thought of
doing anything in return. When she thinks about it now, she wonders
at the person she was then.

It was as if I was looking at this horrible person doing these
things. I'm not that person. You actually stop living when
you are using drugs, because you are not a human being.

Today Tammy understands that in her drug-using days she was no
better than the most down-and-out junkie because of the absence of
thinking and the egotistic pursuit of forgetfulness.

The difference between me and the drug addict that you see
dirty and on the street is the outer package only. I was just

as filthy on the inside. But I had the tools, the ways to stay clean on the outside, to hide it. I ended up in the same place, and no better than any other addict.

It is this self-centeredness, the one-dimensional pursuit of the drug, which the narcotic itself causes, Tammy explains, that brings about the abnormal, uncaring, or immoral behavior that baffles untrained judges and correctional officials. Like the wrapped Christmas presents for the children under the tree on Christmas Eve, but gone on Christmas Day because their parents stole them to get money for drugs in the middle of the night. Or the woman addict agreeing to be gang-raped by thirteen men in exchange for one rock of cocaine. And the male addicts, who after the rapes, give the woman a large bar of soap and run away.

Once she was off heroin, however, Tammy knew she had to change her thinking, but she wasn't quite sure how. So she went to meetings, she went to church, and she took up everything she could to help her "fix all of that garbage that the drug had caused over the years." At the time of Tammy's arrest that garbage cleanup was only just beginning. Her incarceration was to put that important process on hold for about four years.

✳

Not all victims of childhood sexual assault turn to drugs or crime, but sexually victimized children have been found to be three times more apt to become addicted to drugs than nonabused children, and they are also more likely to perpetrate crime, violence, or abuse.[3]

During sexual molestation, the abuser invades and defiles the victim's body; but importantly, far more than the body is affected. The attacked person experiences a sense of powerlessness that destroys her sense of dignity and autonomy. This disrespect of the victims' personhood "constitutes an assault to their sense of self-integrity and affects how they come to view their own human worth."[4] Sexual violence against women and girls is thus more than infliction of physical pain, or even humiliation; it attacks the victims' inner core, leaving them profoundly dehumanized for years afterward. As one survivor describes it, violence should be seen as "anything that interferes or restricts a girl or a woman, of any age, and breaks their self-confidence in themselves as a human being."[5] Researcher Gail Garfield believes this about victims:

"By not fighting back in defense of self they began to lose important pieces of themselves; they lost some of their own sense of value, and their actions become self-destructive."[6]

Tammy's story illustrates how victims who lose this vital sense of self develop coping strategies of aggression and disassociation, both of which are self-destructive. Naturally, this significant loss of self-esteem, the result of shame, humiliation, and helplessness, can cause an aggression that becomes, as in the case of Tammy, a "stable part of the child's personality structure," resulting in more self-hate and antisocial behavior. Child sexual assault expert Judith Herman describes the role of anger.

> Feelings of rage and murderous revenge fantasies are normal responses to abusive treatment. Like abused adults, abused children are often rageful and sometimes aggressive. They often lack verbal and social skills for resolving conflict, and they approach problems with the expectation of hostile attack. The abused child's predictable difficulties in modulating anger further strengthen her conviction of inner badness. Each hostile encounter convinces her that she is indeed a hateful person. If as is common, she tends to displace her anger far from its dangerous source and to discharge it unfairly on those who did not provoke it, her self-condemnation is aggravated still further.[7]

In addition to anger, aggression, and self-hate is disassociation. The anxiety, shame, and fear of the sexual assault can cause children younger than eight or nine to be unable to manage emotions and bring them into equilibrium, resulting in chronic habits of disassociation, which can lead to a sense of complete disengagement from others and thus a disintegration of the self.[8]

And these reactions to trauma may also have a physical basis; scientists now believe that steady exposure to stress also wears away the nervous system, marking a steady deterioration of the brain's ability to cope. Thus violence and stress are thought to actually reconstruct the brain, with long-lasting consequences for neural function and behavior. One expert makes a linkage between stress and reductions in brain cortisol, which destroy the individual's ability to know he (she) is edging toward danger or disaster, and cause depression, impulsive or hostile aggression, or antisocial personality disorders.[9]

Coping strategies in adolescence appear to broaden to include drug use, promiscuity, prostitution, or sexual aggression, as well as running away. Sometimes self-mutilation will follow a profound dissociative state as a way of shocking the system into a more connected state of being.

> Purging and vomiting, compulsive sexual behavior,
> compulsive risk-taking or exposure to danger, and the
> use of psychoactive drugs become the vehicles by which
> abused children attempt to regulate their internal emo-
> tional states. Through these devices, abused children at-
> tempt to obliterate their chronic dysphoria and to stim-
> ulate, however briefly, an internal state of well-being and
> comfort that cannot otherwise be achieved.[10]

As a teen, Tammy employed many of these methods to cope with the anger and low self-esteem she daily experienced. Later, heroin more ef- ficiently helped her regulate her emotions and separate her body from thinking about, confronting, and recovering from the trauma. Thanks to the heroin, she was able to bury all thoughts of her childhood sex- ual molestation and later domestic abuse. Notes one expert:

> For many of these women, the ordinary response to
> trauma is to silence it because it is too difficult to deal
> with. Drugs therefore become the tool for quelling mem-
> ories and feelings, broken dreams, and the inability to live
> up to societal ideals.[11]

But drug-taking for abuse victims is much more than just a means of numbing. If we view drug-induced disassociative states as a response to the anxiety and fear produced by trauma, but broaden the perspec- tive to understand that drugs are also an antidote to the powerlessness trauma induces, then we might begin to understand yet another aspect of women's drug-taking and its connection to crime. For Tammy, using heroin was a method to exert power over her environment, an active way for her to seize the initiative, to reduce the anger, and to wipe away feelings of self-hatred. But drug-taking as a coping strategy, is, in the end, not a true seizure of power, although it may appear so at the time:

> Those who become dependent will be the ones who dis-
> covered drugs at a time when they were better equipped
> to run from their problems rather than resolving them.
> Such people will incorporate drugs into their life-styles
> and come to rely upon them as an effective, if temporary,
> problem-solving device. Drugs become, for these people,
> a way of adapting to and dealing with the inner world
> of feelings and the external world that produces such
> feelings.[12]

At first the approach is effective, but over time the heroin addict becomes more isolated from conventional society and her life more organized around getting the drug; addiction then interferes with legitimate employment, for some women also leading to a critical separation from regular society. Marsha Rosenbaum, one of the few researchers to have studied women's heroin use, summarizes the downward spiral of the addiction process:

> Heroin expands her life options in the initial stages, and
> that is the essence of its social attraction. Yet with pro-
> gressively further immersion in the heroin world, the
> social, psychological, and physiological exigencies of
> heroin use create an option "funnel" for the woman
> addict. Through this funnel the addict's life options are
> gradually reduced until she is functionally incarcerated
> in an invisible prison. Ultimately, the woman addict is
> locked into the heroin life and locked out of the conven-
> tional world . . . the conditions associated with this life
> steadily, almost inevitably, narrow her options further.
> Ultimately, her reduced options outside the heroin world
> become a rationale for continued drug use and even fur-
> ther immersion in deviance.[13]

Part of their allure for abused women may be that drugs are illegal. Using forbidden substances can be a method to exact "revenge" on society for injustices, deprivations, and powerlessness; and crime, as we saw in Tammy's case, can easily result from these antisocial attitudes. In this regard, heroin may have a particular attraction for powerless women. With its reputation as the "hardest drug" (the word heroin comes from the German for "heroic"), male users in the Black community take on an outsider or outlaw status that gives them power, related as it is to race resistance and the quest for racial justice.[14] For women who feel powerless, heroin appears to be an option that can expand their sense of efficacy, providing them with a missing sense of control as well as status.[15]

Even as it represents an attempt to seize power over one's environment, drug taking has to be seen as an act associated with feelings of profound self-hatred and self-abuse. Patrice Gaines, an ex–heroin addict from a middle-class background, arrested while carrying drugs for her boyfriend, believes that the low self-esteem of women addicts cannot be overstated: "To be capable of shooting heroin requires that you do not love yourself at all, do not look upon yourself as a miracle, or a perfect creation of God."[16] Only self-loathing could lead a person to inject herself with heroin, scarring her body, collapsing her veins, risking the threat of an impure hit on a daily basis, sharing dirty needles, and the like.

Lack of self-worth, the effect of violence, can thus propel women into self-destructive acts.

> To varying degrees, that violation and the disrespect that
> is engendered constitutes an assault to their sense of self-
> integrity and affects how they come to view their own
> human worth. . . . [T]hrough their actions they actively
> participated in self-abuse; this abuse was tantamount to
> self-violation; and by not caring about the consequences
> of their actions for their own personhood, self-abuse be-
> came a part of their experiences of violence.[17]

Often the observation is that most women undertake illegal acts to buy drugs; and that is indeed one scenario. But Tammy's crime, committed on behalf of another, is embedded in her dysfunctional and disempowering relationship, which had its origins in her long history of self-destructive acts and her numbing herself from their effects. We are aghast at Tammy's incarceration because her crime, although real, was not at heart an antisocial act, but a natural outcome of a self-destructive lifestyle.

There are other abuse-drug-crime scenarios. All, however, have elements in common with Tammy's story. Experiencing anger and aggression from the loss of power and self-esteem produced by violence, the women search for a sense of empowerment through drugs, and they try to cope with the effects of being trapped in abusive and dysfunctional relationships. In these circumstances, the drugs, the relationships, and the numbing of the self lead to even more self-destructive and antisocial acts.

Consider Rachel, who after being raped and denied a place in a drug treatment program because of lack of insurance, burned her house down.[18]

Or Maxine Breakspear, an eighteen-year-old who had been sexually abused from the age of eight by different men and developed multiple drug habits that temporarily blocked her anger. Why Maxine and another young woman beat and killed a man who was attacking a third youngster remained a mystery to the judge, who sent her to prison. "I took all my anger out on him, I suppose," she said. "I should have got myself sorted out before it got to that, but I had no idea how to help myself."[19]

Or Meredeth, who ended up writing checks on her account when she knew she didn't have the money to cover them. Only later did she understand that the check writing was a response to her earlier abuse; for the first time, it made her feel powerful.[20]

Or Marilyn, serving twenty-two-years-to-life for participating in an armed robbery in which one of the victims was shot and killed. Her boyfriend controlled her by threatening to shoot her if she left him. He coerced her into putting stolen goods into a bag, but she had no gun and was not responsible for the robbery or the shooting. Following her arrest, Marilyn was on a suicide watch. Due to fears for her life, she refused to testify against her partner, who also received time. Later, she had a complete nervous breakdown in prison and was temporarily transferred to a mental hospital.[21]

Based on her many years of research with abused women, psychologist Evelyn Sommers sketches a scenario that could have been written with Tammy in mind. First, the women, already victims of childhood sexual assault, were often in adult abusive relationships. Because these partners were all they had, the women tried to hold on to them, using drugs and alcohol to insulate themselves from the daily pain they experienced. Although they continued to receive no empathy or affirmative responses from the significant others in their lives, they persisted in denying their abuse or victimization and refused to confide in others, in an attempt to ward off feelings of powerlessness. In the end, they were unable to experience themselves as worthy in any way.[22]

Women like these become vulnerable to persons and situations through which they may achieve a false and transitory sense of power, Sommers concludes, and in some cases this empowerment is achieved through antisocial acts. For others, it leads to more self-destructive acts and numbed responses to them, coping strategies that can also lead to crime. "Women," Sommers writes, "must be freed of the burden of victimization, or they will continue to come into conflict with the law."[23]

Formal research studies on women's abuse and crime are few and far between, but those that do exist document these scenarios. Department of Justice research indicates that nearly one in three women serving time in state prisons said they had committed the offense that brought them to prison in order to obtain money for drugs.[24] Two other research studies put the figure closer to 50 percent.

Researcher Beth Richie administered almost three hundred surveys in a large urban jail, followed up with in-depth interviews with thirty-three of the women. All the participants turned out to have suffered abuse from intimate partners and family members, and it was stunning in its depravity.

> That is, the women interviewed for this study were severely assaulted on a regular basis in most of their adult relationships, and they had an average of three assaults. . . . The qualitative data on this theme was full of horrific accounts of brutality that included a woman who was sexually abused with a hot comb, another being locked in a trash dumpster after being beaten, and another who was shot over 40 times.[25]

In close to half the cases, Richie found that the women participated in illegal activity explicitly to support their addiction to alcohol or drugs, and she does not mince her words.

This finding emerged with absolute clarity. The women
sold drugs to buy drugs, they stole property to pay off
drug debts, they violated probation because of drug possession or they failed to appear in court because they
were "drug sick." The extent to which the women felt
illegal behavior was almost inevitable—given the power
of their addiction and the lack of treatment programs—
was a very impressive finding from this research.[26]

She notes too that the violence and the drugs created what she calls a
"desensitization" that caused the women to live "with a sense of numbness, with a very acute sense of tension just below their external identity."[27] This numbness, Richie explains, affected their ability to protect
themselves from either the abuse or from lapsing into criminal acts and
other self-destructive behavior: "The women in this study endured the
abuse and they participated in illegal activity in response to it."[28]

In similar research, the Australian Institute of Criminology found
radically different results for men and women prisoners. The institute
interviewed almost five hundred women in different Australian prisons
to obtain more information about the drug-crime connection in a de-
tailed study largely supporting Richie's conclusions. Eighty-seven percent of the women were victims of abuse in either childhood (63
percent) or adulthood (78 percent), with the majority victims of multiple forms of abuse. Most of the women had committed property and
drug offenses and admitted they did so regularly. Sixty-two percent
considered themselves to be regular drug users in the six months before their arrest. Drug use preceded fraud, property, and prostitution
offenses. Half of the women committing property crimes and 87 percent of those with a preference for heroin attributed their crimes to
the need to obtain money to buy drugs.

Interestingly, for males in the study the outcome was radically different, with only 17 percent using drugs prior to committing any crime.
The researchers' conclusion describes the strong drug-crime connection,
at least for women:

For every type of drug examined in this study, women in
prison reported experimenting at an earlier age than
women in the general population. Early onset of drug use

is also associated with more persistent and regular offending. In addition, drug dependency was indicative of earlier initiation into a criminal career.

In contrast to male prisoners, women in this study tended more often to begin drug use prior to criminal offending. This suggests that for some women, drug use played an important role in the onset and continuation of a criminal career.[29]

✳

For the most part, heroin was the way Tammy coped with her anger and aggression, the residue from abuse that had stripped her of a sense of power and self-esteem. At the same time, the drug facilitated her involvement with abusive men, desensitizing her to the pain they inflicted, which in Tammy's case led to the commission of a crime on behalf of one of them. Once off drugs and out of prison, Tammy then had to contend with the trauma left behind by the pain of incarceration, its effects on her beloved son, and all the earlier abuse issues that heroin had covered up. In that basement she truly hit rock bottom; as she herself has said, her sanity was hanging by a thread. But, Tammy would rise like Phoenix from the ashes. She just didn't know it yet.

CHAPTER TEN

Out of the Basement

We must be the change we wish to see in the world.

— AUDRE LORDE

During her time in the basement—about two years—Tammy started to think about drugs again.

> My thoughts turned to heroin. It would be so easy not to feel
> this hurt and this pain, because the hurt and pain were so
> great, so huge, that I needed to cover it up in order to go
> on. And when I realized that I was thinking about drugging
> again, the only option for me was to die. I either go back to
> drugs or I die. And neither was that appealing to me. Neither
> one appealed to me at all.

In an early entry in her diary from that time, Tammy writes how tempting it would be, now in her inner-city apartment surrounded by drug dealers, to fall back on heroin.

> It would be so easy to mask the pain inside me, but instead
> I choose to feel every sting. Why? I do not know if it will
> get better. I cannot think that far ahead. Sometimes I don't
> think at all.

Tammy made a crucial decision.

It takes a brave soul to even go out and buy drugs, go to
these places. It takes a brave soul to commit suicide, so if
I've got that much bravery, why not do something about it
and change the situation? I can't get any lower than this. I
reached rock bottom. The only way you can go is up when
you reach rock bottom. So I chose to go up. It was either
die or live, no in-between. And I wanted to live.

Moving the computer upstairs out of the basement was the first step.

That was the beginning of the rest of my life, I think. I
moved it up. I opened the shades and I let the sunshine in.
I actually came out on the porch. I can't believe I stayed in
the dark for so long. That time is gone, it was never there.
It's like I didn't exist. Like I died before and came back to
life after.

This moment of transition is a moving part of Tammy's diary.

I will have to start writing in my journal regularly because
if I don't I really don't know what is going to happen to
me. I need someone to talk to. Someone I can trust. I need to
cry, scream, break something, or maybe I just need to pray
harder. I won't lose faith now but I need some hope. Just one
good thing to happen in my life will keep me going.
    It is Friday. This is the very first time I have actually
sat on the back porch and enjoyed the sun. It is becoming
bright and warming my skin but I don't know how much I
am enjoying it. I can hardly see the beautiful scenery through
my tears. This is not healthy. I cry all the time and what is
worse is that I cry alone.

Something jump-started Tammy out of that depression, and that something was Professor Michele McMaster, one of Tammy's university
teachers. Recognizing that she needed to tell someone, Tammy decided
what she needed to do was to talk out her problems and emotions. Up
until now, no one had wanted to hear about it, neither her family
members nor her friends. They would say, "You're home now, it's

okay, forget about it, put that out of your mind." For the past few years, she was never allowed to talk about what was too painful for them to take in.

Professor McMaster noticed that Tammy wore a lot of hats.

> I remember her telling me, "I never saw your hair. You've got a thousand hats." She didn't know I was hiding behind those hats. I didn't want anyone to see me.

In her papers for class Tammy began to write more personally.

> I wanted her to see it. See that I'm hurting, please see that I'm hurting. She told me, "Tammy, you don't like yourself."

So the professor became Tammy's first cheerleader.

> "You can do anything, girl, you can do anything," she would say. "Look in the mirror." She constantly reprimanded me. When I put myself down in class, when I didn't accept compliments, she would say, "Why do you hate yourself so much? What is wrong, why don't you give yourself any credit?"

Finally, one day Tammy went to her professor's office and told her what had happened. She helped Tammy rebuild her confidence and self-esteem.

> She would compliment me so much, "You are such a good writer, you have so much to offer, you have so much to live for, and so much to give." She would tell me this over and over again, she drummed it in my head.
>
> She started the ball rolling. But I would leave her kind words, and I would leave the writing, and I would be right back where I started. I hadn't internalized any of it. Like I needed her all the time. And she couldn't be there all the time. So I had to find the inner power myself.

Later Tammy realized that by numbing herself for so long she had completely lost the inner resources she needed to draw on for recovery. Her resilience had been destroyed, luckily not permanently. But something made Tammy persevere.

> Survival skills are embedded in me. I knew it was not accept-
> able to die or go back to drugs. Drugs would have been
> death. I wanted more.

Professor McMaster's enthusiasm was so very different from the re-action of another professor in whom Tammy had confided earlier. Tammy held the woman in high esteem and wanted her to know so that she could give her some guidance. Since she feared she wouldn't be able to tell her without crying, Tammy sent her a seven-page letter. And her professor never responded.

> She didn't say anything. I noticed that she started looking at
> me and stopped calling on me. And it hurt more than any-
> thing in the world, oh my God, it hurt so much. Because of
> her, of all people, she was African American. I think that
> what she did will stay with me for the rest of my life. No
> one ever hurt me as much as that.

Today Tammy cries when remembering that rebuff.

> I thought that I would have to wear this felony conviction
> for the rest of my life. They put me back in a box. I was
> kept in this box for so many years.

A few friends and some church members gave Tammy the same neg-ative messages, telling her she could never teach school or obtain jobs because of her criminal record. Her former supervisor at Republic Windows (not the woman who hired her) told Tammy she would never amount to much. At the same time that others were stigmatiz-ing her, Tammy continued to imprison herself due to her low self-esteem. She just knew everyone viewed her as an ex-felon and so she stayed away. In church she never heard the benediction because every Sunday she would leave early before anyone else.

> I didn't want to see what they were thinking through their
> eyes, so I never stayed. For years I did that. I was still in
> prison. I never wanted to leave my apartment. I had to leave,
> but I didn't want to. I was more comfortable being confined.

Soon Tammy realized she needed to reach out to new people to help her. So she started sending e-mails to total strangers, individuals and organizations working with ex-prisoners she found on the Internet. Eventually she became hooked up to several local groups. Her e-mail letter was a cry for help: I have been incarcerated, I would like to change my life, and I would like to work. Tell me what to do. Eventually Tammy received an e-mail about a national roundtable for women ex-prisoners to be held in Atlanta in 2004. She applied for a scholarship, got it, and went. That conference proved to be another turning point.

With her exposure to so many successful and inspirational ex-prisoners attending the meeting, Tammy became empowered to think that she could find her rightful place in society.

> When I came back I ferociously started job hunting and in-
> stead of my incarceration being a barrier, I put it out as
> something positive. I no longer felt ashamed of who I was.

Tammy was learning to turn the negative into a positive, and rapidly an employment offer rewarded her efforts. Terry Johnson, vice president of service development at a large southside social services program, hired Tammy only because he had had three failures in the job position before and was impressed by Tammy's energy. He saw her criminal record as neither a particular problem nor as an advantage. Looking back now, he realizes that Tammy came on very strong in the interview.

> Timid is not her. She was really functioning at a feverish
> pitch by that point. Now she is a little more normal.[1]

The major thing Tammy had to do in her first six months on the job was to calm down. She was so anxious to please, wanting to prove to herself and everyone else that she was a valuable employee. Because three others had failed in the job already, Tammy really felt the pressure to succeed.

In the beginning, says Terry Johnson, everything that went wrong was a crisis for Tammy.

> The job means so much to her, probably too much to
> her. What she had to do is to learn how to back off a bit,
> not consider each thing that wasn't working the way she
> wanted it to as the end of the world. She saw I wasn't
> jumping ten feet high when she came in with something
> she thought was a horrendous problem. "They aren't the
> end of the world, you aren't going to lose your job over
> it, just do the best you can."[2]

Because Tammy put in more time on the job than was necessary, Johnson feared she would quickly burn out.

> She was way too busy in my mind. Going to school,
> working here full time, she's involved in all these organi-
> zations that she feels·obligated to contribute to, and it is
> way too much. At this stage and age in her life, it is way
> too much. Maybe when you are twenty-five. She's done
> very well.[3]

But for Tammy the position she now holds is much more than just a job. It also enables her to begin to give back.

> I can help people. The humanistic part of me has to be fed.
> It is like a hunger, an addiction with me, to be helping
> someone. It was always that way but I had to spend so many
> years being selfish and once the selfishness was removed it
> was able to come out.
>
> But more so than anything I think that I do it because
> of how I suffered, the mistakes and the choices that I made.
> The fact that I see the light now and a lot of people are still
> caught in darkness. When I stand there [in front of the class
> of addicts] I remember every emotion that I experienced, the
> fear, the low self-esteem, the worthlessness, so I try to take
> away those fears.

Make no mistake, Tammy is still aggressive, but she has learned to put her energy to good use. By being an advocate for the disadvantaged, she has been able to "turn it around."

At the same time that Tammy had to fight the imprisonment her own low self-esteem created, she continued to confront societal stigmatization that interfered with her inner recovery. When she applied for graduate school, a question on the application asked whether she had ever been convicted of a felony. Her anger ultimately led her to talk with the president of the university about the school's motivation for asking that question and to advise him how such an inquiry dampened hopes and aspirations. Tammy's congressman is a well-known Black activist. She called his local office to discuss the matter. When the aide heard the phrase "ex-felon," he quickly responded, "You can't go to school, you are an ex-felon."

> I said, "I am living proof that what you said is not true."
> He said, "Well, you'll be able to get a job, a lot of ex-felons
> work." I said, "I am not calling you about a job, I have a
> job." He was so rude. He finally said, "What do you want
> from us?" I replied, "I just want the congressman to know,
> to be aware of what is going on in his district, that people
> like me are facing these barriers even after we have been re-
> habilitated in society." When he heard "ex-felon," I was no
> longer important to him. I wasn't anything.

To this day, Tammy believes the societal stigma remains forever and represents the worst part of her incarceration.

> We feel like we are in a box that will never have the lid
> taken off, never, because of that imprisonment. Society makes
> you pay for the rest of your life. You never stop paying.
> There is no cap on it. You pay for the rest of your life.
> One crime and you will pay for the rest of your life.

Expungement, she declares, is the key.

> We shouldn't have to suffer forever. Society wants it open
> forever. Ten years, twenty years, it is still there. It stops you

from achieving your dreams. They talk about paying your debt to society. When is it finally paid?

You may have noticed that Tammy's imagery is always that of boxes; she describes her postprison incarceration as a confinement in a series of boxes, boxes within boxes. "My box has hundreds of little boxes that all fit neatly inside each other," she wrote in her journal. Tammy's goal was to come out of these boxes.

And in one of these boxes was Edward—for the man who saved and helped her many a time over the years now seemed like someone who was trapping Tammy. As you may remember, Tammy took Edward in after he lost his job soon after she departed the work release center. It helped that she was now repaying some of her debt to him, but still she felt her obligation was unmet. And with Edward still in her life, Tammy believed she could not move on.

First, Edward thought he would retire and move to Alabama where the bulk of his family lives, but he later thought better of the plan. Meanwhile, Tammy had moved to a smaller apartment with no room for Edward, who then decided to share living quarters with three other roommates. Tammy believes Edward, now retired, thought about moving to Alabama to get away from her harping on his drinking. Unfortunately, the person who had so often rescued Tammy with financial support returned to drinking upon her arrest, and remains trapped in alcohol abuse. When Tammy was taken to the county jail, Edward simply fell apart. His letters indicated just how much he had organized his life around Tammy. Feeling just as abandoned as Terrence, he turned to drink for solace. For this reason, Tammy believes Edward was yet another victim of her incarceration.

> I don't know what changed his mind about Alabama. I really believe he wanted to move there to get away from me. I don't allow any drinking or drugging in my home and I had become a nag about it. Now that he is away from me, he does not have to answer to me.

Edward's drinking began to cause physical and mental problems; he told Tammy he had fights in his sleep and even punched a hole in the wall while in bed. In May 2006 Edward entered the thirty-day residential alcohol treatment program that employs Tammy.

How Tammy treated Edward and exploited his love for her is a matter of deep regret.

> I would have killed myself if I were him. I was just horri-
> ble. For a long time that also imprisoned me. I couldn't do
> anything because I owed him. I want my debt paid, but how
> long before that debt is paid?

Happily, Tammy has been able to rebuild her relationship with her sisters, Pat and Terri, both of whom state they are delighted with her personality change. Now that Tammy isn't busy keeping all these secrets
and has shared her story, the sisters have returned to their earlier close-
ness; they spend holidays together and talk about moving to the same
city to be with one another.

In another box was Tammy's relationship with Terrence, which
eventually did settle into a more normal pattern. Tammy came to the
realization that she did not have to make up for lost time by round-
the-clock mothering, and has freed Terrence, now a college student
majoring in business administration and dance education, to lead a
normal life. That was not an easy transition. Now she knows that it
was unrealistic and unnatural for mother and son to remain as close as
they had been when Terrence was younger. When she first returned
home, Tammy continually told Terrence that on drugs she was "too
blind" to be a parent, but now she was going to be a real mother for
him. Unfortunately, this decision might have met Tammy's require-
ments but came just at the time that Terrence needed to separate himself from his mother and prepare to leave home.

And when Terrence came back on college vacations, Tammy vocally
worried about where he was going, what he was doing, and when he
was returning home. These concerns are typical for most parents, but
in light of her abandonment of Terrence, trying to find the right bal-
ance was more difficult for Tammy.

Loving son that he is, Terrence feels himself torn.

> I understand that she is trying to make up for abandoning
> me. I see it, but the love is so overpowering. It is such a
> problem. But she is getting better. I'm trying to respect
> that and have my life at the same time. She is trying her
> best. I am trying not to abandon her.

It has taken some time, but Tammy now understands the freedom that
Terrence needs and the trust she must bestow.

> I think most mothers love their sons the way I love mine.
> It is a closeness that I hold in my heart, but my son doesn't
> come to me for everything. He talks to his friends, he doesn't
> talk to me. And I don't mind that. He doesn't talk to me
> anymore. Terrence assures me he is safe. He always says,
> "I know danger when I see it. I lived it."

Terrence's goal is to open a nonprofit dance school for teens while at
the same time pursuing a career in dance and choreography. He has
already taken one step by establishing the Delta Phi Delta Dance Fra-
ternity. A vehicle to provide community youth with an opportunity to
display their talents in venues such as competitions, concerts, and tal-
ent shows, the chapter held its first community concert to benefit the
homeless in the spring of 2006.

Although Tammy knows Terrence is doing extraordinarily well, she
continues to revisit in her mind all the times she put her son's life in
jeopardy; the insights she has now can be paralyzing: "Those are not
easy things to face or admit." In late March 2006, Tammy and this
author discussed putting the guilt about Terrence finally to rest. Terrence was thriving, but Tammy's constant vocalizing of her guilt to him
was actually pulling him down. He so desperately wanted his mother
to move on and be more future oriented. We decided on a symbolic
burial.

She typed the words "guilt," "shame," "low self-esteem," and
"anger" on pieces of paper, and placed them in an empty mayonnaise
jar for burial in the nearby forest preserve. The jar, however, sat for a
week while Tammy procrastinated. One part of her did not really want
to give up wallowing in these feelings.

> These are all things that I relied on to sustain me. Sometimes
> you become so familiar to certain emotions and pain they feel
> comfortable, you feel at home having them. It becomes part
> of you. The guilt was to forever punish me and to ensure
> that I always make choices that I have given a lot of thought
> to. It was of value to me.

152 Finally Tammy buried the jar. Although it was officially spring, the
ground was hard, and for some time she had to chip away at the earth
with the small gardening tool she had brought along.

> It was really a funeral and a burial because I was grieving
> and still grieve for my emotions. I did not want to say good-
> bye to my comfort zones. I prayed to God to forbid me from
> resurrecting the jar and its contents. I know I won't get it
> right immediately, but I will let myself know that what I
> felt for so long is gone forever.
>
> When I look at Terrence today and all that he is doing,
> I realize how long I held onto something that was so un-
> necessary. Despite how the State of Illinois tried to break
> me, abuse me, or humiliate me, me and my son are the best
> we ever were.

Still, she continues to suffer from insomnia.

> In prison, as soon as my head would hit the pillow, I would
> fall asleep. I'm free now and my life is so wonderful, and I
> suffer terribly from insomnia. I numbed myself then, nothing
> was in my head. Now that I'm home, I worry about my
> child, I worry about the bills. I don't know how to accept
> that things are good. I am still struggling with that, because
> I have been in "a things are bad state" for so long that I'm
> afraid. That's what keeps me awake. I'm waiting for the ball
> to drop, instead of trusting that this is the way it is going
> to be and I'll be able to cope with anything.
>
> I don't want to numb myself, I want to feel it, I welcome
> feeling it. If it means giving up three or four nights of sleep
> to do it, then, so be it, because I refuse to do anything to
> make myself go to sleep. This is the first time I have ever
> felt this free in my life.

Today Tammy still struggles to rid herself of what she calls her "self-
esteem issues," comprising the largest box. She is sick and tired of the
battle and more than ready to move on.

> I have to rid myself of many, many demons and fears. I am
> confident that I will do well, finally. The beatings up on
> myself are subsiding and I am conducting damage control of
> my ego. Hallelujah. I am still my own worst enemy and
> critic. I have to find my self-esteem in a bigger way.

What the judge said to Tammy will stay with her the rest of her life. "However," says Tammy today, "the way I process it gets better every day." But Tammy understands that loving herself is only part of the solution. Every human needs approbation from the wider society, and for that to occur the individual must do things worthy of that approval. For her recovery Tammy knows she needs external successes as well.

> I need the external affirmation badly. There have been situa-
> tions where I ran away because I did not get it. I know how
> it makes me feel when I do get it. I feel like I can conquer
> the world.

At long last Tammy has put herself in that place to begin to receive the recognition that will free her. One weekend she attended a workshop at a local college called "African-American Women and Heroin," where, for eight hours, the twenty-five enrollees discussed the issues. At the end, each individual had to talk about what in the class had had the greatest impact on her. That same evening Tammy sent this author an excited e-mail message.

> I was the subject or a mention in all twenty-five students'
> responses. They said things that I could not believe, i.e., I
> was very well spoken and I captivated the class when I spoke,
> I had a friendly and warm spirit, I appeared very stuck up
> at first glance but was a very personable and friendly person.
> They all wanted to keep in touch with me and said they
> would never forget me. Jody, I have to stop beating up on
> myself and recognize the impact that I have on others and
> do something about it.

Now the honor and respect Tammy has always craved appears to be coming her way. Indeed, she seems to be everyone's favorite ex-felon, invited to lecture, serve on boards and committees, and sought out for advice. However, this development also worries her.

> Now I get told that I can do anything I want to. Why? I
> still have the background. What makes me different from all
> the others? They should be given the same hope and encour-
> agement. I am not complaining, I just wish all the others
> were given a chance to correct their mistakes and I really
> wish society would be willing to give them that chance.

By January 2006, Tammy was on a roll. She had earned a bachelor's degree from Purdue University, a masters in communications and a masters in addictions studies from Governor's State University, a certificate as an alcohol and addictions counselor, and another as a criminal justice professional.

Despite these achievements, her application to be a volunteer mentor at the Westside work release center in which she had previously been housed was rejected by the Illinois Department of Corrections due to her "unsuitable background investigation," namely her prior convictions. This time Tammy was secure enough not to take it personally. Presumably a person convicted of manufacturing and delivery of drugs can never volunteer to assist other men and women within the confines of a state correctional facility in Illinois. Because the director of the center asked Tammy to appeal the decision, she wrote back to the department.

> In the letter I said I respected the process and their need to
> keep the prison safe, but I did not understand why they don't
> see that I am bringing something to the table, not taking
> something away. These are the people they need to be role
> models, so they can see someone make it.

A month later Tammy received word that she had been approved.

Tammy's newfound euphoria surprises some of the people with whom she comes in contact. As an icebreaker in one of her certificate classes, each student had to prepare an introduction, telling something unusual or amazing about himself (herself). To her surprise, Tammy heard herself declaring, "I love my job and I love my life. I have the best life in the world to me." After class a woman came up to Tammy, commenting that what Tammy had said would stay with her the rest of her life. With amazement, the woman remarked, "I have never ever heard anyone say they loved their life."

She is now starting her own organization, Behind Every Dark Cloud There is a Silver Lining, or B.E.D.C. Silver Lining. Several years ago when Terrence came home from college, Tammy met his Greyhound bus in the south Chicago suburbs.

> When the bus pulled up, I noticed that it was filled with men wearing white tee-shirts. My son was the only one who did not have on a white tee-shirt. I asked him if that was some kind of special club or fraternity. His reply was, "No, those are prisoners who were just released." I watched in horror as twenty or more formerly incarcerated men got off the bus and went down the street. It was shocking. What was shocking to me was that they were released right back into their communities. I put myself in their place and remembered how lost I was when I was released and how there was no one there to guide me, encourage me, or motivate me to live, let alone live a crime-free life.

B.E.D.C. Silver Lining's purpose is to help dispel that gray cloud hanging over exprisoners and help them find the silver lining as Tammy did.

> I want the same thing for everyone who has ever been in the justice system or who has ever had to spend any time behind the walls of a prison. I want them to know that you can transcend the background and find your way and your calling. I want someone else to be able to say, "I have a nice life."

Newly incorporated, the group now needs to find funding for Tammy's vision to create the only reentry social services program for male exprisoners in the south suburban area of Chicago.

Things are going well at her regular job too. For the first time ever, the program met its contract employment quotas, thanks to Tammy's efforts. But she emphasizes that although she works honestly and hard, she "could not have done that without confidence and without someone believing in me." But perhaps, after all, it was her lack of self-esteem that helped her feel accepted on the job.

> *I received one of the greatest compliments from a coworker that I could have received. As he was introducing me to a new employee, he felt compelled to cite all my accomplishments and credentials and at the end he said, "She is so humble about it all." I sometimes feel it hard to distinguish between my humility and the lack of self-confidence that I carried for so long. The humility is a result of the lack of self-confidence and the knowledge of how easily your life can change overnight. I will never become arrogant, better than those I serve, or too big to do the small things.*

Part of being free, Tammy explains, involves lifting all the veils of secrecy, truly confronting the events of the past. When actress Teri Hatcher finally revealed the secret of her multiyear molestation as a child, she also expressed her relief in coming clean.

> But I'm 41 years old, and it's time for me to stop hiding. It's time for me to accept all the complicated things about me—and if I do that, maybe I'll find someone who wants that whole package, instead of continuing to hide and finding someone who doesn't.[4]

Now that Tammy is starting to become open to the idea of a new romantic relationship, she too is looking for someone who will accept her, warts and all.

> *The first thing that I tell anyone I meet is that "I am completely drama free, don't bring me any drama." I don't want any, I'm not going to bring you any drama. These are peaceful years for me. I have to live in peace. If we can't talk it out, then I'm going to have a problem. I don't want to yell, scream, and fight.*
>
> *He has to let me be me. I have to be able to be me.*
>
> *I want the person to know everything there is to know*

about me. I don't want any secrets. He has to be able to read this book and not be judgmental. He'll be shocked, but I can't blame him for that.

Writer Joan Didion has eloquently written that self-respect is the most prized possession of all.

> To have that sense of one's intrinsic worth which con-
> stitutes self-respect is potentially to have everything:
> the ability to discriminate, to have and to remain
> indifferent. . . . At the mercy of those we cannot but hold
> in contempt, we play roles doomed to failure before they
> are begun, each defeat generating fresh despair at the ur-
> gency of divining and meeting the next demand made
> upon us. . . . To free us from the expectations of others,
> to give us back to ourselves—there lies the great, the sin-
> gular power of self-respect. Without it, one eventually
> discovers the final turn of the screw: one runs away to
> find oneself, and finds no one at home.[5]

And how Tammy ran away for so many years. Recovering her self-esteem will be a long-term process, but Tammy wants it to be over. She yearns to be truly free. Free of disassociating and forgetting. Free of guilt over Terrence and Edward. Free to know that she can makes mistakes and not be punished. Free to take constructive criticism. Free to not care about what people think about her. Free from feelings of low self-worth.

> *I want to be free of my own self-esteem issues. I want to get
> rid of that baggage. I want to be my own self again. I had a
> lot of things that were imprisoning me. I didn't realize until
> we started doing this book how many locked doors I had to
> being free. The prison was a small part, but there were so
> many other doors and so many other imprisonments around
> me everywhere.*
>
> *When this book is over, I want to be able to sit here and
> tell you I am completely free. When we finish, I know that
> I am going to be completely free. I know I am.*

✳

All incarcerated and formerly incarcerated women undoubtedly share Tammy's yearning for a respected place in the world and for peace of mind, freed of feelings of worthlessness. Yet for most it is an inchoate longing, incapable of realization or even of articulation.

Tammy made it. Stuart Shorter, the chronically homeless person in Cambridge, did not. What was the difference? That individual coping skills and resilience could differ, Stuart himself recognized.

> It's something I'm quite philosophical about. Some people
> have grown up, have learned to cope and accept and have
> been very successful, and led a very, in brackets, normal
> competitive life. And then I've met so many people who've
> led the same sort of lifestyle as I have and had the same
> sort of childhood and experiences and they're torn to
> pieces.[6]

So overwhelmed was Stuart by trauma from abuse, that he believed the devil had possessed him. He tried drugs, self-mutilation, and all manner of violence to "cut out" this Devil or to gain a sense of temporary respect from society, but nothing worked for very long. His feelings of low self-worth were so overwhelming that Stuart was incapable of taking Tammy's decision to overcome and banish them. Again and again, his friend Alexander Masters explores this question. Stuart had friends, a job, and a small apartment. Why mess it up? "I don't know Alexander, sometimes it gets so bad you can't think of nothing better to do than make it worse."[7]

Psychologist Craig Haney would call what Tammy and Stuart went through "internalizing the prison experience"; Tammy's burial of the jar was her symbolic expulsion of her former degraded and guilt-ridden personality.

> That is, prisoners may come to think of themselves as the
> kind of person who deserves no more than the degrada-
> tion and stigma to which they have been subjected while
> incarcerated. This degraded identity may be difficult or
> impossible to relinquish upon release from prison, espe-

cially if prisoners return to communities where they continue to be marginalized or stigmatized by others.[8]

In her work, Judith Rumgay focuses on the issue of new external identities; while ex-prisoners continue to suffer from feelings of worthlessness and from dysfunctional syndromes such as post–traumatic stress disorder, at the same time, she finds, they need to go about developing new, conventional identities in the outside world. To succeed they must also have the expectation of being able to fulfill their new roles—and "[r]ecognition and validation by onlookers of the personal identity expressed by those routines will support its maintenance."[9] Rather than stigmatizing the returning prisoner, society should help sustain and encourage the new behaviors that will be necessary, explains Rumgay. This approach can harness the ex-prisoners' innate interest in being valued in the real, noncriminal world.[10] Thus at the same time that Tammy was recovering from her degrading experiences, she was also trying to create a new identity and place in the world, while being stigmatized in that new arena because of her old identity—enough to make anyone crazy.

Penal policy, however, ignores Tammy's experiences, assuming that lawbreakers have no human feelings and need continual shaming and stigma if they are to toe the line. Influenced by theories of crime incorporating themes of good and evil, major segments of the public are convinced ex-prisoners need punitive measures to oversee them on their release, such as frequent drug testing, house arrest, electronic bracelets, and special registries enabling compliance tracking.[11] An ex-prisoner is often held to a standard of behavior with which even law-abiding citizens may experience difficulty, increasing the likelihood of a return to incarceration for a parole violation.

For example, some states require ex-prisoners to pay court costs and various fees upon their release, conditions that those without jobs will be unable to meet. In Washington state, former prisoners cannot vote until such fees are paid; interest at 12 percent accrues. One electronic monitoring company chief executive has indicated that about 70 percent of county agencies employing electronic monitoring charge the users for them on a sliding-fee scale.[12]

Criminologist Elliott Currie views these stern responses as part of our harsh American culture, "a world that is quick to punish and slow to help, a world paradoxically both deeply moralistic and profoundly neglectful."[13] In the end, formerly incarcerated persons are made to feel like failures, losers, and outsiders.

Society's stigmatizing of returning prisoners perpetuates the strange double bind Tammy and all formerly incarcerated individuals experience. Sociologist Erving Goffman puts it in a nutshell when he explains that society is sending mixed messages. "Shape up, you are like everyone else, go out and get a job, and so on." But, on the other hand, "You will always have a felony record and you won't be like everyone else, and it is foolish to deny this difference."

> In brief, he is told he is like anyone else and that he isn't—although there is little agreement among spokesmen as to how much of each he should claim to be. This contradiction and joke is his fate and his destiny.[14]

Of what does this external stigmatization consist? Here's but a brief sampling.

In 1998 federal legislation banned receipt of Pell grants and loans, providing federal financial aid to pursue postsecondary education, for certain periods of time for individuals convicted of possession or sale of controlled substances. Those who complete a drug rehabilitation program meeting certain criteria can regain eligibility, but the delay means that many applicants will be unable to combine education with their recovery efforts, undermining effective drug rehabilitation.[15] The American Council of Education, representing major colleges and universities, has called the restriction "double punishment," pointing out that it discriminates against poor students since the wealthier ones do not need financial aid to pursue higher education.[16] As a result of these provisions, the Government Accountability Office (GAO) estimated that between seventeen thousand and twenty thousand applicants per year would have been denied Pell grants, and between twenty-nine thousand and forty-one thousand were denied student loans for the academic years beginning in 2001 and ending in 2004.[17]

Earlier, in 1994, Congress had denied Pell grants to individuals while in prison on the grounds that the main purpose of prison was punishment and not to reward bad behavior; lawmakers stated they were concerned that the message they were sending was "commit a felony, and get a free education." Reportedly, the law has contributed to a dramatic shrinkage of post–secondary educational programming in U.S. prisons.[18]

When Tammy disappeared into the prison system, she then defaulted on her existing student loans; her unopened mail relating to the loans took up an entire plastic garbage bag. Upon her return to school she was taken out of default and put into deferment, but when she applied for a new grant she was hit with the question about a drug felony. Because her conviction was then so far in the past, Tammy was able to qualify. However, Tammy believes that many ex-prisoners see that question, panic, and fail to follow through.

Federal welfare reform legislation in 1996 imposed a lifetime ban on Temporary Assistance for Needy Families (TANF) and food stamp benefits for individuals with felony drug convictions after August 22, 1996, regardless of subsequent efforts at rehabilitation, unless the state itself passes legislation to opt out or modify the ban. This provision prevents women from obtaining access to temporary benefits to support themselves and their children while they search for a job.[19] By 2005, only eight states and the District of Columbia had opted out of the TANF ban; eighteen states had left the prohibition in place, and all the others had made some modifications involving differentiations between drug sales and possession, or time limitations.[20] In states fully implementing the TANF provision, over a quarter of female drug offenders leaving prison in 2001 would have met TANF eligibility criteria and would have been eligible if not for the ban.[21]

As of 2005, fifteen states fully implemented the federal bar on food stamp benefits for convicted drug felons; although making good estimates is difficult, the GAO says that about 23 percent of those released from prisons in states fully implementing the food stamp prohibition were parents of minor children whose incomes would have qualified them for the program.[22] And the federal government's 1996 "One Strike Initiative" authorized local public housing authorities to obtain conviction records of applicants or tenants for screening purposes, giving them broad discretionary powers to deny public housing or subsidies to households whose members or guests have engaged in drug-related criminal activities, whether convicted or not.[23]

These provisions prevented some households who had lost everything in the aftermath of Hurricane Katrina from obtaining federal financial assistance. Rescued from their porch by a passing boat, the Samsons spent two nights sleeping on a highway overpass and three more in front of the Superdome. Because Antoinette Samson's husband was convicted six years before of crack possession, the family was denied federal housing and welfare assistance; Texas, Alabama, and Mississippi, states initially sheltering many Louisiana evacuees, had all adopted the lifetime bans on federal assistance for felons. "My husband made a mistake in the past, and he admits it," said Samson. "But if you pay your debt to society like he did, it shouldn't come back to haunt you like this."[24]

To remedy this situation, several members of Congress introduced a bill to temporarily restore aid to residents in four states affected by the hurricane. Anticipating a hard sell, the bill's sponsors wrote it so that it would apply only to the hurricane-affected states and would expire after three years. Still, its prospects as of late November 2005 did not appear promising.[25]

About half the states deny licensing or employment to convicted felons, particularly in professions such as education and health care; recently the federal government has introduced conviction-related hiring restrictions into federally regulated areas such as health and child care, transportation, education, and banking.[26] Outright prohibitions preclude individualized licensing and certification decisions providing review of both the individual's crime as well as his or her life since its occurrence. Restrictive federal regulations also guarantee that many ex-prisoners will be barred from working in the helping professions or in situations in which they will come in contact with children, denying them the opportunity to give back to society.

One formerly incarcerated person makes this observation about the kind of work that would help restore self-esteem.

> I also believe community service work would be extremely beneficial. I don't mean picking up garbage and scraping graffiti from walls, which only further adds to a sense of worthlessness. Why not allow them to spend time soothing the cries of a baby born addicted to drugs, or let them read stories to children in hospitals dying of cancer, let them feed the hungry and homeless, let them do something that reaches to the very foundation of their

soul and eventually I believe they will begin to realize and
appreciate the precious gift life is.[27]

Thus, it is no surprise that many low-paying, seasonal industries employ ex-felons who can expect nothing better. One of these areas seems
to be the carnival industry, and apparently even this employment may
be closed to ex-prisoners in the future. A spot check in the summer of
2005 found ex-felons employed in a number of local carnivals in Illinois, working, for example, as merry-go-round operators. State elected
representatives decried the lack of Illinois regulation, frightening parents
that all these workers were a bunch of dangerous child molesters.

> "I hope we get through this [new legislation] without
> somebody being killed or getting raped," said Rep. Bill
> Black (R-Danville), who also has sponsored a failed bill.
> "I'd recommend you stay with [your children] on every
> ride and every attraction on the midway. Your child could
> be getting on a ride that is run by Charles Manson."[28]

Only two states in the U.S., Maine and Vermont, allow persons serving time for a felony to vote, thirty-five states retain the prohibition
during parole, and thirty-one during felony probation. Five states
deny the right to vote permanently, with nine others permitting an
application for a restoration of voting rights after a waiting period.
According to the Sentencing Project, 4.7 million Americans, or one in
forty-three adults, 13 percent of Black males and 2 percent of Black
women (676,730 women), have currently or permanently lost their
voting rights as a result of these provisions. With the increase in the
number of women in prison or on parole or probation, the project concludes that "the disenfranchisement impact will play an increasingly
significant role in women's political participation in coming years."[29]

Recently, the European Court of Human Rights ruled that the disenfranchisement of forty-eight thousand prisoners currently serving
time in the UK violated the European Convention on Human Rights:
"Any departure from the principle of universal suffrage risked undermining the democratic validity of the legislature and its laws."[30] For an
example of just how undemocratic prison disenfranchisement is, consider this letter to a newspaper defending permanent disenfranchisement

164   on the grounds that if prisoners could vote, they would vote to defund
the criminal justice system:

> People contemplating future crimes are likely to vote
> against increased financing for criminal justice agencies,
> against judges who are not lenient toward those convicted
> of crimes, and so on. While there often are many legiti-
> mate reasons to vote against such things, this potential
> motive is not legitimate.[31]

Only eight states have provisions for expungement or record sealing,
and most of these remedies are available only for misdemeanors, first
offenses, or probation.[32]

> It should come as no surprise that not a single U.S. juris-
> diction has attempted a comprehensive assessment of its
> regime of collateral consequences . . . not a single jurisdic-
> tion has considered it necessary or appropriate to develop
> a systematic and accessible way for convicted persons to
> overcome or avoid the legal barriers to reentry and reinte-
> gration. At a time when the front-end mechanics of the
> justice system have become increasingly efficient in pro-
> cessing people in, the mechanics of processing them out
> have become largely ignored. . . . As a practical matter,
> therefore, in most jurisdictions people convicted of a
> crime have no hope of ever being able to fully discharge
> their debt to society.[33]

Shaming of ex-prisoners is one of Tammy's major bugaboos; she finds
her current stigmatization even worse than being in prison. And some
experts agree with Tammy that the practice is counterproductive. In
the end, shaming causes more crime, conclude philosophers John
Braithwaite and Martha Nussbaum, because individuals who are humiliated will become more alienated and troubled than before, and
will certainly be attracted to antisocial groups that will be more accept-
ing of them.[34] Braithwaite: "Shaming that is stigmatizing . . . makes
criminal subcultures more attractive because these are in some sense
subcultures which reject the rejectors."[35] Nussbaum observes, "Using

shame to control crime is, in that sense, like using gasoline to put out a fire."[36]

Even more troubling is the realization that stigmatizing always creates a social class of persons, a subgroup, who are *permanently* different from the others. Political philosopher Hannah Arendt warns that when we create such categories, we force "millions of people into conditions which, despite all appearances, are the conditions of savages."[37] This is because categorizing people obliterates individuality:

> The killing of man's individuality, of the uniqueness
> shaped in equal parts by nature, will, and destiny, which
> has become so self-evident a premise for all human rela-
> tions that even identical twins inspire a certain uneasiness,
> creates a horror that vastly overshadows the outrage of
> the judical-political person and the despair of the moral
> person. . . . For to destroy individuality is to destroy spon-
> taneity, man's power to begin something new out of his
> own resources. . . .[38]

For Tammy that was the worst, both in prison and then when out—to be considered only an evil "inmate" with no consideration for the individual characteristics of her own personhood. Remember how Tammy sat outside the guards' station at the jail and cried, seeking that personal recognition that had been destroyed? All prisoners experience this stigmatization, and it is in reality a blotting out of self, the cruelest penalty of all and the hardest to bear.

Former President Jimmy Carter identifies current punishment and stigmatizing strategies as characteristics of an unacceptable fundamentalism: "I am right and worthy, but you are wrong and condemned."[39] True, compassionate Christians, he says, break through the barrier and reach out to embrace others unlike themselves,[40] a prescription that activist Jane Addams wrote about as early as 1902 as the foundation and guarantee of democracy. "We have learned as common knowledge that much of the insensibility and hardness of the world is due to the lack of imagination which prevents a realization of the experiences of other people," she wrote at that time.[41]

From his current vantage point in the Middle East, Israeli novelist Amos Oz speaks also of a lack of imagination that fuels fanaticism that

166   leads to stigmatization: "A sense of humor, the ability to imagine the other, the capacity to recognize the peninsular quality of every one of us may be at least a partial defense against the fanatic gene that we all contain."[42]

> The essence of fanaticism lies in the desire to force other people to change. The common inclination to improve your neighbor, mend your spouse, engineer your child, or straighten up your brother, rather than let them be. The fanatic is a most unselfish creature. The fanatic is a great altruist. Often the fanatic is more interested in you than in himself. He wants to save your soul, he wants to redeem you, he wants to liberate you from sin, from error, from smoking, from your faith or from your faithlessness, he wants to improve your eating habits, or to cure you of your drinking or you voting habits. The fanatic cares a great deal for you, he is always either falling on your neck because he truly loves you or else he is at your throat in case you prove to be unredeemable.[43]

Epilogue: Back to County

It means, for me, recognizing the enemy outside and the
enemy within, and knowing that my work is part of a
continuum of women's work, of reclaiming this earth
and our power, and knowing that this work did not begin
with my birth nor will it end with my death. And it
means knowing that within this continuum, my life and
my love and my work has particular power and meaning
relative to others.

— AUDRE LORDE

On a rainy November day, Tammy revisits the Cook County jail tier in
which she was incarcerated five years ago. She sees that the cinderblocks
need painting, the linoleum is scuffed and torn, and the lack of ventilation makes the overheated air heavy and fetid. The tier could be easily
and cheaply redecorated, Tammy realizes, but its dilapidated condition
well serves its purpose to punish—although almost all the prisoners
are women only accused of crime, awaiting trial, and unable to make
bail, in some cases as little as one hundred dollars. And the three open
shower stalls, in full view at the end of the cell block—well, Tammy
wonders how she ever took a shower there. One stall is sealed off, out
of order. The cracked, flaking, and rotting tiles on the floor and sides
make a mockery of the idea of sanitation. And where are the shower
curtains? Surely there were shower curtains when she was there.

Next, it is to the dayroom, where masses of women sit after eating
their bologna sandwich lunch. Here Tammy recognizes two women
from the past. Reminding her they met in the work release center,
they surround her admiringly, as if Tammy were visiting royalty. They

admire her looks and her clothing, so at odds with their oversized, blue scrub uniforms stenciled with "DOC" on top and bottom. How loving and gracious and welcoming they are. And, observes Tammy, how much worse for wear these two ladies look since the last time she saw them, burnt out somehow. Their faces show all the pain they have experienced, Tammy thinks. Both are missing most of their top teeth. And since this unit is now devoted to women in the jail's drug treatment program, they had obviously gone back to the drug life.

Over and over again, one of the women tells Tammy, "I knew then you wouldn't be back." Generously, she seems so proud and gratified for Tammy.

The encounters are chilling. Tammy is forced to confront her former self, and also sees what she might have looked like had she not prevailed in her recovery. After all, official statistics show that nearly half of the women (47 percent) in Tammy's prison at any given time return to the facility after their release.[1] No woman would want to come back, Tammy knows. So why do they? Obviously, not becoming another recidivism statistic requires more than just not wanting to. The women are still numbing themselves with drugs, mired in lives of trauma and dysfunction, doomed to repeat the mistakes of the past. Tammy could see it in their faces.

> I saw the lack of hope, I saw the confusion, because they
> didn't have a clue. When I say they don't have a clue, they
> don't have a clue to know that they do have choices. It hurt
> my heart so much to see them there.

A staff member asks Tammy to address the group. In the conclusion to her remarks, punctuated by vociferous clapping, Tammy announces: "Ladies, I have found my place in society."

Later, I ask Tammy what she meant by "place in society." It is, she says, the antithesis of the unbearable loneliness, the dislocation from leading a life disconnected from most people, detached from goals and any sense of achievement, an existence totally dedicated to forgetting.

> "Place in society" means living up to my full potential, using
> the gifts I was given. I had no place. I was doing nothing
> positive, giving nothing to society, nothing to myself. You

have to understand the drugs cloud so much of your thinking, so much of your doing, so much of the true soul of who you are. When I stopped using before prison that wasn't really long enough for me to learn who I was. Then the incarceration came and I was knocked to my knees and couldn't do anything but crawl around. I wanted to stand up and be a productive member of society.

✳

The wonder is that Tammy was able to recover from so much trauma to find a place in society. Others are not so lucky. After receiving clemency, Dorothy Gaines was unable to return to her job as a nurse technician or to any employment in the health care field because of her felony conviction. As a result of these rejections, Gaines found it difficult some days even to leave the house, and never made it back into the labor market. She ended up having to move in with one of her daughters and her four children in a two-bedroom apartment.

Like Tammy, both Dorothy and her son Philip feel themselves confined in "that box."[2] Philip is overwhelmed by bitterness about what happened to him and his mother. He failed eighth grade three times and has already been in trouble with the law himself. Clearly, these confusing and bitter feelings have kept him from moving from adolescence into adulthood.

> "I feel like my mother owes me for what I been through, but she don't," Philip said, in a confused jumble of past and present tense. "That's why I'd get mad about any little thing, 'cause I felt like she owed me something. . . . I'm trying to figure that out right now—to stop stressing mom out just 'cause I'm thinking she owes me. Like when she went to prison, she took my life. And she get back home and she wants her life, but my life's still stuck, so I feel like she owes me a lot."[3]

Unfortunately, in 2005 the travails of the Gaines family of Mobile, Alabama, continued. Lacking funds, they were unable to flee the path of Hurricane Katrina and the entire family had to sit there as the electricity went out and their apartment flooded.[4]

    The Gaineses' experience illustrates just how pain is handed down from one generation to the next. Thankfully, Tammy and Terrence have now avoided this trap, working hard each day not to blame one another, to cut this legacy of suffering, and to stop the intergenerational transmission of blame and pain right in its tracks.

    But Tammy and Terrence's story demonstrates just how hard individuals have to labor to overcome what seems like fate but is the result of earlier constrained choices made in response to specific situations. Early childhood abuse created in Tammy an aggressive, antisocial personality and a habit of disassociation, of splitting herself off, which heroin aided and abetted. Tammy's incarceration created an angry and aggressive son, well on his way toward delinquency. Then history repeated itself: Terrence was sexually assaulted. It was a wake-up call. All Tammy's efforts would be needed to keep Terrence from developing an anti-social personality, a sense of powerlessness and entitlement that can lead to drug addiction and crime.

    After this episode, Tammy and her son purposefully strove to make certain that neither sank back into previous patterns. What would happen in the future, they understood, was in their own hands, and they determined to remain vigilant. Their commitment to work through these issues and to empower themselves in the face of the tremendous odds against them is nothing short of heroic.

> The most important thing in my life, and I give it to my
> son, is being able to have a choice. Maybe because mine was
> taken from me.

Tammy has buried her guilt, and Terrence his regrets: "We are different human beings now," explains Tammy, "and we appreciate life and all that it has to give."

    Tammy's experiences illustrate the difficulties involved in controlling one's destiny within the context of a harsh and judgmental society. She knows she is lucky. Some people, like the Gaines family and Stuart Shorter, seem doomed to repeat the failures of the past; it appears to some to be some kind of moral failing. British barrister and author John Mortimer has wittily described this intergenerational sense of fate.

> Down at the Old Bailey, I had, day in and day out, seen
> sons and daughters of judges, or top barristers, punishing

the sons and daughters of burglars, fraudsters and street-
fighters for what must have seemed to them a natural,
even a preordained way of life.[5]

Mortimer writes that we continue to believe in the doctrine of free will
because so much of our legal system has to rest on such a myth:

> Unless we can assume we are capable of making choices
> and controlling our destiny, laws can't function, politicians
> can't be held to account, great artists can't be praised or
> bad painters and indifferent poets justly criticized. . . . It's
> not vanity but practical necessity that compels us to see
> ourselves as free spirits, capable of taking charge of our
> destiny. Although our freedom in that regard may be far
> narrower than we often like to think.[6]

Tammy has told her story so you can see her suffering and understand
what it feels like to be classified as an outsider for whom rights are denied and only responsibilities imposed. She has spoken so that, as recommended by Amos Oz, you can fully imagine her life, understand
her challenges, and value her struggle. She has shared her experiences
so that you can determine how you want to view her and all the other
women currently incarcerated. Will you see them as immoral individuals in pursuit only of pleasure, women needing to be taught responsibility for their dependencies and choices through continual, harsh
punishment, or will you regard them as persons who did stupid or bad
things because of poor coping strategies to abuse, and who need new
and better opportunities to succeed instead of having the door banged
shut?

You decide.

Notes

Prologue

1. This is her real name. The author interviewed Tammy from August 9, 2004, to May 9, 2006. All interviews were taped. The author interviewed Terrence Johnson, Tammy's son, on November 18, 2004, and July 15, 2005. Patricia ("Pat") Johnson, Tammy's sister, was interviewed on November 30, 2004, and Terri Johnson, her younger sister, on January 22, 2005. All quotes from the Johnson family come verbatim from these interviews. All members of the family have chosen to use their real names. The names of some non-family members in this narrative have been changed to protect their identities. These are "Maurice," "Edward," "Brenda," and "Auntie White."

2. Shari Zavala, interview by author, March 17, 2005.

3. Jody Raphael, Saving Bernice: Battered Women, Welfare, and Poverty (Boston: Northeastern University Press, 2000).

4. Jody Raphael, Listening to Olivia: Violence, Poverty, and Prostitution (Boston: Northeastern University Press, 2004).

5. Alexander Masters, Stuart: A Life Backwards (London: Fourth Estate, 2005), 103.

6. Jonathan Coe, Like a Fiery Elephant: The Story of B. S. Johnson (London: Picador, 2004), 35.

7. Joane Martel, "Policing Criminological Knowledge: The Hazards of Qualitative Research on Women in Prison," Theoretical Criminology 8, no. 2 (2004): 157–89.

8. Recent academic approaches have included Lori Girshick, No Safe Haven: Stories of Women in Prison (Boston: Northeastern University Press, 1999), and Paula C. Johnson, Inner Lives: Voices of American Women in Prison (New York: New York University Press, 2003). Recent journalistic efforts include Jennifer Gonnerman, Life on the Outside: The Prison Odyssey of Elaine Bartlett (New York: Farrar, Straus and Giroux, 2004), and Alan Elsner, Gates of Injustice: The Crisis in America's Prisons (Upper Saddle River, N.J.: Prentice Hall: 2004).

9. Cristina Rathbone, *A World Apart: Women, Prison, and Life behind Bars* (New York: Random House, 2005).

10. Ibid., 33.

11. Ibid., 4.

12. See, for example, Renny Golden, *War on the Family: Mothers in Prison and the Families They Leave Behind* (New York: Routledge, 2005), and Cynthia Martone, *Loving through Bars: Children with Parents in Prison* (Santa Monica, Calif.: Santa Monica Press, 2005).

13. Audre Lorde, *A Burst of Light: Essays* (Ithaca, N.Y.: Firebrand Books, 1998), 130. Lorde was never charged with a crime and never served time in prison.

CHAPTER THREE

1. Shelley Williams, "To the Girls at the Audy," in *Real Conditions: Writings from Cook County Jail, Women's Division 4 and the Cook County Juvenile Temporary Detention Center* 2, no. 3 (2001):19.

2. Steve Bogira, *Courtroom 302: A Year behind the Scenes in an American Criminal Courthouse* (New York: Knopf Publishing Group, 2005), 7.

3. Ibid.

4. Ibid., 8.

5. Ibid., 91.

6. Ibid., 7.

7. Craig Haney, "Prison Overcrowding: Harmful Consequences and Dysfunctional Reactions," testimony given on July 19, 2005, to the Vera Institute of Justice Commission on Safety and Abuse in America's Prisons, http://www.prisoncommission.org.

8. Malcolm M. Feeley and Jonathan Simon, "The New Penology: Notes on the Emerging Strategy of Corrections and Its Implications," *Criminology* 30, no. 4 (1992): 452. For a thorough discussion of the new, nonrehabilitative penology and its causes, see also Craig Haney, *Reforming Punishment: Psychological Limits to the Pains of Imprisonment* (Washington, D.C.: American Psychological Association, 2006).

9. Paige M. Harrison and Allen J. Beck, "Prisoners in 2004," 2005 Bulletin from the U.S. Department of Justice, Bureau of Justice Statistics, 1, http://www.ojp.usdoj.gov/bjs/abstract/p04.htm.

10. Ibid., 4.

11. Meda Chesney-Lind, "Patriarchy, Crime, and Justice: Feminist Criminology in an Era of Backlash," *Feminist Criminology* 1, no. 1 (2006): 17.

12. Lauren E. Glaze and Seri Palla, "Probation and Parole in the United States, 2004," 2005 Bulletin from the U.S. Department of Justice, Bureau of Justice Statistics, 6, http://www.ojp.usdoj.gov/bjs/abstract/ppus04.htm.

13. Ibid.

14. Ibid., 9.

15. Lawrence A. Greenfeld and Tracy L. Snell, "Women Offenders," 1999 Special Report from the U.S. Department of Justice, Bureau of Justice Statistics, 7, http://www.ojp.usdoj.gov/bjs/pub/pdf/wo.pdf.

16. Christopher J. Mumola, "Incarcerated Parents and Their Children," 2000 Special Report from the U.S. Department of Justice, Bureau of Justice Statistics, 2, http://www.ojp.usdoj.gov/bjs/abstract/iptc.htm.

17. Harrison and Beck, "Prisoners," 8.

18. This statistic was computed from data found at the Web site of the U.S. 2000 census, at http://www.factfinder.census.gov.

19. Harrison and Beck, "Prisoners," 8.

20. Greenfeld and Snell, "Women Offenders," 8.

21. Don Stemen, Andres Rengifo, and James Wilson, "Of Fragmentation and Ferment: The Impact of State Sentencing Policies on Incarceration Rates, 1975–2002," 2006 report to the National Institute of Justice, 144, http://www.ncjrs.gov/pdffiles1/nij/grants/213003.pdf.

22. Arthur J. Lurigio, Mary Harkenrider, and Pamela Loose, "The Disproportionate Incarceration of African Americans for Drug Crimes: The Illinois Perspective," 2005 report to the U.S. Department of Justice, 16, http://www.nicic.org/Library/021255.

23. Ibid., 7.

24. Greenfeld and Snell, "Women Offenders," 8. It is important to remember that although women continue to be arrested and incarcerated at higher rates than men, women's drug use, according to national surveys, has not been accelerating and still remains half that of men; almost 13 percent of men and 6.2 percent of women reported current drug usage in 2004. Department of Health and Human Services, Substance Abuse and Mental Health Services Administration, "Overview of Findings from the 2004 National Survey of Drug Use and Health," 2005 report, http://www.oas.samhsa.gov.

25. Ibid., 9.

26. Office of National Drug Control Policy, "Women and Drugs," Fact sheet at http://www.whitehousedrugpolicy.gov/drugfact/women.

27. Harrison and Beck, "Prisoners," 9.

28. The project found that in 1986 in New York State, one out of every twenty women arrested for a drug offense was sentenced to prison, but by 1995 that rate had risen to one in seven. In California, the researchers found a 316 percent growth in the number of women sentenced to prison for drug crimes, a rise fully ten times the increase in the number of arrests. The increases in prison sentences outpaced rises in arrests and convictions in all three states studied. Marc Mauer, Cathy Potler, and Richard Wolf, "Gender and Justice: Women, Drugs, and Sentencing Policy," 1999 report from the Sentencing Project, http://www.sentencingproject.org.

29. In the late 1980s the Cook County Circuit Court shifted most of its

176   drug cases to five courtrooms that began business at 4:00 p.m., leaving other judges time to dispose of more serious cases. This change, creating specialized drug courtrooms, resulted in more minor cases going through the system rather than being dismissed. Bogira, Courtroom 302, 117–18.

30. Joel Anderson, "Furcal Lives for the Present: Braves Shortstop Must Begin Jail Term after Season," Chicago Tribune, 9 October 2004.

31. Nancy D. Campbell, Using Women: Gender, Drug Policy and Social Justice (New York: Routledge, 2000), 43, 199. In the summer of 2004, then UK Home Secretary David Blunkett warned that women were no longer exerting the good influence they had in the past to curb drinking to excess and fighting in pubs; with their own drinking and drunken antics, they were declining their historical role and becoming part of the problem itself. Matthew Hickley, "Lager Loutettes 'Fuel Pub Violence,'" (London) Daily Mail, 19 July 2004.

32. Elizabeth Ettore, Women and Substance Use (New Brunswick, N.J.: Rutgers University Press, 1992), 9–10.

33. Jill McCorkel, "Embodied Surveillance and the Gendering of Punishment," Journal of Contemporary Ethnography 32, no. 1 (2003): 69.

34. Ibid.

35. Margaret Pereira, "Women and Drugs: Destruction by Incarceration," Hecate 28, no. 1 (2002): 155.

36. Pat Carlen and Anne Worrall, Analysing Women's Imprisonment (Portland, Ore.: Willan Publishing, 2004), 83.

37. Angela P. Harris, "Criminal Justice as Environmental Justice," 1 Journal of Gender Race and Justice (1997–98): 17.

38. Lynne Haney, "Introduction: Gender, Welfare, and States of Punishment," Social Politics: International Studies in Gender, State and Society 11, no. 3 (2004): 344.

39. Ibid., 345.

40. Jill McCorkel, "'Criminally Dependent'? Gender, Punishment, and the Rhetoric of Welfare Reform," Social Politics: International Studies in Gender, State, and Society 11, no. 3 (2004): 387.

41. Ibid., 405. Emphasis in original.

42. Patricia Hill Collins, Black Feminist Thought: Knowledge, Consciousness, and the Politics of Empowerment (New York: Routledge, 2000), 69.

43. Julia Sudbury, "A World Without Prisons: Resisting Militarism, Globalized Punishment, and Empire," Social Justice 31, nos. 1–2 (2004): 24.

44. Wahneema Lubiano, "Black Ladies, Welfare Queens, and State Minstrels: Ideological War by Narrative Means," in Race-Ing Justice, En-Gendering Power, ed. Toni Morrison, (New York: Pantheon Books, 1992), 336.

45. Ibid., 339. Emphasis in original. This stereotype of the tough Black female criminal easily leads to a belief in strong punishment. As crime-committing drug addicts, for example, Black women may be seen as domineering, assertive, and masculine, needing strong punishment, which will not

harm them. As a female rape victim, the Black woman is seen as loose and immoral, not a believable complainant, and merely vindictive; and as a Black victim of domestic violence, she probably precipitated the abuse. See Harris, "Criminal Justice," which traces the multitude of common references to criminals as animals, and Sharon Angella Allard, "Rethinking Battered Woman's Syndrome: A Black Feminist Perspective," in *Domestic Violence at the Margins: Readings on Race, Class, Gender, and Culture*, ed. Natalie Sokoloff (Piscataway, N.J.: Rutgers University Press, 2005), 200. Also embedded in these attitudes is the idea that the poor are so different from others that they are incapable of suffering in the same way as the majority do, justifying harsher approaches to "deviancy." Barbara Bush's remarks about the persons relocated during Hurricane Katrina into the former Houston Astrodome ("And so many of the people in the arena here, you know, were underprivileged anyway, so this is working very well for them") are one example. "Barbara Bush Calls Evacuees Better Off," *New York Times*, 7 September 2005. Critic Margery Sabin explains that writer George Orwell, most notably in *The Road to Wigan Pier*, forces one to discard the convenient rationalization that other kinds of people somehow do not mind their poverty or imprisonment; that unlike oneself, they prefer or choose to live that way. Margery Sabin, "Outside/Inside: Searching for Wigan Pier," in *George Orwell into the Twenty-First Century*, eds. Thomas Cushman and John Rodden (Boulder, Colo.: Paradigm Publishers, 2004), 249.

46. Lenora Lapidus, Namita Luthra, Anjuli Verma, Deborah Small, Patricia Allard, and Kirsten Levingston, "Caught in the Net: The Impact of Drug Policies on Women and Families," 2004 report from the American Civil Liberties Union, the Brennan Center for Justice, and Break the Chains: Communities of Color and the War on Drugs, 35, http://www.fairlaws4families.org/publications.html.

47. Ibid., 36–37.

48. Ibid., 41.

49. Ibid., 35.

50. Ibid., 1.

51. Tim Whitney, "Disproportionate Sentencing of Minority Drug Offenders in Illinois," report to the U.S. Department of Justice, 10, http://www.icjia.state.il.us/public/pdf/ResearchReports/Disproportionate%Sentencing%20Report.pdf.

CHAPTER FOUR

1. Ruth Wyner, "Letters," on the Cambridge Two Web site, letter of February 2000, http://www.cambridgetwo.com/rj/fruth.htm.

2. Ruth Wyner, *From the Inside: Dispatches from a Women's Prison* (London: Aurum Press, 2003), 5.

3. Ibid., 149.

4. Ibid., 155. After her release from prison, Wyner developed a serious case of breast cancer that she attributes to the stress of her prison experience.

178   5. Susan McDougal, jailed for contempt of court when she failed to provide testimony to a grand jury investigating Whitewater abuses under special prosecutor Ken Starr, describes many harrowing incidents in which guards publicly humiliated the prisoners at the Sybil Brand Institute for Women in California. Here is but one example.

> On one particularly memorable trip back from court, a female guard
> took it upon herself to teach me a lesson in humility, a recurring theme
> between Sybil Brand's guards and inmates. As I stepped off the bus,
> she yanked out of my hands the manila envelope I was carrying, then
> dumped its contents—my glasses and some court documents—onto the
> sidewalk. My glasses broke and the guard, unapologetic, then refused to
> remove my handcuffs, as was required. Instead, she put me in a locked
> waiting room with several other women—none of whom were hand-
> cuffed. As she left, the guard loudly announced that I had just told her I
> shouldn't be placed in that room, as I was better than the other women
> there. The guard was clearly expecting the other women to administer a
> first-class beating, but thankfully, no one took her seriously and they just
> ignored her. (Susan McDougal and Pat Harris, *The Woman Who Wouldn't
> Talk* [New York: Carroll & Graf, 2003], 267.)

Jean Harris's two books also eloquently describe the effects of the guards' deliberate policies of humiliation and degradation. Jean Harris, *Marking Time: Letters from Jean Harris to Shana Alexander* (New York: Charles Scribner's Sons, 1991) and *"They Always Call Us Ladies": Stories from Prison* (New York: Charles Scribner's Sons, 1988). Prisoner Judee Norton relates a particularly sadistic episode. Her son, who had traveled a great distance to visit her in prison, was initially turned away because he was not in compliance with the prison dress code. After standing outside in the Arizona sun for three and a half hours without water, he was let in twenty minutes before the end of the visitation period. Then Norton was summoned to the guard captain.

> "It is my feeling that for the continued secure operation of this institu-
> tion, it will be necessary to discontinue your son's visits until further
> notice. Perhaps he only needs time away from you to learn to deal with
> the fact of your incarceration in a mature and sensible manner. An atti-
> tude adjustment period." He smiles.
>
> I am consumed by impotent rage. I wrestle with a crushing and
> mighty urge to rise and beat that superior face of his into a bleeding
> pulp of unrecognizable jutting bones and torn flesh. That desire is so
> intense as to be palpable. I can hear the dull wet crunch of gristle and
> cartilage, can feel his warm slippery brains between my fingers, can
> smell the dark coppery odor of his blood, can see it splashing up, up,
> onto the walls, the carpet, the desk, my face, my hair, crimson and
> joyous.
>
> I am dazed and shaken by this vision. I sit for a moment gripping the

chair bottom with white-knuckled horror. Then I push the chair back gently, like a woman preparing to excuse herself from the dinner table and say softly, "May I leave, sir?" (Judee Norton, "Norton #59900," in *Doing Time: 25 Years of Prison Writing*, ed. Bell Chevigny [New York: Arcade Publishing, 1999], 228–35.)

In his 1961 study sociologist Erving Goffman famously details the "mortification" practices total institutions employ so that "cooperation from persons who often have cause to be uncooperative" is achieved. Erving Goffman, *Asylums: Essays on the Social Situation of Mental Patients and Other Inmates* (Garden City, N.Y.: Anchor Books, 1961), 52. The comment of one woman prisoner summarizes the situation: "You're all trash; you know they talk to you like you're a dog. . . . I don't do anything to deserve that. Yes I made a mistake, and I'm here and I'm paying for my time. If I was acting in an unordered fashion or like an animal, I would expect to be treated like that. But I'm not. I don't disrespect them, and they still want to treat you like that." Candace Kruttschnitt, "The Politics of Confinement: Women's Imprisonment in California and the UK," in *The Effects of Imprisonment*, eds. Alison Liebling and Shadd Maruna (Portland, Ore.: Willan Publishing, 2005), 161.

6. James Gilligan, "Punishment and Violence: Is the Criminal Law Based on One Huge Mistake?" *Social Research* 67, no. 3 (2000): 755.

7. Erwin James, "A Life Again," (London) *Guardian*, 5 September 2005.

8. Craig Haney, "Psychology and the Limits to Prison Pain: Confronting the Coming Crisis in Eighth Amendment Law," *Psychology, Public Policy, and Law* 3, no. 4 (1997): 531.

9. Ibid.

10. Ibid., 573.

11. Patricia McConnel, essay, in *Wall Tappings: An International Anthology of Women's Prison Writings 200 to the Present*, ed. Judith Scheffler (New York: The Feminist Press, 2002), 263.

12. Dot Goulding, "Severed Connections: An Exploration of the Impact of Imprisonment on Women's Familial and Social Connectedness," 2004 report, Murdoch University Centre for Social and Community Research, 37, http://www.cscr.murdoch.edu.au/impact_of_prison_.pdf.

13. Jimmy Santiago Baca, "Coming Into Language," in Chevigny, *Doing Time*, 105.

14. David Rohde and Christopher Drew, "Prisoners Evacuated after Hurricanes Allege Abuse," *New York Times*, 2 October 2005.

15. Ibid.

16. Haney, "Psychology," 528.

17. Franz Kafka, *The Trial* (New York: Alfred A. Knopf, 1986), 264.

18. For a provocative description of the "clandestine legal organization" or "strange jurisprudence" in this novel, see Scott Finet, "Franz Kafka's Trial as Symbol in Judicial Opinions," *Legal Studies Forum* 12, no. 1 (1988): 23–35.

Chapter Five

1. Caroline Wolf Harlow, "Prior Abuse Reported by Inmates and Probationers," 1999 Selected Findings from the U. S. Department of Justice, Bureau of Justice Statistics, 1, available at http://www.ojp.usdoj.gov/bjs/abstract/parip.htm.

2. Ibid.

3. Angela Browne, Brenda Miller, and Eugene Maguin, "Prevalence and Severity of Lifetime Physical and Sexual Victimization among Incarcerated Women," International Journal of Law and Psychiatry 22, nos. 3–4 (1999): 313. In a study in the Cook County (Chicago) Jail, researchers found that over one-third of the sample (35.3 percent) reported a history of childhood sexual abuse, with the mean age of abuse at 10.6 years. Susan F. McClanahan, Gary M. McClelland, Karen M. Abram, and Linda A. Teplin, "Pathways into Prostitution among Female Jail Detainees and Their Implications for Mental Health Services," Psychiatric Services 50, no. 12 (1999): 1609.

4. Harlow, "Prior Abuse," 3.

5. Ibid.

6. Ibid.

7. Danielle Dirks, "Sexual Revictimization and Retraumatization of Women in Prison," Women's Studies Quarterly 32, no. 3/4 (2004): 107. Several women prisoners relate how spending time in maximum security brought back horrific memories of being locked in closets as children by family members. To cope, one woman lay on the floor and looked out under the door at the light. Luana Ross, Inventing the Savage: The Social Construction of Native American Criminality (Austin: University of Texas Press, 1998), 144.

8. Barbara H. Zaitzow, "Pastel Fascism: Reflections of Social Control Techniques Used with Women in Prison," Women Studies Quarterly 32, no. 3/4 (2004): 41. See also Jan Heney and Connie M. Kristiansen, "An Analysis of the Impact of Prison on Women Survivors of Childhood Sexual Abuse," in Breaking the Rules: Women in Prison and Feminist Therapy, eds. Judy Harden and Marcia Hill, 29–44 (Binghamton, N.Y.: The Haworth Press, 1998). One woman, serving life in prison without parole for killing her abuser, and suffering daily humiliation and abuse in prison, has written, "I sometimes wonder if I should have stayed with my abuser. Even if he had succeeded in killing me, my life sentence would be done." Darcy K. War Bonnet, "Women in Prison Tell It Like It Is," Off Our Backs, February 2001, http://www.kersplebedeb.com/mystuff/feminist/wip_oob.html.

9. Jasbir K. Puar, "Abu Ghraib: Arguing against Exceptionalism," Feminist Studies 30, no. 2 (2004): 533. For a full discussion see Teresa A. Miller, "Sex Surveillance: Gender, Privacy and the Sexualization of Power in Prison," 10 Geo. Mason U. Civ. Rts. L.J. (2000): 291. Miller describes how guards relate to prisoners in many sexually derogative ways that emphasize the prisoner's subor-

dinate position. For example, male prisoners are addressed with titles such as "pussy," "sissy," "cunt," and "bitch," and in prison riots, male prisoners frequently sexually assault guards.

10. Andrea Dworkin, *Life and Death* (New York: Free Press, 1997), 55–56.

11. Anannya Bhattacharjee, "Private Fists and Public Force: Rape, Gender, and Surveillance," in *Policing the National Body: Race, Gender, and Criminalization*, eds. Jael Silliman and Anannya Bhattacharjee (Cambridge, Mass.: South End Press, 2002), 26–27.

12. Christy Marie Camp, "I'm Going In . . . ," *Cell Door Magazine* (on-line publication), 1, no. 6 (1999), http://www.lairdcarlson.com/celldoor/00106/Camp00106GoingIn.htm.

13. Interview with Mark Merin on 24 August 2004 on Democracy NOW!, a daily radio and TV news program, http://www.democracynow.org/article.pl?sid=04/08/24/2110246.

14. Judy Haney, Statement to the Commission on Safety and Abuse in America's Prisons, 19 April 2005, 3, http://www.prisoncommission.org.

15. Abdon M. Pallasch, "Lawsuit Challenges County Jail's Invasive Checks for Sex Diseases," *Chicago Sun-Times*, 10 August 2005.

16. Pete Rose, *My Prison without Bars*, (New York: Rodale Press, 2004), 193.

17. See Judge Richard Posner's dissent in *Johnson v. Phelan*, 69 F. 3d 144 (7th Circuit Court of Appeals, 1995), in which he disagreed with the Seventh Circuit Court of Appeals's holding that cross-sex prison monitoring did not violate the U.S. Constitution: "The nudity taboo retains great strength in the United States. It should not be confused with prudery. It is a taboo against being seen in the nude by strangers, not by one's intimates. . . . The taboo is particularly strong when the stranger belongs to the opposite sex." bell hooks finds nakedness a particular issue for Black women: "After the branding all slaves were stripped of any clothing. The nakedness of the African female served as a constant reminder of her sexual vulnerability." bell hooks, *Ain't I a Woman: Black Women and Feminism* (Boston: South End Press, 1981), 18.

18. Joane Martel, "Policing Criminological Knowledge: The Hazards of Qualitative Research on Women in Prison," *Theoretical Criminology* 8, no. 2 (2004): 160.

19. Adam Liptak, "Pregnant Inmates Often Shackled During Labor," *New York Times*, 2 March 2006. One prisoner relates another incident that demonstrates the insensitivity of the guards to women's medical conditions. The woman was being transferred from the hospital back to prison following a hysterectomy. "When I was leaving the hospital, they did a full body search to make sure I wasn't trying to bring anything back with me. The guard rammed her hand up me. I still had stitches and everything hurt like hell." Mark R. Pogrebin and Mary Dodge, "Women's Accounts of Their Prison Experiences: A Retrospective View of Their Subjective Realities," *Journal of Criminal Justice* 29, no. 6 (2001): 537.

20. Amber Richelle Dean, "Prisoners' Rites?" *e.Peak Lastword* 13, no. 105 (2000), http://www.peak.sfu.ca/the-peak/2000–2/issue13/op-lw.html.

21. Elizabeth Fernandez, "Improper Strip Searches Alleged; 2 Women Sue, Claim They Were Left Naked in S.F. Jail Cells," *San Francisco Chronicle*, 4 September 2003.

22. Alan Elsner, *Gates of Injustice: The Crisis in America's Prisons* (Upper Saddle, N.J.: Prentice Hall, 2004), 133.

23. Elizabeth Fernandez, "Stories of Anguish: Jail Has Man Disrobe to Photograph His Tattoos," *San Francisco Chronicle*, 16 November 2003.

24. Ibid.

25. Kathryn Watterson, *Women in Prison: Inside the Concrete Womb* (Boston: Northeastern University Press, 1996), 98.

26. Karlene Faith, "Transformative Justice versus Re-entrenched Correctionalism: The Canadian Experience," in *Harsh Punishment: International Experiences of Women's Imprisonment*, eds. Sandy Cook and Susanne Davies (Boston: Northeastern University Press, 1999), 101–2. The filming of strip searches seems to be a practice that compounds the women's humiliation. In the UK, ten prisoners were subject to disciplinary measures for refusing to be strip-searched on the grounds that the process would be videotaped. The filming has now been halted, but, in response to a parliamentary question, the government admitted that the strip search tapes had not been destroyed. House of Commons Hansard Written Answers for 26 February 1997, http://www.parliament. the-stationery-office.co.uk/pa/cm199697/cmhansrd/vo970226/debindx/ 70226-x.htm.

27. Faith, "Transformative Justice," 103.

28. Debbie Kilroy, "Sisters Inside: Speaking Out against Criminal Injustice," in *Global Lockdown: Race, Gender, and the Prison-Industrial Complex*, ed. Julia Sudbury (New York: Routledge, 2005), 290.

29. Stop Prisoner Rape, a national human rights organization, recently investigated allegations of sexual abuse and harassment in the Ohio Reformatory for Women. Three former staff members reported that sex between prisoners and staff was the subject of almost daily discussion, and that staff members routinely abused women inside of locked broom closets and kept a mattress in a boiler room for the purpose of sexual misconduct. Retaliation for reporting sexual assaults can also be horrific. After prisoner Amy Hale reported an assault she was transferred for her own protection, but even then male correctional officers frequently entered her cell, held her down on the bed, choked her, and spat in her face. "The Sexual Abuse of Female Inmates in Ohio," 2003 report of Stop Prisoner Rape, http://www.spr.org. The Web site contains a number of other publications and firsthand accounts.

30. Pogrebin and Dodge, "Women's Accounts," 538.

31. "PREA Update," fact sheet on the Stop Prisoner Rape Web site, http:// www.spr.org.

32. Allen J. Beck and Timothy H. Hughes, "Sexual Violence Reported by Correctional Authorities, 2004," 2005 Special Report from the U.S. Department of Justice, Bureau of Justice Statistics, http://www.ojp.usdoj/gov/bjs/abstract/dvsal.htm.

33. Mona Lynch, "Punishing Images: Jail Cam and the Changing Penal Enterprise," *Punishment and Society: The International Journal of Penology* 6, no. 3 (2004): 258, 265. Lynch summarizes Sheriff Arpaio's practices: "With simple imagery, they tell a story about the need to use old-fashioned discipline and austerity, hierarchized power, shaming and humiliation and even physical force in order to restore social order." Ibid., 258.

CHAPTER SIX

1. Jeffrey Archer, *Purgatory: A Prison Diary, Volume II* (New York: St. Martin's Press, 2004), 257.

2. Mark R. Pogrebin and Mary Dodge, "Women's Accounts of Their Prison Experiences: A Retrospective View of Their Subjective Realities," *Journal of Criminal Justice* 29, no. 6 (2001): 534.

3. Ibid.

4. For a complete description of this thesis, see Loic Wacquant, "Deadly Symbiosis: When Ghetto and Prison Meet and Mesh," *Punishment and Society* 3, no. 1 (2001): 95–134.

5. Barbara Lane, "Puzzle Pieces," in *Couldn't Keep It to Myself: Testimonies from Our Imprisoned Sisters*, ed. Wally Lamb (New York: Regan Books, 2003), 237.

6. Christy Marie Camp, "Sleep with One Eye Open," *Cell Door Magazine* (on-line magazine) 2, no. 1 (2000), http://www.lairdcarlson.com/celldoor/00201/camp00201Sleep/htm.

7. James Gilligan, "Punishment and Violence: Is the Criminal Law Based on One Huge Mistake?" *Social Research* 67, no. 3 (2000): 762.

8. Primo Levi, *The Drowned and the Saved* (New York: Vintage Books, 1989), 44.

9. For many pages of brilliant description of this phenomenon, see Hannah Arendt, *The Origins of Totalitarianism* (New York: Harcourt Brace, 1973).

10. Levi, *The Drowned*, 38.

11. Craig Haney, "Psychology and the Limits to Prison Pain: Confronting the Coming Crisis in Eighth Amendment Law," *Psychology, Public Policy, and Law* 3 (1997): 539.

12. "Prison Gangs Target Martha Stewart," *National Enquirer*, 22 March 2004.

13. Ron Scherer and Sara B. Miller, "Martha Stewart Preps for Prison, Consultant in Tow," *Christian Science Monitor*, 15 July 2004.

14. "Martha Prison No 'Camp Cupcake,'" CBSNews.com, http://www.cbsnews.com/stories/2004/10/07/earlyshow/main647995.shtml.

15. "Mass Incarceration and Rape: The Savaging of Black America," *Black Commentator* (on-line magazine), reprinted at the Stop Prisoner Rape website: 17 June 2004, http://www.spr.org/en/sprnews/2004.

184   16. Deirdre Golash, *The Case against Punishment: Retribution, Crime Prevention, and the Law* (New York: New York University Press, 2005), 3.

17. Adam Liptak, "Inmate Was Considered 'Property' of Gang, Witness Tells Jury in Prison Rape Lawsuit," *New York Times*, 25 September 2005.

18. Ibid.

CHAPTER SEVEN

1. Nell Bernstein, *All Alone in the World: Children of the Incarcerated* (New York: New Press, 2005), 20.

2. Ibid., 196.

3. Jeremy Travis, "Families and Children," *Federal Probation* 69, no. 1 (2005), http://www.uscourts.gov/fedprob/jun2005/families.html.

4. Alison Cunningham and Linda Baker, "Invisible Victims: The Children of Women in Prison," 2004 report from the Centre for Children and Families in the Justice System," http://www.voicesforchildren.ca/report-Dec2004-1htm. See also, Ross D. Parke and Alison Clarke-Stewart, "The Effects of Parental Incarceration on Children: Perspectives, Promises, and Policies," in *Prisoners Once Removed: The Impact of Incarceration and Reentry on Children, Families, and Communities*, eds. Jeremy Travis and Michelle Waul, 189–232 (Washington, D.C.: The Urban Institute Press, 2003).

5. Ibid.

6. Ibid.

7. Joanne Archibald, author interview, 20 October 2004.

8. Nell Bernstein, "Motherless Children," *Salon*, 25 October 2000, http://www.dir.salon.com/mwt/feature/2000/10/25drug_families/index.html.

9. Ibid.

10. Sarah Karnasiewicz, "Love under Lock and Key," *Salon*, 25 November 2005, http://www.salon.com/mwt/feature/2005/11/15/bernstein/print.html.

11. Emani Davis, author interview, 2 March 2005.

12. Christopher J. Mumola, "Incarcerated Parents and Their Children," 2000 Special Report from the U.S. Department of Justice, Bureau of Justice Statistics, 5, http://www.ojp.usdoj.gov/bjs/abstract/iptc.htm.

13. Ibid.

14. All these details were found on the campaign's Web site, http://www.etccampaign.com.

15. Bernstein, *All Alone*, 87.

16. Mumola, "Incarcerated Parents," 4.

17. Mariely Downey, "Policy Watch: Losing More Than Time: Incarcerated Mothers and the Adoption and Safe Families Act of 1997," 9 Buff. *Woman's L. J.* 41 (2001). This article reviews all the provisions of the act in great detail.

18. Ibid., 46.

19. Travis, "Families and Children."

20. Mumola, "Incarcerated Parents," 2.

21. Downey, "Policy Watch," 47.

22. Nell Bernstein, "Terminating Motherhood: How the Drug War Has Stamped an Entire Class of Parents as Permanently Unfit," http://www.asentenceoftheirown.com/Essays%20%20Terminating.html. In recent research, child removal appeared to accelerate criminal activity among the study group's mothers. Timothy Ross, Ajay Khashu, and Mark Wamsley, "Hard Data on Hard Times: An Empirical Analysis of Maternal Incarceration, Foster Care, and Visitation," 2004 report from the Vera Institute of Justice, http://www.vera.org/publications.

23. Mumola, "Incarcerated Parents," 5. This research finds that parents in state prison were more likely to be serving a sentence for drug offenses (24 percent) than nonparents (17 percent) and reported mothers having more serious drug use histories than fathers. Mothers in state prison were more likely than fathers to report drug use in the month before their arrest and were more likely to report being under the influence of drugs when they committed the crime. In addition, 32 percent of mothers in state prison reported committing their crime to get drugs or money for drugs, compared to 19 percent of fathers.

24. Elaine Lord, former superintendent of the Bedford Hills Correctional Facility, New York State's maximum security prison for women, draws this conclusion: "Imprisonment should be the absolute last resort—for use when all else has failed and when there is concern for the safety of others. This is not the case for the majority of women who are sent to prison. They would be expected to do well in settings where they could be with their children and where the majority of the budget is not spent on staff or sophisticated security paraphernalia—where direct and necessary services are provided." Elaine Lord, "A Prison Superintendent's Perspective on Women in Prison," *Prison Journal* 75, no. 2 (1995): 257–69.

CHAPTER EIGHT

1. Nell Bernstein, *All Alone in the World: Children of the Incarcerated* (New York: New Press, 2005), 181.

2. Alexander Masters, *Stuart: A Life Backwards* (London: Fourth Estate, 2005), 6.

3. Ibid.

CHAPTER NINE

1. Alexander Masters, *Stuart: A Life Backwards* (London: Fourth Estate, 2005), 272.

2. Renny Golden, *War on the Family: Mothers in Prison and the Families They Leave Behind* (New York: Routledge, 2005), 97.

3. David Finkelhor and Jennifer Dziuba-Leatherman, "Victimization of

186   Children," *American Psychologist* 49, no. 3 (1994): http://www.gateway.ut.ovid/com/gw2/ovidweb.cgi.

4. Gail Garfield, *Knowing What We Know: African American Women's Experiences of Violence and Violation* (New Brunswick, N.J.: Rutgers University Press, 2005), 245.

5. Ibid., 33.

6. Ibid., 27.

7. Judith Lewis Herman, *Trauma and Recovery* (New York: Basic Books, 1997), 104.

8. Ibid., 111. "Children victimized during preschool years, when children experiment with normal dissociative skills, may be those who become most likely to use dissociation as a defense mechanism and to develop a pattern of dissociation that becomes chronic." David Finkelhor, "The Victimization of Children and Youth: Developmental Victimology," in *Victims of Crime*, 2nd ed. eds. Robert C. Davis, Arthur J. Lurigio, and Wesley G. Skogan (Thousand Oaks, Calif.: Sage Publications, 1997), 103.

9. Debra Niehoff, *The Biology of Violence: How Understanding the Brain, Behavior, and Environment Can Break the Vicious Circle of Aggression* (New York: The Free Press, 1999): 183–85.

10. Herman, *Trauma and Recovery*, 109.

11. Annette M. Mahoney and Carol Ann Daniel, "Bridging the Power Gap: Narrative Therapy with Incarcerated Women," *The Prison Journal* 86, no. 1 (2006): 83.

12. Barbara Kerr, *Strong at the Broken Places: Women Who Have Survived Drugs* (Chicago: Follett Publishing, 1974), 307. Many abused women describe their drug usage in terms of control. Nina, a homeless twenty-five-year-old daily crack smoker, explains: "I need to do what I want to do. I need to be in control. I feel better and happy when I'm high. Drugs give me control. I've been hurt too many times. I've learned from the streets—don't trust anyone, protect yourself." Carol A. Roberts, "Drug Use Among Inner-City African American Women: The Process of Managing Loss," *Qualitative Health Research* 9, no. 5 (1999): 631.

13. Marsha Rosenbaum, *Women on Heroin* (New Brunswick, N.J.: Rutgers University Press, 1981), 11.

14. Regina Austin, "The Black Community: Its Lawbreakers, and a Politics of Identification," *Southern California Law Review* 65 (1992): 1774.

15. Elliott Currie, *Reckoning: Drugs, the Cities, and the American Future* (New York: Hill and Wang, 1993), 110. See also Rosenbaum, *Women on Heroin*, 41.

16. Patrice Gaines, *Laughing in the Dark: From Colored Girl to Woman of Color; A Journey from Prison to Power* (New York: Crown Publishers, 1994), 96. "At that moment when Ben offered me drugs, I loved him more than I did myself. I was too addicted to him to do anything other than what he suggested. I followed men. What they did, I did. What they told me to do, I did. I wanted

their approval, an ounce of care I could pass off as love. It made me higher than any heroin I ever shot into my veins." Ibid.

17. Garfield, *Knowing What We Know*, 198.

18. Dana D. DeHart, "Pathways to Prison: Impact of Victimization in the Lives of Incarcerated Women," 2004 report submitted to the U.S. Department of Justice, National Institute of Justice, http://www.nicic.org/library/020226.

19. Julie Bindel, "I Took All My Anger out on Him," (London) *Guardian*, 16 August 2005. Sometimes the criminal act is the end product of a relationship of such violence and marginality that the criminal justice system's response seems especially harsh and certainly irrelevant. Such is the case of Emma Humphreys, released from a mandatory life sentence after seven years of imprisonment following a campaign on her behalf in the UK. Emma's stepfather repeatedly beat her; as a teen she engaged in prostitution and was battered by her pimp, Trevor Armitage, if she didn't go out and make money, and brutalized if she would not have sex with him as well. When her pimp demanded sex, Emma could not carry on anymore. She started to cut her wrists with a knife, thinking that he would not demand sex or hit her and would have to take her to the hospital. But she was interrupted and she cut him with the knife instead, although she had no real wish for him to die. The women who helped with Emma's appeal described the situation: "Emma's condition following Armitage's death, and the life which had led up to that night—her feelings of remorse, bereavement and confusion—should by any standards have suggested an environment where she would be carefully contained; debriefed by someone skilled in understanding the effects of both acute and chronic trauma; given physical and medical care; fed with nourishing and non-toxic food and medication; and gradually surrounded by a therapeutic intervention." What she got instead, was prison. Julie Bindel and Harriet Wistrich, *The Map of My Life: The Story of Emma Humphreys* (London: Astraia Press, 2003), 141.

20. Elizabeth Comack, *Women in Trouble: Connecting Women's Law Violations to Their Histories of Abuse* (Halifax, Nova Scotia: Fernwood Publishing, 1996), 84–85.

21. Paula C. Johnson, *Inner Lives: Voices of African American Women in Prison* (New York: New York University Press, 2003), 124–30.

22. Evelyn K. Sommers, *Voices from Within: Women Who Have Broken the Law* (Toronto: University of Toronto Press, 1995), 120.

23. Ibid., 129–30.

24. Lawrence A. Greenfeld and Tracy L. Snell, "Women Offenders," 1999 Special Report from the U.S. Department of Justice, Bureau of Justice Statistics, 9, http://www.ojp.usdoj.gov/bjs/pub/pdf.wo.pdf.

25. Beth E. Richie, "Understanding the Links Between Violence against Women and Women's Participation in Illegal Activity," 2003 report to the U.S. Department of Justice, 35, http://www.ncjrs.gov/pdffiles1/nij/grants/199369.pdf.

26. Ibid., 33.

27. Ibid., 40.

28. Ibid., 43.

29. Holly Johnson, "Key Findings from the Drug Use Careers of Female Offenders Study," 2004 report from the Australian Institute of Criminology, http://www.aic.gov.au/publications/tandi2/tandi289t.html. For good qualitative research on this topic, see DeHart, "Pathways"; Comack, *Women in Trouble*; and Johnson, *Inner Lives*; as well as Sommers, *Voices from Within*.

CHAPTER TEN

1. Terry Johnson, author interview, 3 February 2006.

2. Ibid.

3. Ibid.

4. Leslie Bennetts, "Teri Hatcher's Desperate Hour," *Vanity Fair*, April 2006, 244.

5. Joan Didion, "On Self-Respect," in *Journalistas: 100 Years of the Best Writing and Reporting by Women Journalists*, ed. Eleanor Mills (New York: Carroll & Graf Publishers, 2005), 280.

6. Alexander Masters, *Stuart: A Life Backwards* (London: Forth Estate, 2005), 284.

7. Ibid., 39.

8. Craig Haney, *Reforming Punishment: Psychological Limits to the Pains of Imprisonment* (Washington, D.C.: American Psychological Association, 2006), 177–78.

9. Judith Rumgay, "Scripts for Safer Survival: Pathways out of Female Crime," *The Howard Journal* 43, no. 4 (2004): 409.

10. Ibid., 416.

11. On the way to visit a rural Midwest prison, psychologist Craig Haney saw a religious message on the signboard of a small church at the turn-off to the institution: "Compassion in the face of evil is no virtue." This reminded Haney that this is the belief that has been at the core of much prison policy in the United States for several decades now: that "evil is a tangible thing that inheres inside persons who have done bad, reprehensible things." Haney then goes on to demonstrate that this theory ignores all we have learned about the psychological and societal causes of crime. Craig Haney, "The Contextual Revolution in Psychology and the Question of Prison Effects," in *The Effects of Imprisonment*, ed. Alison Liebling and Shadd Maruna (Portland, Ore.: Willan Publishing, 2005), 67. That this concept of good and evil has a religious basis cannot be denied. Consider this statement from Supreme Court Justice Antonin Scalia:

> Besides being *less* likely to regard death as an utterly cataclysmic punishment, the Christian is also *more* likely to regard punishment in general as deserved. The doctrine of free will—the ability of man to resist temptations to evil, which God will not permit beyond man's capacity to

resist—is central to the Christian doctrine of salvation and damnation, heaven and hell. The post-Freudian secularist, on the other hand, is more inclined to think that people are what their history and circumstances have made them, and there is little sense in assigning blame. (Antonin Scalia, "God's Justice and Ours," *First Things*, [May 2002]: 19.) Philosopher Stephen Duguid summarizes this world view, which seems to have taken over the penal discourse:

The lesson learned from "nothing works" is that the criminal did not *want* the treatment to work, that the criminal had entered the Sadean and anti-Socratic utopia in which pleasure alone guided action, and individuals could willingly and with knowledge choose to do evil . . . Believing that the criminal commits crime because it gives him or her pleasure and identity, the public in turn is thereby freed to derive equal pleasure in punishing the criminal. The Sadean circle is complete and potentially perpetual. (Stephen Duguid, *Can Prisons Work? The Prisoner as Object and Subject in Modern Corrections* [Toronto: University of Toronto Press, 2000], 262.)

12. Adam Liptak, "Debt to Society is Least of Costs for Ex-Convicts," *New York Times* 23 February 2006. The issue is being litigated.

13. Elliott Currie, *The Road to Whatever: Middle-Class Culture and the Crisis of Adolescence* (New York: Metropolitan Books, 2004), 254. Currie believes that this delineation of "good and evil" means we have created a harsh culture that has abdicated its responsibilities of nurture and support, leaving adolescents, in particular, in a "sink or swim" ethos of punitive individualism. Ibid., 255. This harsh worldview is exemplified by Judge Dan Locallo, presiding in the Cook County Courthouse, courtroom 302:

"Yeah, some people have a bad start," Locallo concedes. "If you don't have parents who stress hard work, and getting an education, and being a productive citizen, it might be harder to go down the right road. But at some point—assuming there are no mental problems—you make a choice. You take the high road, or you take the low road." Steve Bogira, *Courtroom 302: A Year behind the Scenes in an American Criminal Courthouse* (New York: Knopf Publishing Group, 2005), 86.

14. Erving Goffman, *Stigma: Notes on the Management of Spoiled Identity* (New York: Simon & Shuster, 1963), 124. In a diary kept during his recovery from heroin and a life of crime, published in the *Guardian*, Andrew Constantine, like Tammy, suffers from the conflict Goffman identified: "The stigma of my addiction and my criminal past cling to me and no matter how normal a person I become, I think this will always be so." Andrew Constantine, "My Comeback," (London) *Guardian*, 1 March 2004.

15. For all the details of these complicated provisions, see United States Government Accountability Office (GAO), "Drug Offenders: Various Factors May Limit the Impacts of Federal Laws That Provide for Denial of Selected Benefits," 2005 report to Congress, http://www.gaoaccess.gov/gaoreports.

16. Amy E. Hirsch, et al., "Every Door Closed: Barriers Facing Parents with Criminal Records," 2002 report from Community Legal Services (Philadephia, Penn.) http://www.clasp.org/publications/every_door_closed.pdf.

17. GAO, "Drug Offenders," 12.

18. Joshua Page, "Eliminating the Enemy: The Import of Denying Prisoners Access to Higher Education in Clinton's America," Punishment and Society 6, no. 4 (2004): 358–59.

19. For details on the ban, see GAO, "Drug Offenders," 8.

20. Ibid., 17–18.

21. Ibid., 19.

22. Ibid., 20.

23. Ibid., 8.

24. Vince Beiser, "Punishment Delayed: Thousands of Katrina Victims Are Being Denied Help—Because of Long-Ago Drug Convictions," American Prospect, Web Exclusive, 22 November 2005, http://www.prospect.org/web//view-web.ww?id=10660.

25. Ibid.

26. Margaret Colgate Love, "Relief from the Collateral Consequences of a Criminal Conviction: A State-by-State Resource Guide," 2005 report of the Sentencing Project, http://www.sentencingproject.org.

27. Charon Schwartz, "Rehabilitation vs. Incarceration: Non-Violent Women Drug Offenders," http://www.prisonerlife.com/.

28. Tom Rybarczyk, "Probe Finds Ex-convicts at Carnivals," Chicago Tribune, 6 September 2005.

29. The Sentencing Project, "Felony Disenfranchisement Rates for Women," 2004 report, http://www.sentencingproject.org.

30. Simon Jeffery, "UK Prisoners Should Get Vote, European Court Rules," (London) Guardian, 6 October 2005.

31. Dan Kevin, "Ex-Felons and the Vote," letter to the editor, New York Times, 16 January 2006.

32. Love, "Relief," 8.

33. Ibid., 2.

34. Martha C. Nussbaum, Hiding from Humanity: Disgust, Shame, and the Law (Princeton, N.J.: Princeton University Press, 2004), 236.

35. John Braithwaite, Crime, Shame and Reintegration (New York: Cambridge University Press, 1989), 102.

36. Nussbaum, Hiding, 236. Moral philosopher Avishai Margalit reminds us that a "decent society is one whose institutions do not humiliate people." Humiliation, he writes, is serious, because it "involves acting towards persons 'as if'—as if they were inanimate objects, as if they were tools, as if they were beasts." Animals are treated better than most prisoners, because, lacking humanity, there is no way to humiliate them by treating them as animals: the key concept for humiliation is rejection from the human commonwealth.

Avishai Margalit, *The Decent Society* (Cambridge, Mass.: Harvard University Press, 1996), 108, 121.

37. Hannah Arendt, *The Origins of Totalitarianism* (New York: Harcourt Brace, 1973), 302.

38. Ibid., 451, 455.

39. Jimmy Carter, *Our Endangered Values: America's Moral Crisis* (New York: Simon & Schuster, 2005), 79.

40. Ibid., 30–31.

41. Jane Addams, *Democracy and Social Ethics* (New York: MacMillan, 1902); on-line at http://www.gutenberg.org/files/15497/15487-h/15487-h.htm.

42. Amos Oz, *How to Cure a Fanatic* (Princeton, N.J.: Princeton University Press, 2006), 71.

43. Ibid., 57.

Epilogue

1. Information presented by Warden Alyssa Williams at a public presentation in Chicago on 12 August 2004.

2. Nell Bernstein, *All Alone in the World: Children of the Incarcerated* (New York: New Press, 2005), 182.

3. Ibid.

4. Nell Bernstein, "Narratives of Storm Survivors—'The One That's Left Behind,'" *Pacific News Service*, 6 September 2005, http://www.news.ncmonline.com/news.

5. John Mortimer, *Where There's a Will* (London: Penguin Books, 2004), 24.

6. Ibid., 25.

Bibliography

Abramsky, Sasha. *Hard Time Blues*. New York: St. Martin's Press, 2002.

Adams, Jay. "The Consequences of Damaged Sexuality: Observations from the Prison Population." *HopeDance* (on-line journal) 21 (2000). http://www.hopedance.org/archive/issue 21/articles21/damaged.htm.

Addams, Jane. *Democracy and Social Ethics*. New York: MacMillan, 1902, on-line at http://www.gutenberg.org/files/15497/15487-h/15487-h.htm.

Allard, Sharon Angella. "Rethinking Battered Woman's Syndrome: A Black Feminist Perspective." In *Domestic Violence at the Margins: Readings on Race, Class, Gender, and Culture*, edited by Natalie Sokoloff, 194–205. Piscataway, N.J.: Rutgers University Press, 2005.

Anderson, Joel. "Furcal Lives for the Present: Braves Shortstop Must Begin Jail Term after Season." *Chicago Tribune*, 9 October 2004.

Archer, Jeffrey. *Heaven: A Prison Diary, Volume III*. New York: St. Martin's Press, 2005.

———. *A Prison Diary*. New York: St. Martin's Press, 2002.

———. *Purgatory: A Prison Diary, Volume II*. New York: St. Martin's Press, 2004.

Archibald, Joanne. Author interview, 20 October 2004.

Arendt, Hannah. *The Origins of Totalitarianism*. New York: Harcourt Brace, 1973.

Arnold, Regina. "Black Women in Prison: The Price of Resistance." In *Women of Color in U.S. Society*, edited by Maxine Zinn and Bonnie Thornton Dill, 171–84. Philadelphia: Temple University Press, 1994.

Austin, Regina. "The Black Community: Its Lawbreakers, and a Politics of Identification." *Southern California Law Review* 65 (1992): 1769.

Ayre, Richard V. "The Prison Crisis: An Essay on the Social and Political Foundations of Criminal Justice Policy." *Public Administration Quarterly* 19, no. 1 (1995): 41–57.

Baca, Jimmy Santiago. "Coming Into Language." In *Doing Time: 25 Years of Prison Writing*, edited by Bell Chevigny, 100–6. New York: Arcade Publishing, 1999.

194   "Barbara Bush Calls Evacuees Better Off." New York Times 7 September 2005.

Baunach, Phyllis Jo. Mothers in Prison. New Brunswick, N.J.: Transaction Books, 1985.

Bean, Philip. Drugs and Crime. Portland, Ore.: Willan Publishing, 2002.

Beck, Allen J., and Timothy A. Hughes. "Sexual Violence Reported by Correctional Authorities, 2004." 2005 Special Report from the U.S. Department of Justice, Bureau of Justice Statistics. Available at http://www.ojp.usdoj/gov/bjs/abstract/dvsal.htm.

Beiser, Vince. "Punishment Delayed: Thousands of Katrina Victims Are Being Denied Help—Because of Long-Ago Drug Convictions." American Prospect Web Exclusive, 22 November 2005. http://www.prosepct.org/web/view-web.ww?id=10660.

Beitchman, Joseph H., Kenneth J. Zucker, Jane E. Hood, Granville A. DaCosta, Donna Akman, and Erika Cassavia. "A Review of the Long-Term Effects of Child Sexual Abuse." Child Abuse and Neglect 16, no. 1 (1992): 101–18.

Bennetts, Leslie. "Terri Hatcher's Desperate Hour." Vanity Fair, April 2006, 190–94, 239–44.

Bernstein, Nell. All Alone in the World: Children of the Incarcerated. New York: New Press, 2005.

———. "Motherless Children." Salon. 25 October 2000. http://www.dir.salon.com/mwt/feature/2000/10/25/drug_families/index.html.

———. "Narratives of Storm Survivors—'The One That's Left Behind.'" Pacific News Service, 6 September 2005. On-line news service. http://www.news.ncmonline.com/news.

———. "Terminating Motherhood: How the Drug War Has Stamped an Entire Class of Parents as Permanently Unfit." http://www.asentenceoftheirown.com/Essays%20%20Terminating.html.

Bhattacharjee, Anannya. "Private Fists and Public Force: Race, Gender, and Surveillance." In Policing the National Body: Race, Gender, and Criminalization, edited by Jael Silliman and Anannya Bhattacharjee, 1–48. Cambridge, Mass.: South End Press, 2002.

Bindel, Julie. "'I Took All My Anger out on Him.'" (London) Guardian, 16 August 2005.

Bindel, Julie, and Harriet Wistrich. The Map of My Life: The Story of Emma Humphreys. London: Astraia Press, 2003.

Bloom, Barbara. Introduction. In Gendered Justice: Addressing Female Offenders, edited by Barbara Bloom, 3–24. Durham, N.C.: Carolina Academic Press, 2003.

Bogira, Steve. Courtroom 302: A Year behind the Scenes in an American Criminal Courthouse. New York: Knopf Publishing Group, 2005.

Bosworth, Mary. "Confining Femininity: A History of Gender, Power and Imprisonment." Theoretical Criminology 4, no. 3 (2000): 265–84.

———. Engendering Resistance: Agency and Power in Women's Prison. Brookfield, Vt.: Ashgate Publishing, 1999.

Boyd, Susan C. From *Witches to Crack Moms: Women, Drug Law, and Policy*. Durham, N.C.: Carolina Academic Press, 2004.

Braithwaite, John. *Crime, Shame and Reintegration*. New York: Cambridge University Press, 1989.

Browne, Angela, Brenda Miller, and Eugene Maguin. "Prevalence and Severity of Lifetime Physical and Sexual Victimization among Incarcerated Women." *International Journal of Law and Psychiatry* 22, nos. 3–4 (1999): 301–22.

Burke, Anna Celeste. "Triple Jeopardy: Women Marginalized by Substance Abuse, Poverty, and Incarceration." In *Women at the Margins: Neglect, Punishment, and Resistance*, edited by Josephina Figuerira-McDonough and Rosemary C. Sarri, 175–201. New York: The Haworth Press, 2002.

Bush-Baskette, Stephanie R. "The War on Drugs as a War against Black Women." In *Crime Control and Women: Feminist Implications of Criminal Justice Policy*, edited by Susan Miller, 113–29. Thousand Oaks, Calif.: Sage Publications, 1998.

Camp, Christy Marie. "I'm Going In . . ." *Cell Door Magazine* (on-line magazine) 1, no. 6 (1999). http://www.lairdcarlson.com/celldoor/00106GoingIn.htm.

———. "Sleep with One Eye Open." *Cell Door Magazine* (on-line magazine) 2, no. 1 (2000). http://www.lairdcarlson.com/celldoor/00201/Campoo201Sleep.htm.

Campbell, Nancy D. *Using Women: Gender, Drug Policy and Social Justice*. New York: Routledge, 2000.

Carlen, Pat. *Alternatives to Women's Imprisonment*. Philadelphia: Open University Press, 1990.

———. *Women, Crime and Poverty*. Philadelphia: Open University Press, 1988.

Carlen, Pat, and Anne Worrall. *Analysing Women's Imprisonment*. Portland, Ore.: Willan Publishing, 2004.

Carnwath, Tom, and Ian Smith. *Heroin Century*. New York: Routledge, 2002.

Carter, Jimmy. *Our Endangered Values: America's Moral Crisis*. New York: Simon & Schuster, 2005.

Chesney-Lind, Meda. "Imprisoning Women: The Unintended Victims of Mass Imprisonment." In *Invisible Punishment: The Collateral Consequences of Mass Imprisonment*, edited by Marc Mauer and Meda Chesney-Lind, 79–94. New York: The New Press, 2002.

———. "Patriarchy, Crime, and Justice: Feminist Criminology in the Era of Backlash." *Feminist Criminology* 1, no. 1 (2006): 6–26.

Chesney-Lind, Meda, and Lisa Pasko. *The Female Offender: Girls, Women, and Crime*. Thousand Oak, Calif.: Sage Publications, 2004.

Chesney-Lind, Meda, and Joycelyn M. Pollock. "Women's Prisons: Equality with a Vengeance." In *Women, Law, and Social Control*, edited by Alida Merlo and Joycelyn Pollock, 155–75. Needham Heights, Ma.: Allyn & Bacon, 1995.

Chevigny, Bell Gale, ed. *Doing Time: 25 Years of Prison Writing*. New York: Arcade Publishing, 1999.

Chigwada-Bailey, Ruth. "Black Women and the Criminal Justice System." In *Women Who Offend*, edited by Gill McIvor, 183–206. New York: Jessica Kingsley Publishers, 2004.

Clark, Judith. "The Impact of the Prison Environment on Mothers." *Prison Journal* 75, no. 3 (1995): 306–29.

Coe, Jonathan. *Like a Fiery Elephant: The Story of B. S. Johnson*. London: Picador, 2004.

Collins, Catherine Fisher. *The Imprisonment of African American Women: Causes, Conditions, and Future Implications*. Jefferson, N.C.: McFarland & Company, 1997.

Collins, Patricia Hill. *Black Feminist Thought: Knowledge, Consciousness, and the Politics of Empowerment*. New York: Routledge, 2000.

———. *Black Sexual Politics: African Americans, Gender, and the New Racism*. New York: Routledge, 2004.

———. *Fighting Words: Black Women and The Search for Justice*. Minneapolis: University of Minnesota Press, 1998.

Comack, Elizabeth. *Women in Trouble: Connecting Women's Law Violations to Their Histories of Abuse*. Halifax, Nova Scotia: Fernwood Publishing, 1996.

Constantine, Andrew. "My Comeback." (London) *Guardian*, 1 March 2004.

Covington, Stephanie S. "The Relational Theory of Women's Psychological Development: Implications for the Criminal Justice System." In *Female Offenders: Critical Perspectives and Effective Interventions*, edited by Ruth T. Zaplin, 113–31. Gaithersburg, Md.: Aspen Publishers, 1998.

———. "A Woman's Journey Home: Challenges for Female Offenders." In *Prisoners Once Removed: The Impact of Incarceration and Reentry on Children, Families, and Communities*," edited by Jeremy Travis and Michelle Waul, 67–104. Washington, D.C.: The Urban Institute Press, 2003.

Cunningham, Alison, and Linda Baker. "Invisible Victims: The Children of Women in Prison." 2004 report from the Centre for Children and Families in the Justice System. Available at http://www.voicesforchildren.ca/report-Dec2004-1.htm.

———. "Waiting for Mommy: Giving a Voice to the Hidden Victims of Imprisonment." 2003 report from the Centre for Children and Families in the Justice System. Available at http://www.lfcc.on.ca/CCFJS_researchreports.html.

Currie, Elliott. *Crime and Punishment in America*. New York: Henry Holt and Company, 1998.

———. *Reckoning: Drugs, the Cities, and the American Future*. New York: Hill and Wang, 1993.

———. *The Road to Whatever: Middle-Class Culture and the Crisis of Adolescence*. New York: Metropolitan Books, 2004.

Davis, Emani. Author interview, 2 March 2005.

Dean, Amber Richelle. "Prisoners' Rites?" *e. Peak Lastword* 13, no. 105 (2000).
http://www.peak.sfu.ca/the-peak/2000-2issue13/op-lw.html.

DeHart, Dana D. "Pathways to Prison: Impact of Victimization in the Lives of Incarcerated Women." 2004 report submitted to the National Institute of Justice. Available at http://www.nicic.org/Library/020226.

Dennehy, Kathleen M. Testimony to the Commission on Safety and Abuse in America's Prisons, November 1, 2005. Available at http://www.prison commission.org.

Department of Health and Human Services, Substance Abuse and Mental Health Services Administration. "Overview of Findings from the 2004 National Survey of Drug Use and Health." 2005 report. Available at http://www.oas .samhsa.gov.

Didion, Joan. "On Self-Respect." In *Journalistas: 100 Years of the Best Writing and Reporting by Women Journalists*, edited by Eleanor Mills, 277–80. New York: Carroll & Graf Publishers, 2005.

Dirks, Danielle. "Sexual Revictimization and Retraumatization of Women in Prison." *Women's Studies Quarterly* 32, no. 3/4 (2004): 102–15.

Dodge, L. Mara. *"Whores and Thieves of the Worst Kind": A Study of Women, Crime, and Prisons, 1835–2000*. DeKalb: Northern Illinois University Press, 2002.

Dougherty, Joyce. "Female Offenders and Childhood Maltreatment: Understanding the Connections." In *Female Offenders: Critical Perspectives and Effective Interventions*, edited by Ruth T. Zaplin, 227–44. Gaithersburg, Md.: Aspen Publishers, 1998.

———. "Power-Belief Theory: Female Criminality and the Dynamics of Oppression." In *Female Offenders: Critical Perspectives and Effective Interventions*, edited by Ruth T. Zaplin, 133–59. Gaithersburg, Md.: Aspen Publishers, 1998.

Downey, Mariely. "Policy Watch: Losing More than Time: Incarcerated Mothers and the Adoption and Safe Families Act of 1997." 9 Buff. Woman's L.J. 41 (2001).

Duguid, Stephen. *Can Prisons Work? The Prisoner as Object and Subject in Modern Corrections*. Toronto: University of Toronto Press, 2000.

Durose, Matthew R., and Christopher J. Mumola. "Profile of Nonviolent Offenders Exiting State Prisons." 2004 Fact Sheet from the U.S. Department of Justice Bureau of Justice Statistics. Available at http://www.ojp.usdoj. gov/bjs/abstract/pnoesp.htm.

Dworkin, Andrea. *Life and Death*. New York: Free Press, 1997.

Eddy, Mark J., and John B. Reid. "The Antisocial Behavior of the Adolescent Children of Incarcerated Parents: A Developmental Perspective." 2002 report prepared for the U.S. Department of Health and Human Services. Available at http://www.urban.org/uploadedPDF/410631-AntisocialBevhavior.pdf.

Ellis, Eddie. Testimony to the Commission on Safety and Abuse in America's Prisons, November 1, 2005. Available at http://www.prisoncommission. org.

198   Elsner, Alan. *Gates of Injustice: The Crisis in America's Prisons.* Upper Saddle River, N.J.:
        Prentice Hall, 2004.

Ettore, Elizabeth. *Women and Substance Use.* New Brunswick, N.J.: Rutgers University Press, 1992.

Faith, Karlene. "The Politics of Confinement and Resistance: The Imprisonment of Women." In *Criminal Injustice: Confronting the Prison Crisis,* edited by Elihu Rosenblatt. 165–83. Boston: South End Press, 1996.

———. "Transformative Justice versus Re-entrenched Correctionalism: The Canadian Experience." In *Harsh Punishment: International Experiences of Women's Imprisonment,* edited by Sandy Cook and Susanne Davies, 99–122. Boston: Northeastern University Press, 1999.

———. *Unruly Women: The Politics of Confinement and Resistance.* Vancouver: Press Gang Publishers, 1993.

Feeley, Malcolm M., and Jonathan Simon. "The New Penology: Notes on the Emerging Strategy of Corrections and Its Implications." *Criminology* 30, no. 4 (1992): 449–74.

Fernandez, Elizabeth. "Improper Strip Searches Alleged; 2 Women Sue, Claim They Were Left Naked in S.F. Jail Cells." *San Francisco Chronicle,* 4 September 2003.

———. "Stories of Anguish: Jail Has Man Disrobe to Photograph His Tattoos." *San Francisco Chronicle,* 16 November 2003.

Ferraro, Kathleen J., and Angela M. Moe. "Women's Stories of Survival and Resistance." In *Women in Prison: Gender and Social Control,* edited by Barbara Zaitzow and Jim Thomas, 65–93. Boulder, Colo.: Lynne Rienner Publishers, 2003.

Finet, Scott. "Franz Kafka's Trial as Symbol in Judicial Opinions." *Legal Studies Forum* 12, no. 1 (1988): 23–35.

Finkelhor, David. "The Victimization of Children: A Developmental Perspective." *American J. Orthopsychiatry* 65, no 2 (1995): 177–93.

———. "The Victimization of Children and Youth: Developmental Victimology." In *Victims of Crime,* 2nd ed. edited by Robert C. Davis, Arthur J. Lurigio, and Wesley G. Skogan, 86–107. Thousand Oaks, Calif.: Sage Publications, 1997.

Finkelhor, David, and Jennifer Dziuba-Leatherman. "Victimization of Children." *American Psychologist* 49, no. 3 (1994): 173–83. Available at http://www.gateway.ut.ovid/com/gwz/ovidweb.cgi.

Finkelhor, David, and Kathy Kendall-Tackett. "A Developmental Perspective on the Childhood Impact of Crime, Abuse, and Violent Victimization." In *Developmental Perspectives on Trauma: Theory, Research, and Intervention,* edited by Dante Cicchetti and Sheree L. Toth, 1–32. New York: University of Rochester Press, 1997.

Foucault, Michel. *Discipline and Punish: The Birth of the Prison.* New York: Vintage Books, 1995.

Friedman, Jennifer, and Marixsa Alicea. *Surviving Heroin: Interviews with Women in*   199
Methadone Clinics. Gainesville: University Press of Florida, 2001.

Gaines, Patrice. *Laughing in the Dark: From Colored Girl to Woman of Color; A Journey from Prison to Power.* New York: Crown Publishers, 1994.

Garfield, Gail. *Knowing What We Know: African American Women's Experiences of Violence and Violation.* New Brunswick, N.J.: Rutgers University Press, 2005.

Gelsthorpre, Lorraine. "Female Offending: A Theoretical Overview." In *Women Who Offend,* edited by Gill McIvor, 13–37. New York: Jessica Kingsley Publishers, 2004.

George, Amanda. "Strip Searches: Sexual Assault by the State." Available at http://www.aic.gov.au/publications/proceedings/20/george.pdf.

Gilbert, Paul. "Bullying in Prisons: An Evolutionary and Biophyschosocial Approach." In *Bullying among Prisoners: Innovations in Theory and Research,* edited by Jane L. Ireland, 176–99. Portland, Ore.: Willan Publishing, 2005.

Gilfus, Mary E. "From Victims to Survivors to Offenders: Women's Routes of Entry and Immersion into Street Crime." *Women and Criminal Justice* 4, no. 1 (1992): 63–89.

Gilligan, James. *Preventing Violence.* New York: Thames and Hudson, 2001.

———. "Punishment and Violence: Is the Criminal Law Based on One Huge Mistake?" *Social Research* 67, no. 3 (2000): 745–73.

Girshick, Lori B. "Abused Women and Incarceration." In *Women in Prison: Gender and Social Control,* edited by Barbara Zaitzow and Jim Thomas, 95–117. Boulder, Colo.: Lynne Rienner Publishers, 2003.

———. *No Safe Haven: Stories of Women in Prison.* Boston: Northeastern University Press, 1999.

Glaze, Lauren E., and Seri Palla. "Probation and Parole in the United States, 2004." 2005 Bulletin from the U.S. Department of Justice, Bureau of Justice Statistics. Available at http://www.ojp.usdoj.gov/bjs/abstract/ppus04.htm.

Goffman, Erving. *Asylums: Essays on the Social Situations of Mental Patients and Other Inmates.* Garden City, N.Y.: Anchor Books, 1961.

———. *Stigma: Notes on the Management of Spoiled Identity.* New York: Simon & Shuster, 1963.

Golash, Deirdre. *The Case against Punishment: Retribution, Crime Prevention, and the Law.* New York: New York University Press, 2005.

Golden, Renny. *War on the Family: Mothers in Prison and the Families They Leave Behind.* New York: Routledge, 2005.

Gonnerman, Jennifer. *Life on the Outside: The Prison Odyssey of Elaine Bartlett.* New York: Farrar, Straus and Giroux, 2004.

Gordon, Diana R. *The Return of the Dangerous Classes: Drug Prohibition and Policy Politics.* New York: W. W. Norton & Company, 1994.

Goulding, Dot. "Severed Connections: An Exploration of the Impact of Imprisonment on Women's Familial and Social Connectedness." 2004 report,

200   Murdoch University Centre for Social and Community Research. Available at http://www.cscr.murdoch.edu.au.

Greenfeld, Lawrence A., and Tracy L. Snell. "Women Offenders." 1999 Special Report from the U.S. Department of Justice, Bureau of Justice Statistics. Available at http://www.ojp.usdoj.gov/bjs/pub/pdf/wo.pdf.

Hallinan, Joseph T. Going Up River: Travels in a Prison Nation. New York: Random House, 2001.

Haney, Craig. "The Contextual Revolution in Psychology and the Question of Prison Effects." In The Effects of Imprisonment, edited by Alison Liebling and Shadd Maruna, 66–93. Portland, Ore.: Willan Publishing, 2005.

———. "Prison Overcrowding: Harmful Consequences and Dysfunctional Reactions." Testimony given to the Commission on Safety and Abuse in America's Prisons on July 19, 2005. Available at http://www.prisoncommission.org.

———. "The Psychological Impact of Incarceration: Implications for Post-Prison Adjustment," In Prisoners Once Removed: The Impact of Incarceration and Reentry on Children, Families, and Communities, edited by Jeremy Travis and Michelle Waul, 33–66. Washington, D.C.: Urban Institute Press, 2004.

———. "Psychology and the Limits to Prison Pain: Confronting the Coming Crisis in Eighth Amendment Law." Psychology, Public Policy, and Law 3, no. 4 (1997): 499–588.

———. Reforming Punishment: Psychological Limits to the Pains of Imprisonment. Washington, D.C.: American Psychological Association, 2006.

Haney, Judy. Statement to the Commission on Safety and Abuse in America's Prisons. April 19, 2005. Available at http://www.prisoncommission.org.

Haney, Lynne. "Introduction: Gender, Welfare, and States of Punishment." Social Politics: International Studies in Gender, State and Society 11, no. 3 (2004): 333–62.

Hanks, Eva Evelyn. Test of Faith: Hope, Courage and the Prison Experience. Toronto: Canadian Scholars' Press, 2000.

Harlow, Caroline Wolf. "Prior Abuse Reported by Inmates and Probationers." 1999 Selected Findings from the U.S. Department of Justice, Bureau of Justice Statistics. Available at http://www.ojp.usdoj.gov/bjs.abstract/po4.htm.

Harris, Angela P. "Criminal Justice as Environmental Justice." 1 Journal of Gender, Race and Justice. (1997–98): 1–46.

Harris, Jean. Marking Time: Letters from Jean Harris to Shana Alexander. New York: Charles Scribner's Sons, 1991.

———. "They Always Call Us Ladies": Stories from Prison. New York: Charles Scribner's Sons, 1988.

Harrison, Paige M., and Allen J. Beck. "Prisoners in 2004." 2005 Bulletin from the U.S. Department of Justice, Bureau of Justice Statistics. Available at http://www.ojp.usdoj.gov/bjs/abstract/po4.htm.

Heney, Jan, and Connie M. Kristiansen. "An Analysis of the Impact of Prison on Women Survivors of Childhood Sexual Abuse." In *Breaking the Rules: Women in Prison and Feminist Therapy*, edited by Judy Harden and Marcia Hill, 29–44. Binghamton, N.Y.: The Haworth Press, 1998.

Herman, Judith Lewis. *Trauma and Recovery*. New York: Basic Books, 1997.

Hickley, Matthew. "'Lager Loutettes' Fuel Pub Violence." (London) *Daily Mail*, 19 July 2004.

Hirsch, Amy E., Sharon M. Dietrich, Rue Landau, Peter D. Schneider, and Irv Ackelsberg. "Every Door Closed: Barriers Facing Parents with Criminal Records." 2002 Report from Community Legal Services (Philadelphia). Available at http://www.clasp.org/publications/every_door_closed.pdf.

hooks, bell. *Ain't I a Woman: Black Women and Feminism*. Boston: South End Press, 1981.

———. *Sisters of the Yam: Black Women and Self-Recovery*. Boston: South End Press, 1993.

House of Commons Hansard Written Answers for 26 February 1997. Available at http://www.parliament. The-stationery-office.co.uk/pa/cm199697. cmhansrd/vo970226/debindx/70226-x.htm.

Howe, Adrian. *Punish and Critique: Towards a Feminist Analysis of Penalty*. New York: Routledge, 1994.

Interview with Mark Merin. *Democracy Now!* 24 August 2004. Available at http://www.democracynow.org/article.pl?sid=04/08/24/2110246.

Irwin, John. "The Jail." In *Incarcerating Criminals: Prisons and Jails in Social and Organizational Context*, edited by Timothy J. Flanagan, James W. Marquart, and Kenneth G. Adams, 227–35. New York: Oxford University Press, 1998.

James, Erwin. "All Mod Cons." (London) *Guardian*, 18 July 2002.

———. "Does Prison Work?" (London) *Guardian*, 29 January 2001.

———. "A Life Again." (London) *Guardian*, 5 September 2005.

———. "Never a Luxury." (London) *Guardian*, 24 June 2005.

Jeffery, Simon. "UK Prisoners Should Get Vote, European Court Rules." (London) *Guardian*, 6 October 2005.

Johnson, Holly. "Key Findings from the Drug Use Careers of Female Offenders Study." November 2004 report from the Australian Institute of Criminology. Available at http://www.aic.gov.au/publications/tandi2/tandi289t.html.

Johnson, Paula C. *Inner Lives: Voices of African American Women in Prison*. New York: New York University Press, 2003.

Johnson, Robert, and Hans Toch, eds. *Crime and Punishment: Inside Views*. Los Angeles: Roxbury Publishing, 2000.

Johnson, Terry. Author interview, 3 February 2006.

Kafka, Franz. *The Trial*. New York: Alfred A. Knopf, 1986.

Kaplan, John. *The Hardest Drug: Heroin and Public Policy*. Chicago: University of Chicago Press, 1983.

202 Karnasiewicz, Sarah. "Love under Lock and Key." *Salon*, 25 November 2005. http://www.salon.com/mwt/feature/2005/11/15/bernstein/print.html.

Kelly, Judith. "Prison Witness: Called to Bold Action for Peace." Available at http://www.soaw.org/new/newswire_detail.php?id=567.

Kendall-Tackett, Kathleen A., Linda Meyer Williams, and David Finkelhor. "Impact of Sexual Abuse on Children: A Review and Synthesis of Recent Empirical Studies." *Psychological Bulletin* 113, no. 1 (1993): 164–80.

Kerr, Barbara. *Strong at the Broken Places: Women Who Have Survived Drugs.* Chicago: Follett Publishing, 1974.

Kevin, Dan. "Ex-felons and the Vote." Letter to the editor, *New York Times*, 16 January 2006.

Kilroy, Debbie. "Sisters Inside: Speaking Out against Criminal Injustice." In *Global Lockdown: Race, Gender, and the Prison-Industrial Complex*, edited by Julia Sudbury, 285–93. New York: Routledge, 2005.

———. "Strip-Searching: Stop the State's Sexual Assault of Women in Prison." 2005 report from Sisters Inside, Inc. Available at http://www.sistersinside.com.au/media/antistripsearchingInfo.pdf.

King, Ryan S., and Marc Mauer. "Distorted Priorities: Drug Offenders in State Prisons." 2002 Report from the Sentencing Project. Available at http://www.sentencingproject.org.

Klofas, John M. "The Jail and the Community." In *Incarcerating Criminals: Prisons and Jails in Social and Organizational Context*, edited by Timothy J. Flanagan, James W. Marquart, and Kenneth G. Adams, 244–58. New York: Oxford University Press, 1998.

Knight, Louise W. *Citizen: Jane Addams and the Struggle for Democracy.* Chicago: University of Chicago Press, 2005.

Kruttschnitt, Candace. "The Politics of Confinement: Women's Imprisonment in California and the UK." In *The Effects of Imprisonment*, edited by Allison Liebling and Shadd Maruna, 146–73. Portland, Ore.: Willan Publishing, 2005.

Kruttschnitt, Candace, Rosemary Gartner, and Amy Miller. "Doing Her Own Times? Women's Responses to Prison in the Context of the Old and the New Penology." *Criminology* 38, no. 3 (2000): 681–718.

Lane, Barbara. "Puzzle Pieces." In *Couldn't Keep It to Myself: Testimonies from Our Imprisoned Sisters*, edited by Wally Lamb, 211–43. New York: Regan Books, 2003.

Lapidus, Lenora, Namita Luthra, Anjuli Verma, Deborah Small, Patricia Allard, and Kirsten Levingston. "Caught in the Net: The Impact of Drug Policies on Women and Families." Report from the American Civil Liberties Union, the Brennan Center for Justice, and Break the Chains: Communities of Color and the War on Drugs, 2004. Available at http://www.fairlaws4families.org/publications.html.

Levi, Primo. *The Drowned and the Saved.* New York: Vintage Books, 1989.

Liptak, Adam. "Debt to Society is Least of Costs for Ex-Convicts." *New York Times*, 203
23 February 2006.

———. "Inmate Was Considered 'Property' of Gang, Witness Tells Jury in
Prison Rape Lawsuit." *New York Times*, 25 September 2005.

———. "Pregnant Inmates Often Shackled during Labor." *New York Times*,
2 March 2006.

Lord, Elaine. "A Prison Superintendent's Perspective on Women in Prison."
Prison Journal 75, no. 2 (1995): 257–69.

Lorde, Audre. *A Burst of Light: Essays*. Ithaca, N.Y.: Firebrand Books, 1988.

Love, Margaret Colgate. "Relief from the Collateral Consequences of a Criminal Conviction: A State-by-State Resource Guide." July 2005 report of the
Sentencing Project. Available at http://www.sentencingproject.org.

Lubiano, Wahneema. "Black Ladies, Welfare Queens, and State Minstrels:
Ideological War by Narrative Means." In *Race-Ing Justice, En-Gendering Power*,
edited by Toni Morrison, 323–63. New York: Pantheon Books, 1992.

Lurigio, Arthur J. "Disproportionate Incarceration of African Americans for
Drug Offenses in the U.S." 2004 Research Bulletin from the Illinois Crim-
inal Justice Information Authority. Available at http://www.nicic.org/
Library/019393.

Lurigio, Arthur J., Mary Harkenrider, and Pamela Loose. "The Disproportionate Incarceration of African Americans for Drug Crimes: The Illinois
Perspective." 2005 report to the U.S. Department of Justice. Available at
http://www.nicic.org/library/021255.

Lynch, Mona. "Punishing Images: Jail Cam and the Changing Penal Enterprise." *Punishment and Society: The International Journal of Penology* 6, no. 3 (2004):
255–70.

McClanahan, Susan F., Gary M. McClelland, Karen M. Abram, and Linda A.
Teplin. "Pathways into Prostitution among Female Jail Detainees and Their
Implications for Mental Health Services." *Psychiatric Services* 50, no. 12 (1999):
1606–13.

McConnel, Patricia. Essay. In *Wall Tappings: An International Anthology of Women's
Prison Writings 200 to the Present*, edited by Judith Scheffler, 261–70. New York:
The Feminist Press, 2002.

McCorkel, Jill. "'Criminally Dependent'? Gender, Punishment, and the Rhetoric
of Welfare Reform." *Social Politics: International Studies in Gender, State, and Society*
11, no. 3 (2004): 386–410.

———. "Embodied Surveillance and the Gendering of Punishment." *Journal of
Contemporary Ethnography* 32, no.1 (2003): 41–76.

McDougal, Susan, and Pat Harris. *The Woman Who Wouldn't Talk*. New York: Carroll & Graf, 2003.

McGinnis, Kenneth. "Make 'em Break Rocks." In *Building Violence: How America's
Rush to Incarcerate Creates More Violence*, edited by John P. May, 34–38. Thousand
Oaks, Calif.: Sage Publications, 2000.

204　McMurtry, John. "Caging the Poor: The Case against the Prison System." In *The Case for Penal Abolition*, edited by W. Gordon West and Ruth Morris, 167–86. Toronto: Canadian Scholars' Press, 2000.

Maeve, M. Katherine. "Speaking Unavoidable Truths: Understanding Early Childhood Sexual and Physical Violence among Women in Prison." *Issues in Mental Health Nursing* 21, no. 5 (2000): 473–98.

Mahoney, Annette M. and Carol Ann Daniel. "Bridging the Power Gap: Narrative Therapy with Incarcerated Women." *The Prison Journal* 86, no. 1 (2006): 75–88.

Malloch, Margaret S. "Not 'Fragrant' at All: Criminal Justice Responses to 'Risky' Women." *Critical Social Policy* 24, no. 3 (2004): 385–405.

Mancuso, Richard F. and Brenda A. Miller. "Crime and Punishment in the Lives of Women Alcohol and Other Drug (AOD) Users: Exploring the Gender, Lifestyle, and Legal Issues." In *Women, Crime, and Criminal Justice: Original Feminist Readings*, edited by Claire Renzetti and Lynne Goodstein, 93–110. Los Angeles, Calif.: Roxbury Publishing Company, 2001.

Margalit, Avishai. *The Decent Society*. Cambridge, Mass.: Harvard University Press, 1996.

Markowitz, Michael W. "Theoretical Explanations of the Nexus between Race and Crime." In *The System in Black and White: Exploring the Connections between Race, Crime, and Justice*, edited by Michael Markowitz and Delores D. Jones-Brown, 3–13. Westport, Conn.: Praeger, 2000.

Marlowe, Ann. *How to Stop Time: Heroin from A to Z*. New York: Basic Books, 1999.

Martel, Joane. "Policing Criminological Knowledge: The Hazards of Qualitative Research on Women in Prison." *Theoretical Criminology* 8, no. 2 (2004): 157–89.

"Martha Prison No 'Camp Cupcake.'" CBSNEWS.com, 7 October 2004. Available at http://www.cbsnews.com/stories/2004/10/07/early-show/main 647995.shtml.

Martone, Cynthia. *Loving through Bars: Children with Parents in Prison*. Santa Monica, Calif.: Santa Monica Press, 2005.

"Mass Incarceration and Rape: The Savaging of Black America." *Black Commentator* (on-line magazine) 17 June 2004. Available at http://www.spr.org.

Masters, Alexander. *Stuart: A Life Backwards*. London: Fourth Estate, 2005.

Mauer, Marc, Cathy Potler, and Richard Wolf. "Gender and Justice: Women, Drugs, and Sentencing Policy." 1999 report from the Sentencing Project. Available at http://www.sentencingproject.org.

Miller, Teresa A. "Sex Surveillance: Gender, Privacy and the Sexualization of Power in Prison," 10 Geo. Mason U. Civ. Rts. L.J. (2000): 291–356.

Moe, Angela M. "Blurring the Boundaries: Women's Criminality in the Context of Abuse." *Women's Studies Quarterly* 32, no. 3/4 (2004): 116–38.

Mortimer, John. *Where There's a Will*. London: Penguin Books, 2004.

Moss, Barbara Robinette. *Fierce: A Memoir.* New York: Scribner, 2004.

Mullings, Janet L., Joycelyn Pollock, and Ben M. Crouch. "Drugs and Criminality: Results from the Texas Women Inmates Study." *Women and Criminal Justice* 13, no. 4 (2002): 69–96.

Mumola, Christopher J. "Incarcerated Parents and Their Children." 2000 Special Report from the U.S. Department of Justice, Bureau of Justice Statistics. Available at http://www.ojp.usdoj.gov/bjs/abstract/iptc.htm.

———. "Suicide and Homicide in State Prisons and Local Jails." 2005 Special Report from the U.S. Department of Justice, Bureau of Justice Statistics. Available at http://www.ojp.jusdoj.gov/bjs/abstract/shsplj.htm.

National Institute of Corrections. "Annual Issue 2000: Responding to Women Offenders in the Community." Available at http://www.nicic.org.

Niehoff, Debra. *The Biology of Violence: How Understanding the Brain, Behavior, and Environment Can Break the Vicious Circle of Aggression.* New York: The Free Press, 1999.

Norton, Judee. "Norton #59900." In *Doing Time: 25 Years of Prison Writing,* edited by Bell Chevigny, 228–35. New York: Arcade Publishing, 1999.

Nussbaum, Martha C. *Hiding from Humanity: Disgust, Shame, and the Law.* Princeton, N.J.: Princeton University Press, 2004.

O'Brien, Patricia. *Making It in the "Free World": Women in Transition from Prison.* Albany: State University of New York Press, 2001.

O'Faolain, Naula. *The Story of Chicago May.* New York: Riverhead Books, 2005.

Office of National Drug Control Policy. "Women and Drugs," Fact Sheet. Available at http://www.whitehousedrugpolicy.gov/drugfact/women.

Orwell, George. *The Road to Wigan Pier.* New York: Harcourt, 1958.

Owen, Barbara. *"In the Mix": Struggle and Survival in a Women's Prison.* Albany: State University of New York Press, 1998.

Oz, Amos. *How to Cure a Fanatic.* Princeton, N.J.: Princeton University Press, 2006.

Page. Joshua. "Eliminating the Enemy: The Import of Denying Prisoners Access to Higher Education in Clinton's America." *Punishment and Society* 6, no. 4 (2004): 357–78.

Pallasch, Abdon M. "Lawsuit Challenges County Jail's Invasive Checks for Sex Diseases." *Chicago Sun-Times,* 10 August 2005.

Parke, Ross D., and K. Alison Clarke-Stewart. "The Effects of Parental Incarceration on Children: Perspectives, Promises, and Policies." In *Prisoners Once Removed: The Impact of Incarceration and Reentry on Children, Families, and Communities,* edited by Jeremy Travis and Michelle Waul, 189–232. Washington, D.C.: The Urban Institute Press, 2003.

Pereira, Margaret. "Strip Searching as Sexual Assault." *Hecate* 27, no. 2 (2001): 187–96.

———. "Women and Drugs: Destruction by Incarceration." *Hecate* 28, no. 1 (2002): 154–63.

206   Pimlott, Sheryl, and Rosemary C. Sarri. "The Forgotten Group: Women in Prisons and Jails." In *Women at the Margins: Neglect, Punishment, and Resistance*, edited by Josephina Figueira-McDonough and Rosemary C. Sarri, 55–85. New York: The Haworth Press, 2002.

Pogrebin, Mark R., and Mary Dodge. "Women's Accounts of Their Prison Experiences: A Retrospective View of Their Subjective Realities." *Journal of Criminal Justice* 29, no. 6 (2001): 531–41.

Pollock, Jocelyn M. *Women, Prison, and Crime*. Belmont, Calif.: Wadworth Thomson Learning, 2002.

"PREA Update." Fact sheet from the Web site of Stop Prisoner Rape. Available at http://www.spr.org.

"Prison Gangs Target Martha Stewart." *National Enquirer*, 22 March 2004.

Puar, Jasbir K. "Abu Ghraib: Arguing against Exceptionalism." *Feminist Studies* 30, no. 2 (2004): 522–34.

Rafter, Nicole Hahn. *Partial Justice: Women, Prisons, and Social Control*. New Brunswick, N.J.: Transaction Publishers, 1990.

Raphael, Jody. *Listening to Olivia: Violence, Poverty, and Prostitution*. Boston: Northeastern University Press, 2004.

———. *Saving Bernice: Battered Women, Welfare, and Poverty*. Boston: Northeastern University Press, 2000.

Rathbone, Cristina. *A World Apart: Women, Prison, and Life behind Bars*. New York: Random House, 2005.

Reiman, Jeffrey. *The Rich Get Richer and the Poor Get Prison: Ideology, Class, and Criminal Justice*. Needham Heights, Mass.: Allyn & Bacon, 1998.

Richie, Beth. *Compelled to Crime: The Gender Entrapment of Battered Black Women*. New York: Routledge, 1996.

———. "The Social Impact of Mass Incarceration on Women." In *Invisible Punishment: The Collateral Consequences of Mass Imprisonment*, edited by Marc Mauer and Meda Chesney-Lind, 137–49. New York: The New Press, 2002.

———. "Understanding the Links between Violence against Women and Women's Participation in Illegal Activity." 2003 report to the U. S Department of Justice. Available at http://www.ncjrs.gov/pdffiles1/nij/grants/199369.

Rierden, Andi. *The Farm: Life inside a Women's Prison*. Amherst: University of Massachusetts Press, 1997.

Ripstein, Arthur. "Responses to Humiliation: The Decent Society." Available at http://www.findarticles.com/p/articles/mi_m2267/is_nl_v64/ai_19382728/print.

Roberts, Carol A. "Drug Use Among Inner-City African American Women: The Process of Managing Loss." *Qualitative Health Research* 9, no. 5 (1999): 620–38.

Rohde, David, and Christopher Drew. "Prisoners Evacuated After Hurricanes Allege Abuse." *New York Times*, 2 October 2005.

Rose, Pete. *My Prison without Bars*. New York: Rodale Press, 2004.

Rosenbaum, Marsha. *Women on Heroin*. New Brunswick, N.J.: Rutgers University Press, 1981.

Ross, Luana. *Inventing the Savage: The Social Construction of Native American Criminality*. Austin: University of Texas Press, 1998.

Ross, Timothy, Ajay Khashu, and Mark Wamsley. "Hard Data on Hard Times: An Empirical Analysis of Maternal Incarceration, Foster Care, and Visitation." 2004 report from the Vera Institute of Justice. Available at http://www.vera.org/publication.

Rumgay, Judith. "Scripts for Safer Survival: Pathways out of Female Crime." *The Howard Journal* 43, no. 4 (2004), 405–19.

———. "When Victims Become Offenders: In Search of Coherence in Policy and Practice." Report from the Fawcett Society. http://www.fawcettsociety.org.

Russell-Brown, Kathryn. *Underground Codes: Race, Crime, and Related Fires*. New York: New York University Press, 2004.

Rybarczyk, Tom. "Probe Finds Ex-convicts at Carnivals." *Chicago Tribune*, 6 September 2005.

Sabin, Margery. "Outside/Inside: Searching for Wigan Pier." In *George Orwell into the Twenty-First Century*, edited by Thomas Cushman and John Rodden, 243–51. Boulder, Colo.: Paradigm Publishers, 2004.

Scalia, Antonin. "God's Justice and Ours." *First Things*, (May 2002): 17–21.

Scheffler, Judith A., ed. *Wall Tappings: An International Anthology of Women's Prison Writings 200 to the Present*. New York: The Feminist Press, 2002.

Scherer, Ron, and Sara B. Miller, "Martha Stewart Preps for Prison, Consultant in Tow." *Christian Science Monitor*, 15 July 2004.

Schwartz, Charon. "Rehabilitation vs. Incarceration: Non-Violent Women Drug Offenders." Available at http://www.prisonerlife.com.

The Sentencing Project. "Felony Disenfranchisement Rates for Women." 2004 report. Available at http://www.sentencingproject.org.

Shelden, Randall G. *Controlling the Dangerous Classes: A Critical Introduction to the History of Criminal Justice*. Needham Heights, Mass.: Allyn & Bacon, 2001.

Siegel, Jane A. and Linda M. Williams. "The Relationship between Child Sexual Abuse and Female Delinquency and Crime: A Prospective Study." *Journal of Research in Crime and Delinquency* 40, no. 1 (2003): 71–94.

Sokoloff, Natalie J. "Women Prisoners at the Dawn of the 21st Century." *Women and Criminal Justice* 16, nos. 1–2 (2005): 127–37.

Sommers, Evelyn K. *Voices from Within: Women Who Have Broken the Law*. Toronto: University of Toronto Press, 1995.

Steffensmeier, Darrell, and Emilie Alan. "The Nature of Female Offending: Patterns and Explanation." In *Female Offenders: Critical Perspectives and Effective Interventions*, edited by Ruth T. Zaplin, 5–29. Gaithersburg, Md.: Aspen Publishers, 1998.

Steman, Don, Andres Rengifo, and James Wilson. "Of Fragmentation and

Ferment: The Impact of State Sentencing Policies on Incarceration Rates, 1975–2002." 2006 report to the National Institute of Justice. Available at http://www.ncjrs.gov/pdffiles1/nij/grants/213003.pdf.

Sterk, Claire E. *Fast Lives: Women Who Use Crack Cocaine*. Philadelphia: Temple University Press, 1999.

Stern, Vivien. *A Sin against the Future: Imprisonment in the World*. Boston: Northeastern University Press, 1998.

Stop Prisoner Rape. "The Sexual Abuse of Female Inmates in Ohio." 2003 report. Available at http://www.spr.org.

Street, Paul. "Color Blind." In *Prison Nation: The Warehousing of America's Poor*, edited by Tara Herivel and Paul Wright, 30–40. New York: Routledge, 2003.

Sudbury, Julia. "A World without Prisons: Resisting Militarism, Globalized Punishment, and Empire." *Social Justice* 31, nos. 1–2 (2004): 9–30.

Taylor, Avril. *Women Drug Users: An Ethnography of a Female Injecting Community*. New York: Oxford University Press, 1993.

Tonry, Michael. *Thinking about Crime*. New York: Oxford University Press, 2004.

Travis, Jeremy. "Families and Children." *Federal Probation* 69, no. 1 (2005). Available at http://www.uscourts.gov/fedprob/jun2005/families.html.

Travis, Jeremy, and Michelle Waul. "Prisoners Once Removed: The Children and Families of Prisoners." In *Prisoners Once Removed: The Impact of Incarceration and Reentry on Children, Families, and Communities*, edited by Jeremy Travis and Michelle Waul, 1–32. Washington, D.C.: The Urban Institute Press, 2003.

United States Government Accountability Office. "Drug Offenders: Various Factors May Limit the Impacts of Federal Laws That Provide for Denial of Selected Benefits." 2005 Report to Congress. Available at http://www.gpoaccess.gov/gaoreports.

Virella, Kelly. "Trapped by the System: Parole in America." In *Prison Nation: The Warehousing of America's Poor*, edited by Tara Herivel and Paul Wright, 100–105. New York: Routledge, 2003.

Wacquant, Loic. "Deadly Symbiosis: When Ghetto and Prison Meet and Mesh." *Punishment and Society* 3, no. 1 (2001): 95–134.

Walters, Glenn D. *Drugs and Crime in Lifestyle Perspective*. Thousand Oaks, Calif.: Sage Publications, 1994.

War Bonnet, Darcy K. "Women in Prison Tell It Like It Is." *Off Our Backs*, February 2001. Available at http://www.kersplebedib.com/mystuff/feminist/wp_oob.html.

Watterson, Kathryn. *Women in Prison: Inside the Concrete Womb*. Boston: Northeastern University Press, 1996.

Websdale, Neil. *Policing the Poor: From Slave Plantation to Public Housing*. Boston: Northeastern University Press, 2001.

West, Traci C. *Wounds of the Spirit: Black Women, Violence, and Resistance Ethics*. New York: New York University Press, 1999.

Weston-Henriques, Zelma, and Delores D. Jones-Brown. "Prisons as 'Safe

Havens' for African-American Women." In *The System in Black and White: Exploring the Connections between Race, Crime, and Justice*, edited by Michael W. Markowitz and Delores D. Jones-Brown, 267–73. Westport, Conn.: Praeger, 2000.

Whitehead, Tony L. "Epidemic and Cultural Legends of Black Male Incarceration: The Socialization of African American Children to a Life of Incarceration." In *Building Violence: How America's Rush to Incarcerate Creates More Violence*, edited by John P. May, 82–89. Thousand Oaks, Calif.: Sage Publications, 2000.

Whitney, Tim. "Disproportionate Sentencing of Minority Drug Offenders in Illinois." 2005 Report to the U.S. Department of Justice. Available at http://www.icjia.state.il.us/public/pdf/ResearchReports/Disproportionate%Sentencing%20 Report.pdf.

Williams, Shelley. "To the Girls of the Audy." Poem in *Real Conditions: Writings from Cook County Jail, Women's Division 4 and the Cook County Juvenile Temporary Detention Center* 2, no. 3 (2001): 19.

Worrall, Anne. *Offending Women: Female Lawbreakers and the Criminal Justice System.* New York: Routledge, 1990.

Wurtzel, Elizabeth. *More, Now, Again: A Memoir of Addiction.* New York: Simon & Shuster, 2002.

Wyner, Ruth. *From the Inside: Dispatches from a Women's Prison.* London: Aurum Press, 2003.

———. "Letters." from the Cambridge Two Web site, http://www.cambridge two.com/rj/fruth.htm.

Young, Vernetta D. "Gender Expectations and Their Impact on Black Female Offenders and Victims." *Justice Quarterly* 3, no. 3 (1986): 305–27.

Zaitzow, Barbara H. "Doing Gender." In *Women in Prison: Gender and Social Control*, edited by Barbara Zaitzow and Jim Thomas, 21–38. Boulder, Colo.: Lynne Rienner Publishers, 2003.

———. "Pastel Fascism: Reflections of Social Control Techniques Used With Women in Prison." *Women Studies Quarterly* 32, no. 3/4 (2004): 33–48.

Acknowledgments

I extend grateful thanks to:

The awesome Tammy Johnson, who from the very first day trusted me with her story;

Tammy's wonderful son, Terrence, and gracious sisters, Patricia and Terri, who so readily agreed to speak candidly with me, sometimes at length, about their lives with Tammy;

Terry Johnson, Tammy's supervisor, who so generously allowed Tammy to work on this book with me during "company time";

Dorenda Dixon, Director of Women's Programs, Department of Women's Justice Services, Cook County Sheriff's Office, who suggested Tammy to me, arranged our first meeting, and also made it possible for us to revisit the site of Tammy's jail incarceration;

Scholars Lisa Brush, Marc Mauer, Jennifer Wesely, and Barbara Zaitzow, who gave an early draft of the manuscript a close reading and made valuable suggestions for improvements;

Phyllis Deutsch, brilliant editor-in-chief of University Press of New England, whose editorial suggestions, based on multiple readings of the draft and individual rewritten chapters (well beyond the call of duty), resulted in a major revamping of the book's structure, resulting in a far clearer, cleaner, and more powerful narrative; copy editor Leslie Cohen, whose close reading removed many inaccuracies from the text; and managing editor Mary Crittendon and assistant production editor Elizabeth Rawitsch, who made the entire process a delight.

Jane Rutherford and Barbara Hausman at the Schiller DuCanto &

212   Fleck Family Law Center, DePaul University College of Law, who have so enthusiastically supported my work in so many ways;

Rachel Durchslag, Nathan Cummings Community Foundation; Jennifer Rosenkranz and Dorothy Gardner, Michael Reese Health Trust; and Kim Riordan, Field Foundation of Illinois, who have generously supported my work over the past few years;

The staff at the DePaul College of Law library, without whose assistance this book would not exist: Deidre Dieffenbacher, Drusilla Dillard, Mark Giangrande, Milta Hall, Zachary Rouse, and Daniel Ursini; and

Shay-Ann Heiser Singh, whose cheerful assistance made clearing the hurdles of the university's Institutional Review Board a breeze.

If you've already read *Freeing Tammy* you will understand that this book owes a large debt to three authors. I found and read Alexander Masters's *Stuart: A Life Backwards*, just as Tammy was telling me her life story backwards. I have gained immeasurably from Masters's trials and tribulations as he labored to capture Stuart for his readers and to understand his story. Journalist Nell Bernstein's tracking of Dorothy Gaines and her family, along with her profound insights into the relationship of Ms. Gaines and her son Philip, also assisted me in better appreciating Tammy and Terrence's struggles. Psychologist Craig Haney's immense erudition and his courageous campaign against "prison pain" have influenced every chapter in this book.

Like the other two books in the trilogy, this volume is dedicated to the editor of the Northeastern University Press Series on Gender, Crime, and Law, Claire Renzetti. Claire has always believed in this project and from the very beginning did everything to make it a reality, including finding a publisher. As Tammy has said, you have to believe in yourself, but you also have to have someone out there who believes in you. For me, Claire is that person.

Lastly, my deep thanks to Alan Raphael (who prepared the index), who truly makes everything possible.

Index